PRACTICAL DEPLOYMENT OF CISCO IDENTITY SERVICES ENGINE (ISE)

PRACTICAL DEPLOYMENT OF CISCO IDENTITY SERVICES ENGINE (ISE)

Real-World Examples of AAA Deployments

ANDY RICHTER

JEREMY WOOD

ELSEVIER

AMSTERDAM • BOSTON • HEIDELBERG • LONDON
NEW YORK • OXFORD • PARIS • SAN DIEGO
SAN FRANCISCO • SINGAPORE • SYDNEY • TOKYO

Syngress is an imprint of Elsevier

Acquiring Editor: Chris Katsaropoulos
Editorial Project Manager: Anna Valutkevich
Project Manager: Punithavathy Govindaradjane
Designer: Mark Rogers

Syngress is an imprint of Elsevier
225 Wyman Street, Waltham, MA 02451, USA

Copyright © 2016 Elsevier Inc. All rights reserved.

No part of this publication may be reproduced or transmitted in any form or by any means, electronic
or mechanical, including photocopying, recording, or any information storage and retrieval system,
without permission in writing from the publisher. Details on how to seek permission, further information about the Publisher's permissions policies and our arrangements with organizations such as
the Copyright Clearance Center and the Copyright Licensing Agency, can be found at our website:
www.elsevier.com/permissions.

This book and the individual contributions contained in it are protected under copyright by the
Publisher (other than as may be noted herein).

Notices
Knowledge and best practice in this field are constantly changing. As new research and experience
broaden our understanding, changes in research methods, professional practices, or medical treatment
may become necessary.

Practitioners and researchers must always rely on their own experience and knowledge in evaluating
and using any information, methods, compounds, or experiments described herein. In using such information or methods they should be mindful of their own safety and the safety of others, including parties
for whom they have a professional responsibility.

To the fullest extent of the law, neither the Publisher nor the authors, contributors, or editors, assume
any liability for any injury and/or damage to persons or property as a matter of products liability,
negligence or otherwise, or from any use or operation of any methods, products, instructions, or ideas
contained in the material herein.

ISBN: 978-0-12-804457-5

British Library Cataloguing-in-Publication Data
A catalogue record for this book is available from the British Library

Library of Congress Cataloging-in-Publication Data
A catalog record for this book is available from the Library of Congress

For information on all Syngress publications
visit our website at http://store.elsevier.com/Syngress

Working together
to grow libraries in
developing countries

www.elsevier.com • www.bookaid.org

Contents

Acknowledgments

I have to first thank my wife Jenn for being incredibly supportive through this. To my daughter Grace for keeping everything important in perspective.

My colleagues at Presidio have been so helpful to me over the years through many projects. Thanks to especially Jonathan, Ron, Colum, Gareth, and Tom.

The AAA TAC team out of RTP incredibly still takes my calls and they have always been polite while fixing any of my mistakes. Thanks guys.

http://bit.ly/1JYMtma

Andy Richter

The support of family and friends while writing this book is what made it possible for me; thank you to all of you. The IT group at Norwich University as well deserves a special mention because without them I wouldn't have most of the experience needed for this. Finally my coauthor Andy, it was his drive to do this book that really got it off the ground.

Jeremy Wood

1

Introduction

Thank you for opening to the first page, as this is a step many people don't take in a technical manual. I have a few technical books on my shelf that I use exclusively to flip through to specific chapters and have never read the introduction. In that spirit, let's keep the intro short so we can get into the meat of what you're here for.

In this book we hope to bring a practical perspective to deploying the Cisco Identity Services Engine (ISE) system that may otherwise be elusive to the uninitiated in the arts of edge authentication or those who don't have lots of time to spend in the lab playing.

A little history: Before ISE was a product, if you were a Cisco customer and you wanted to deploy edge authentication that used 802.1x, enforce policy based on the posture of a personal computer (PC), deploy robust guest provisioning/web authentication, and profile what connected devices physically, you'd need to buy four separate products. These included:

- Cisco Access Control Server (ACS)
- Cisco Clean Access
- Network Admission Control (NAC) Guest
- NAC Profiler

Someone at Cisco (whose hand we'd really like to shake) decided that having so many products in a design was a really poor idea and Cisco went about creating a product that brought each of those together.

ISE provides edge authentication services for networks in a variety of ways:

- IEEE 802.1x authentication
- Media access control (MAC) Authentication Bypass (MAB)
- Web authentication
- Posture assessment
- Device profiling
- External mobile device management (MDM) integration
- Authentication via application program interface (API)

To accomplish these functions, ISE integrates into network access devices (switches, wireless controllers, virtual private network (VPN) concentrators) with Remote Authentication Dial-In User Service (RADIUS). Not only is it simply RADIUS integration, but also the great majority of what ISE provides is standards-compliant RADIUS. Being that Cisco is a large manufacturer (let's point out the obvious), there are some proprietary features ISE provides; we'll address some of those individually later.

Because ISE is a RADIUS server at its core, when you configure it, you have to remember the three A's (aka AAA or triple A):

- Authentication
- Authorization
- Accounting

Each of these not only need to be configured on your network access devices but are also the process that ISE goes through in processing devices that are connecting to the network.

When a RADIUS authentication request first comes in, it goes to "authentication" policy. This is where ISE determines if the identity of the user or device is who they say they are. This process could involve 802.1x authentication, MAB, or a web authentication.

For the authentication to be successful, a few possible things could be validated, which depends on what is happening for the specific device. If a password is used in the authentication, the password is validated against the Active Directory (AD) and/or Lightweight Directory Access Protocol (LDAP) database. If a certificate is used, it is validated against the certification authority (CA) certificate chain; perhaps its validity is also checked for revocation status. If the MAC address is presented for an authentication bypass, MAB authentication is processed, meaning the MAC address is checked against the MAC addresses in a database of known MAC addresses.

At the end of the authentication process we should know who the user is who is asking for network access. This would mean that the password presented is valid, or the certificate is valid in our database, or the MAC address is in our database. If this is the case, then the process proceeds. If the password or certificate or MAC address is invalid, ISE will stop the process and send a RADIUS access-reject.

Now it's important to realize that just because a device or user is authenticated doesn't mean they're necessarily going to be authorized for network access. This is an important concept. Again, the purpose of authentication is only to determine the identity of the user or device and not necessarily to determine what we would like to do with them; that's the role of the authorization in ISE.

Authorization takes place after authentication and while the rules look very similar to authentication (for those already accustomed to ISE), the purpose is to say, now that I know who this is, what level of access do I wish to give them to my network? That level of access may be all sorts of things:

- Unfettered access to network resources
- No network access
- Access to network resources with some limitations

The first two of these examples are pretty easy to break down.

In the case of unfettered network access, this may be most applicable to information technology (IT) administrators who do need access to all resources to perform job duties.

No network access may come about when we know who or what the user or endpoint is, but we don't want them to have any access. In that case the device would have succeeded in authenticating, but failed to authorize.

Access with limitations is really where some of the magic can happen. You then have the ability to deploy policy and impose it on users to ensure that the correct people and devices have appropriate access. The example that is often brought up to customers may be something like:

- Marketing users should have access to marketing servers and email servers but not finance servers.
- Finance users should have access to finance servers and email servers but not marketing servers.

But what if you want to know whether the marketing users are connecting to the network with an Android phone? Would you want them to have access to their corporate servers then?

That's a common situation that ISE can help provide a solution for. ISE has a built-in profiler that helps answer the following question: What kind of device is the user connecting with? ISE develops the endpoint profile by learning a variety of things about it. Does the device Organizationally Unique Identifier (OUI) tell us who manufactured the device? How does it ask for an Internet Protocol (IP) address and is there something that gives us a clue about what a device is as it asks for an address? What kind of browser is it using? Is it running a protocol that will announce what it is (Cisco Discovery Protocol (CDP) or Link Layer Discovery Protocol (LLDP))?

Based on a combination of a variety of things like this we can, with some certainty, understand what the endpoint device is and then potentially apply policy based on that information. The policy may look like the following:

- Marketing users coming in with Android phones don't get access to corporate servers but do get access to the internet and the mail server.
- Marketing users connecting with Microsoft Windows PCs are allowed access to marketing servers and email servers.

You see where we're going with this; we are looking to deploy policy based on a range of criteria based on who the person may be and what kind of device they are connecting with. Let's take this a step further and look into another example. Say you have a third party coming to work at your office, someone like an outside auditor. You need to provide this person some level of internal access for them to perform the job functions they've been hired by your company to do, and they're going to be using the PC that their employer issued to them. Given that his or her machine is not a member of your domain, and this user is not indoctrinated into your security policy, you need to understand more about what the device is and who may be using them. ISE can help with this in that we can perform a posture assessment of the device. With this posture assessment we can obtain really useful information about the PC including specific Windows versions, what version of antivirus is deployed and whether it has been updated recently, and other arbitrary things such as: are certain patches installed, are registry keys set, do files exist, and are applications or services running? This lets us create network policy that may read something like:

- Auditors connecting with PCs that are running recently an up-to-date antivirus are permitted access to finance servers and the internet.
- Auditors connecting with PCs that are running out-of-date antivirus applications are permitted access to the internet in order to obtain definition updates but are not permitted access to internal resources.

This provides us really in-depth policy creating functionality all from one user interface (UI) and one product to integrate into your network. From a single authorization policy we can deploy policy about who the user is and what they're connecting with, and we can apply policy based on the running state of the end system. That is what we're able to bring all together with ISE.

In our opinion, most important piece of ISE (for the uninitiated) is the concept of "Change of Authorization" (CoA). This is the magical part of ISE that lets our advanced functionality work. CoA is a RADIUS datagram that is sent from the RADIUS server to the authentication device (switch, controller, etc.) that can change the state of an edge client device (PC, phone, printer, etc.). Previously for a device to have its RADIUS authentication state changed, it would have to be entirely disconnected and authenticated from the start. There was simply no RADIUS mechanism for the RADIUS server to send an unsolicited update to an authenticator about a client that was previously allowed onto the network. This allows ISE to actually manipulate the live network access state of clients in a variety of ways:

- The administrator may revoke a user's access in real time from a central authentication server.
- ISE may require a login to a website. Once the login is successful, access may be granted to a user. CoA is required to present the website redirect, and then remove it after the user enters authorized credentials.
- A previously unknown device is connected to the network. ISE may learn that this is actually valid and it may authorize the device onto the network.

If a network device does not support CoA, the utility of deploying ISE is greatly reduced, but not entirely negated; we just lose the ability to do things like the above.

In this book we're going to spend some time at a variety of points going through useful design options that we've found to be helpful in our deployments. The configurations will include really important broad design points, such as how to design strong authentication for corporate assists or how to configure enforcement in a wired environment. We'll also go through much smaller points such as how to design ISE rules efficiently or what ISE settings may be particularly useful.

Lastly, once you've finished designing and deploying your ISE implementation, we're going to spend some time going over monitoring, reporting, and troubleshooting. What's the point of having all this identity information on your network if you don't bother reporting and looking to see who is authenticated where and when and with what? ISE has built-in reporting capabilities but depending on what you're looking to get out of it there are capabilities with syslog and third-party products that give you additional capabilities that augment your network viability.

We want to get something out of the way early here—ISE has a reputation of being a challenging product to deploy. This is an unfair characterization because the challenges come mostly from complexity that the administrator has created for themselves. This complexity can be broken down into a few categories:

- Cumulative effect of design requirements
- Gratuitous design requirements that may or may not increase security
- Numerous complex integrations
- Trying to fit old paradigms into a new product

There are a few ways we want to help you out here. One, we want to give you good design options with the tools you need to deploy them in your environment. We also want to call out the popular, but not necessarily effective, design elements.

Lastly, we hope to demystify integrations because broken down to individual components the concepts in any particular ISE deployment are not challenging. Complexity in ISE deployments comes from the cumulative sum of small manageable problems in a variety of disciplines (e.g., Cisco Internetworking Operating System (IOS) and Microsoft AD and public key infrastructure (PKI)). By breaking down the configuration and design elements individually we hope you'll have a good grasp on how ISE may be deployed in your environment by the time you get through this book.

Our goal is to focus on practice examples of how ISE is configured and practical tips for ISE design. ISE is extraordinarily configurable and there is simply no way to get through every possibly design; therefore, we intend to cover common and useful designs and configurations. Since ISE is extremely flexible in design it can seem daunting when you first start out; taking things in small sections can make much easier. We've endeavored to design this book to do just that. One of the sales guys at my company has said to a variety of our customers: "ISE can boil the ocean, but we don't want to do that." At the risk of giving a sales guy too much credit, he's exactly right.

We also will not cover every feature available in ISE because some provide very narrow-use cases, or others are useful to only a very small handful of customers and are generally impractical for most environments. It's not that we don't like these features; some we really like but they are practical for a small sliver of deployments out there and are not practical for most users. If we don't mention a specific ISE feature or functionality that you think is practical for your organization, don't be shy; use it! Every deployment is different; we're just sharing what we think and you're welcome to disagree with us.

In any case, we hope you enjoy this book and find it helpful.

2

ISE Clustering and Basic Setup

INTRODUCTION

You're ready to start building your Identity Services Engine (ISE) environment; that's great. You'll need to figure out how large a cluster you need to deploy and what sized nodes in order to support your environment. We say you need a cluster of ISE servers because while you technically can install ISE in a stand-alone fashion, almost every organization is going to need redundancy for authentication so nearly everyone is going to install at least two ISE nodes.

ISE can be installed on both hardware appliances and VMware virtual machines (VMs). At the time of this writing there a few different models of hardware appliances you can use.

From the old legacy NAC server hardware you may use:

- NAC-3315
- NAC-3355
- NAC-3395

These systems are end of sale and are not recommended and not discussed in detail.

For newer Unified Computing System (UCS)-based hardware there are two models that are available:

- SNS-3415
- SNS-3495

For details of their specific hardware please refer to the ISE 1.4 hardware installation guide located at http://bit.ly/1LVSkst.

For convenience there are Open Virtual Appliances (OVAs) of comparable hardware configuration for both SNS models when ISE is deployed in VMware. In the following section the hardware and VMware versions may be interchangeable for scalability.

ISE requires the following VMware disk performance:

- 50 MB/s write
- 300 MB/s read

The following types of disks are supported in VMware environments:

- Local disk
- Fiber Channel (FC)/Fiber Channel over Ethernet (FCOE)
- Internet Small Computer System Interface (iSCSI)

As to what releases of VMware are supported platforms, at the time of this writing ESXi 5.x is supported.

SIZING AND PREPARATION

When selecting hardware (size and quantity) for deployment, you're going to need to understand how high you need to scale the cluster, which is based on how many concurrent active endpoints you're going to have and how you will install the ISE personas. Let's address personas first.

ISE servers are allocated with roles in the cluster. An ISE node in a cluster may have only a single persona, or it may have more than one persona. The personas include:

- Administration
- Monitoring
- Policy
- Platform Exchange Grid (pxGrid)

The Administration persona is the persona that provides for the administrative graphical user interface (GUI) for the IT guy to login to and deploy ISE policy and integrate the ISE software into the environment. There may be up to two ISE servers with the Administration persona, there must be one. They're set primary/secondary roles but will not automatically failover by default.[1]

The Monitoring persona is the persona in the ISE cluster that receives logging data from all other nodes, and stores it for retrieval in monitoring and reporting. There may be up to two ISE servers with the Monitoring persona in the cluster and a cluster must always have at least one monitor node. If there are two, they are set in primary/secondary roles and will automatically failover if one node goes down.

The Policy persona is the persona in the ISE cluster that does the real work of ISE. The policy node is the RADIUS server, provides web pages for guest login, and holds the self-service websites, the Sponsor portal and My Devices portal. There may be up to 40 policy nodes in an ISE cluster.

pxGrid is a feature of ISE that allows for third-party applications to integrate with and share information with ISE. The pxGrid persona is what would be the point of contact(s) for any pxGrid clients you may choose to deploy. In keeping with other APIs it's normally a good idea to assign this role to your monitor nodes but like other personas it can be assigned to any server you wish as well as dedicated nodes.

To determine how many and of what persona you need to build, you need to first determine how to scale your ISE deployment.

The most important factor to evaluate when determining how many ISE nodes you're going to need is the number of concurrent active endpoints that are on line at one time.

---

[1]There is a capability in ISE 1.4 or later to have automated Admin role failover in the event of a server failure. We haven't seen this widely deployed yet so we're not covering it. If you feel like it makes sense in your deployment, by all means deploy this feature.

When we say concurrent endpoints, we mean devices that have been authenticated and are maintaining an authenticated session with a switch or wireless controller or VPN concentrator.

If you're going to have no more than 5000 active concurrent endpoints, you may use 2 SNS-3415 servers, each with all 3 personas. This would be characterized as a small deployment.

- Host: ISE1—SNS-3415: Admin (primary), Monitoring (secondary), Policy
- Host: ISE2—SNS-3415: Admin (secondary), Monitoring (primary), Policy

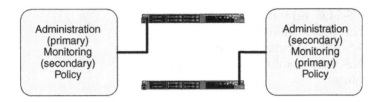

For more concurrent active endpoints up to 10,000 you have a couple of options. You should most likely set up nodes with the Administration and Monitoring personas, and then some nodes dedicated for policy. With Administration and Monitoring personas being coresident on two nodes you can have up to five dedicated policy nodes.[2] The specific number of policy nodes would be depend on your redundancy requirements.

- Host: ISE1—SNS-3495: Admin (primary), Monitoring (secondary)
- Host: ISE2—SNS-3495: Admin (secondary), Monitoring (primary)
- Host: ISE3—SNS-3415: Policy
- Host: ISE4—SNS-3415: Policy
- Host: ISE5—SNS-3415: Policy

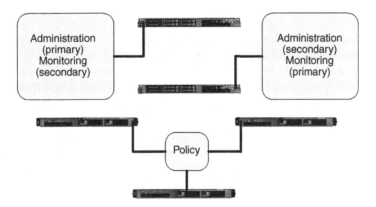

[2]It's possible to do this with two SNS-3495 servers without dedicated policy nodes, but for many thousands of concurrent endpoints, it's our opinion that dedicated policy nodes are a much better design.

An important thing to keep in mind is the following scalability requirements when procuring ISE policy nodes. When a server is dedicated as a policy node these are the maximum concurrent authenticated endpoints per-node:

- SNS-3415: 5000
- SNS-3495: 20,000

For deployments that are larger than 10,000 concurrent active endpoints, you will need nodes that are dedicated for administration, monitoring, and policy where no nodes have coresident personas (every node has a single persona).

- Host: ISE1—SNS-3495: Admin (primary)
- Host: ISE2—SNS-3495: Admin (secondary)
- Host: ISE3—SNS-3495: Monitoring (primary)
- Host: ISE4—SNS-3495: Monitoring (Secondary)
- Host: ISEx—Policy

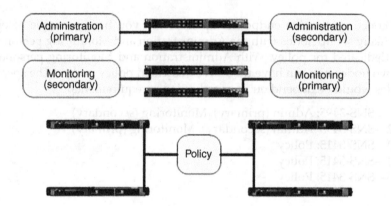

In the fully distributed ISE cluster you may have up to 40 ISE policy nodes and scalability to 250,000 concurrent active authenticated endpoints.

Another important variable in designing your ISE implementation is placement of your ISE nodes in an enterprise that has multiple data centers. It is absolutely a best practice to distribute your ISE nodes across data centers if you have redundant data centers available. ISE replication occurs with Transmission Control Protocol (TCP) and can definitely handle wide area network (WAN) speeds and interconnects. When ordering ISE you should consult with the Cisco ISE Authorized Technology Partner (ATP)-certified partner about what the ISE cluster bandwidth requirements are. They will have a bandwidth calculated provided by Cisco to assist you with identifying any bandwidth requirements. The most important factor when designing multisite ISE nodes is typically latency. ISE nodes should not be separated by WAN links that exceed 200 ms round trip latency in normal operation. This typically excludes single ISE clusters being distributed between North America and Asia-Pacific, but the specifics of your deployment may be different.

If your network security requirements stipulate that a firewall must be between your ISE nodes, that is supported but do take care to ensure that the required ports are open between your ISE nodes. Here is the port reference: http://bit.ly/1I0amW8.

SERVER/NODE DEPLOYMENT

When you have determined how many ISE nodes you're going to need, let's set about building some.

Here are the pieces of information you're going to need before you get started:

- Hostname[3]
- IP address
- Subnet mask
- Default gateway
- Domain Name System (DNS) suffix
- Name servers (up to three of them)
- Network Time Protocol (NTP) servers (up to three of them)
- Time zone[4]
- SSH (enabled yes/no)
- Administrator username
- Administrator password

Once you've got the above-mentioned information and ISE server stood up, either from OVA deployment or from spinning up a server fresh out of the box, type "setup" at the initial login prompt to go through the initial setup wizard.

---

[3]It's important to keep in mind when you're creating ISE nodes that the hostname cannot be longer than 15 characters if the host is to be integrated into Active Directory (AD). As such, we recommend keeping hostnames simple and straightforward.

[4]Under the hood it's important to remember that ISE 1.3 is just RedHat 6.x and that any time zone supported by RedHat may be configured in ISE. Example: America/New_York may be used if you're on the Eastern time zone of the United States so that you get valid daylight saving time.

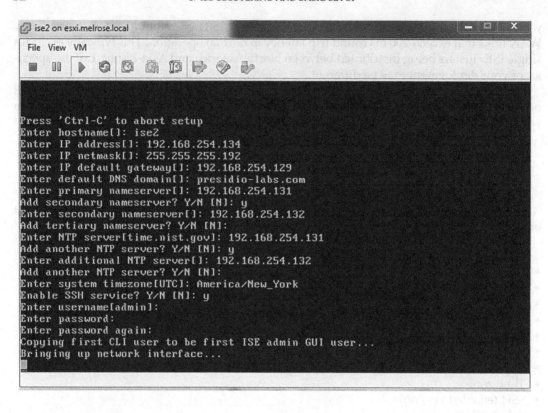

Once you've input that information, ISE will proceed to check if the network configuration is correct. The system will attempt to ping its default gateway, DNS, and NTP servers. If any of those fail, ISE will give you an opportunity to fix an issue. If you need to restart the wizard, just hit "Ctrl + C" and it will bring you back to the login prompt.

If everything succeeds, ISE will then install VMware tools if VMware hardware is detected. Once VMware tools are deployed, the ISE installation process is checked to see if the performance of the disk I/O is sufficient. If your VMware hardware is like my lab environment (not totally fit for production), ISE will display an error kind of like what is seen in the following figure:

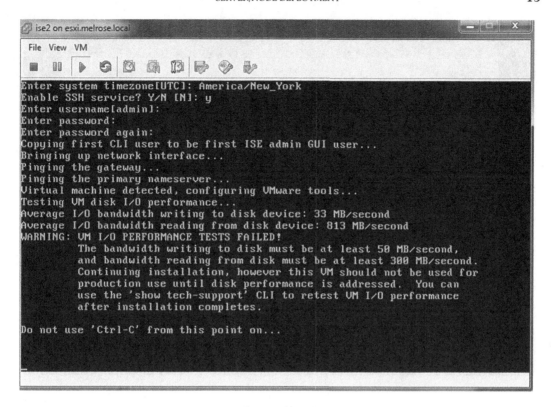

```
ise2 on esxi.melrose.local

File  View  VM

Enter system timezone[UTC]: America/New_York
Enable SSH service? Y/N [N]: y
Enter username[admin]:
Enter password:
Enter password again:
Copying first CLI user to be first ISE admin GUI user...
Bringing up network interface...
Pinging the gateway...
Pinging the primary nameserver...
Virtual machine detected, configuring VMware tools...
Testing VM disk I/O performance...
Average I/O bandwidth writing to disk device: 33 MB/second
Average I/O bandwidth reading from disk device: 813 MB/second
WARNING: VM I/O PERFORMANCE TESTS FAILED!
         The bandwidth writing to disk must be at least 50 MB/second,
         and bandwidth reading from disk must be at least 300 MB/second.
         Continuing installation, however this VM should not be used for
         production use until disk performance is addressed.  You can
         use the 'show tech-support' CLI to retest VM I/O performance
         after installation completes.

Do not use 'Ctrl-C' from this point on...
```

If you're installing in the lab like me, feel free to disregard and move on. If this is for production, do follow-up and ensure you have adequate VMware performance. Your user community will thank you later.

Now that you have the setup script done, this is a good time to run and grab lunch. ISE will now install on your server and this process can take 30 min or so.

After you're done with your lunch, it is time to get into the ISE system.

Point your browser to the hostname or IP of the ISE server with either Internet Explorer (IE) or Firefox. Chrome is not supported for ISE administration at the time of this writing. I find that ISE user interface (UI) works best when you use the Firefox, and the fewest bugs are in the extended support release (ESR) update channel.

The username will be the Admin username you configured during the initial setup wizard on the command-line interface (CLI).

Before you get into ISE policy, it's a good idea to get through a few things. First, you want to integrate each ISE node into a cluster. To join the ISE nodes together there are a few things that need to be done:

1. ISE nodes must be added to DNS so they may resolve each other forward and reverse.
2. The ISE Admin node must have certificate trust to all other nodes (preferably mutual trust).

If you're using Microsoft Active Directory (AD) as your DNS server, the configuration could look something like this (I have four nodes in my lab: ise1, ise2, ise3, ise4).

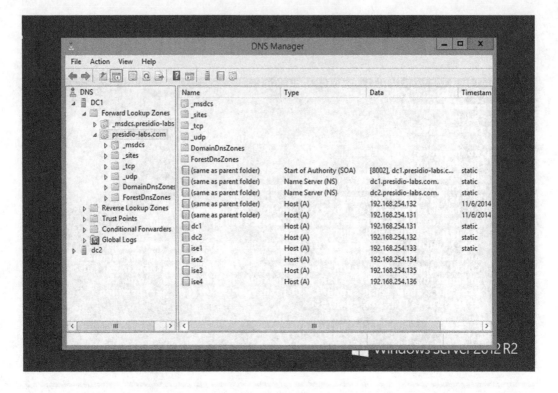

CERTIFICATES

Next you need to issue your ISE node certificates. The easiest way to do this is to create Certificate Signing Request (CSR) on each of them. To do that, click Administration → System → Certificates → Certificate Signing Requests.

You'll notice that there are a few different types of certificates under the Usage menu:

1. Multi-Use
2. Admin
3. Extensible Authentication Protocol (EAP)
4. Portal
5. pxGrid
6. ISE Root CA
7. Online Certificate Status Protocol (OCSP)

To start with, we need an Admin-type certificate (which could easily be used for EAP and Portal also).

Select the node type Admin and the ISE node you're on. And fill out the form with subject information you wish to include.[5]

---

[5]Wildcard certificates are supported for some ISE functions. They do have their use case in some deployments but it's generally recommended to use individual certificates per node whenever possible. It leads to a more compatible deployment and typically certificates are inexpensive, or free in the case of an internal CA from AD.

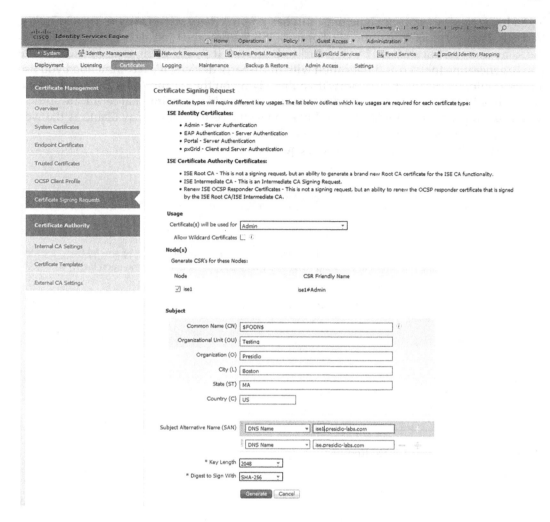

Take note that Subject Alternative Names (SANs) are available for various uses including custom portal configurations and Canonical Names (CNAMEs).[6]

For non-wildcard certificates the fully qualified domain name (FQDN) must be in the common name of the certificate but should that be long, it may be useful to add a shorter name for logging into the primary Admin node. For example, it's commonly recommended that customers make a DNS CNAME record of ise.fqdn.com pointing to the primary Admin node, and if the certificate of the primary Admin node also has ise.fqdn.com included, then there is no certificate error.

Once you've clicked "Generate," you're prompted to export the certificate.

Export the CSR and open it in your favorite text editor and save it to your local machine. Generating CSRs for all your ISE nodes at the same time and having them signed by a CA is

[6] I highly recommend carefully and liberally using SANs where you can. When you have multiple portals implemented in ISE, each can have a different hostname associated to it and as such you'd want a SAN configured. I also like adding "ise.localdomain" to my Admin nodes to simplify connecting to your primary Admin node if you have complicated actual hostnames.

a good way to save yourself some time. ISE has no preference what CA you use, GoDaddy, Verisign, Thawte, or a CA in your AD. For most ISE features the type of certificate required is the same exact certificate used by standard web servers. If you're going to use the certificate you're generating for web authentication with third-party devices, it's recommended you use a trusted internet certificate authority. If you're relying on the certificate for EAP authentication with only company-owned Windows clients, you could use an internal certificate authority like the one provided by Microsoft. I like to use the certsrv website available as the web enrolling role in the Windows Server CA role.

Browse to the CA website. And click "Request Certificate".

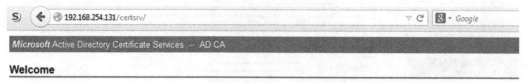

Select Advanced Certificate Request:

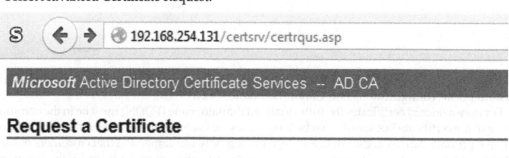

Select "Web Server" as your certificate template and paste your CSR into the "Saved Request" field and click Submit:

Submit a Certificate Request or Renewal Request

To submit a saved request to the CA, paste a base-64-encoded CMC or PK external source (such as a Web server) in the Saved Request box.

Saved Request:

Base-64-encoded certificate request (CMC or PKCS #10 or PKCS #7):

```
VbvCaqbtDmz2MUAeNHYkeTMCIAVrgunbPTJq4vfK
op0Lbavzc3E6dNXAUNn7YvyMGV2kiXpIoptfJPWv
9jyNGpDffZQHr9u3ilyZ4gvH9PfkBSyJQeynD97f
G1xA4i07x6EXoiOzdTmojzljNpPxSZ4OvdwEG1H4
-----END CERTIFICATE REQUEST-----
```

Certificate Template:

Web Server

Additional Attributes:

Attributes:

Submit >

Select Base 64 Encoded and Download Certificate.

  192.168.254.131/certsrv/certfnsh.asp

Microsoft Active Directory Certificate Services -- AD CA

Certificate Issued

The certificate you requested was issued to you.

  ○ DER encoded or ◉ Base 64 encoded

 Download certificate
Download certificate chain

The certificate will be named "certnew.cer" when you download. Be sure to give it a logical name before requesting your next certificate. Once you've got your certificate named properly, go and repeat the certificate request process for each of your other other ISE nodes.

When you have fully downloaded all your certificates, it's time to log back into each of your ISE nodes; go back into the "Certificate Signing Requests" page. Select the CSR saved and click "Bind Certificate".

Select your certificate file and click Submit. You'll be warned that the application will be restarted when you change the Admin certificate; click "Yes." Complete this task for all your ISE nodes you're going to be integrating into your cluster at this point.

Next, you'll want to import the CA certificate of the PKI the certificates you're using were generated from. This allows the ISE cluster to trust nodes as they are joined to the cluster.

ISE comes with the major public CA certificates installed but if you're using another CA, public or internal, you'll need to download the CA certificate. In a Microsoft CA go back to the CA website and click "Download CA Certificate, Certificate Chain, or CRL".

Microsoft Active Directory Certificate Services -- AD CA

Welcome

Use this Web site to request a certificate for your Web browser, e-mail client, or other program. By using a certificate, you can verify your i you communicate with over the Web, sign and encrypt messages, and, depending upon the type of certificate you request, perform other :

You can also use this Web site to download a certificate authority (CA) certificate, certificate chain, or certificate revocation list (CRL), or to of a pending request.

For more information about Active Directory Certificate Services, see Active Directory Certificate Services Documentation.

Select a task:
Request a certificate
View the status of a pending certificate request
Download a CA certificate, certificate chain, or CRL

Select Download CA Certificate (it will save again as certnew.cer so give it a meaningful name). Then browse in ISE Administration → System → Certificates → Trusted Certificates.

Select Import, and select your CA file. Ensure that "Trust for Authentication within ISE" is selected.[7]

---

[7]Depending on the PKI you're using you will likely have to import multiple certificates as part of a whole trusted certificate chain. In the case where you have a multi-tiered PKI it's recommended you import the certificates in the chain individually and not many in a PKCS file.

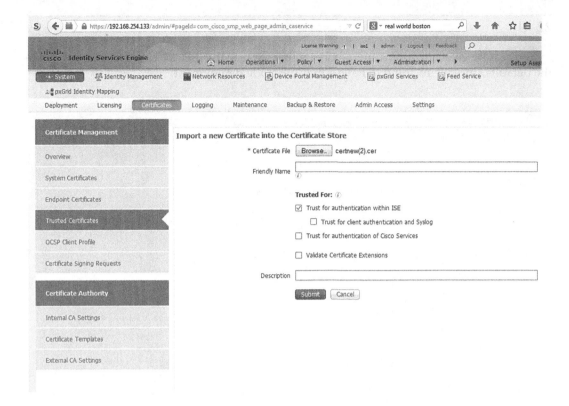

CLUSTER CONFIGURATION

Now that you've done that, you're ready to register another ISE node to your cluster:

Browse: Administration → System → Deployment
Select: Register → Register ISE Node

Enter the FQDN of the ISE node you want to join and the username/password.

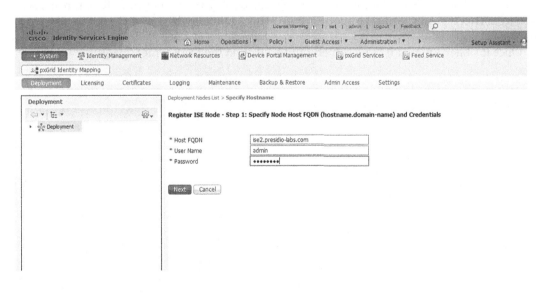

You're now given an opportunity to assign personas to the ISE node. In this case we'll take the defaults since we're going to have a two-ISE-node deployment.

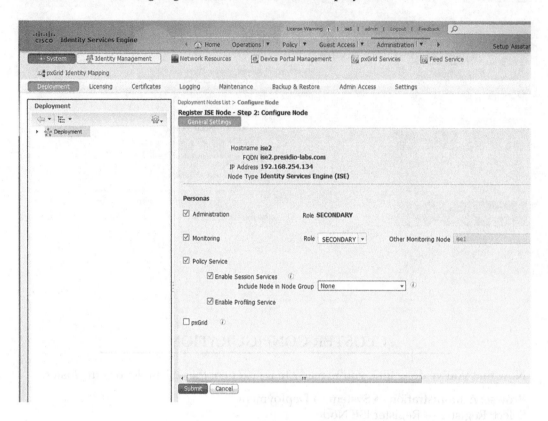

The secondary ISE node will replicate the database (DB) from the primary Admin node and a green check box will appear next to it in the deployment page; after this, it restarts its services. This typically will take about 15 min. This again may be a nice chance to take a coffee break.

Once it's back up, you'll have something like this on the Deployment page:

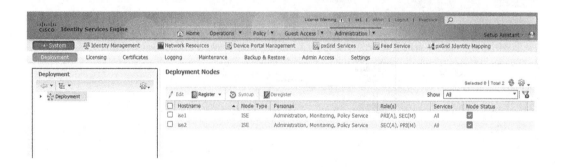

Before making the nodes do any heavy lifting it's recommended to always wait for the "Node Status" to go green indicating that all services are started and replication has completed. Once the primary and secondary Admin nodes are configured in a cluster it is typically time to install their licenses.

If you run into a situation where you are trying to integrate ISE nodes into a cluster and you're unable to join them, there are a few common things to check before you call our friends at TAC:

- Double-check your network, virtual local area network (VLAN) configuration, if the nodes are able to ping each other and that there are no missing firewall rules between the nodes.
- Be sure that your ISE nodes are resolvable to both forward and reverse in DNS and that there are no spelling errors in their hostname.
- Be sure NTP is functioning and synced.
- Validate that the primary Admin node has the trusted CA chain installed from the CA used to issue the ISE nodes their server certificates on the HTTP service.

REPLICATION OPTIMIZATION

While you're deploying ISE nodes if they're going to be in different data centers across WAN links you'll want to ensure that you have the "Endpoint Attribute Filter" feature configured. This is under: Administration → System → Settings → Profiling.

Profiler Configuration

* CoA Type:	Reauth
Current custom SNMP community strings:	•••••• [Show]
Change custom SNMP community strings:	(For NMAP, comma separated. Field will be cleared on successful saved change.)
Confirm changed custom SNMP community strings:	(For NMAP, comma separated. Field will be cleared on successful saved change.)
EndPoint Attribute Filter:	☑ Enabled ⓘ

[Save] [Reset]

The purpose of this is to allow ISE to delay replication of endpoint profiling attributes that are not used in the actual implementation of ISE policy. Unchecked, all profiling information of every client is replicated in real time. Checked, ISE will replicate only profiling data in real time that is required for the implementation of policy.

If you aren't deploying ISE across WAN links and you're inclined to replicate all profiling data in real time, feel free to leave this box unchecked.

LICENSING

ISE licensing is deceptively simple. There are several different kinds of licenses:

- VM node
- Evaluation
- Base user
- Plus user
- Apex user
- Mobility
- Mobility upgrade

Yes we did say that seven license types are actually simple. Let's break them down one at a time:

- VM node licenses are simply right-to-use (RTU) licenses you must purchase when you create ISE VMs and integrate them into your cluster. This is not a license you are required to install but you're required to procure as part of the ISE licensing agreement.
- Evaluation licensing is the licensing that comes with your ISE installation. When you install a new ISE node, it comes with a 100 user license valid for base, plus, and apex that will expire in 90 days.
- Base user license provides the basic functionality in ISE. This includes basic MAB, 802.1x authentication, Web authentication, TrustSec, and MACsec. At the time of this writing these licenses are perpetual.
- Plus user licensing includes some additional features that are not necessarily included in base. This includes Bring Your Own Device (BYOD) (NSP/CA) functionality, Endpoint Protection Service, pxGrid, and device profiling. When a device uses one of these functions in an authorization rule, a plus license is consumed along with a base license.
- Apex user license includes the most advanced features offered by ISE. These features include posture assessment and MDM integration. When a device uses one of these functions in an authorization rule, an apex license is consumed along with plus and base licenses.
- The mobility license is simply a stock keeping unit (SKU) available to provide the Apex level of functionality in ISE for VPN and wireless-only deployments but would not allow ISE functionality on a wired network. Mobility upgrade licensing can be applied to an existing ISE deployment with the mobility licensing to add wired support. These are rare.

The user-type licenses—base, plus, and apex—are consumed by ISE with concurrent authorized users. Specifically ISE will consume the license based on RADIUS accounting transactions. Once a user is authorized, and the NAD sends an accounting start message, the license is consumed based on what features were used during the device authorization. The license is released when ISE receives a RADIUS accounting stop message from the NAD.[8]

---

[8]To get an accurate license consumption it's important to have RADIUS accounting configured properly. If you believe your license count is off, always first check to make sure you don't have accounting misconfigured. If it's configured correctly, check to see if you had any NAD reboots which can cause stale license in the DB when ISE doesn't see an accounting stop message. If you do have stale licenses you believe, they will be flushed from the DB eventually, or you can call Cisco TAC and they can look in the DB for you to troubleshoot.

In any case, you have presumably already had your licenses ordered and have them in hand to install. The licenses are either PDF files or physical paperwork that have Product Authorization Keys (PAK) provided by Cisco. Go to the Cisco License portal[9] and start the process of registering them. The portal will ask you to provide a few things:

- PAK you're trying to register
- Primary Admin Unique Device Identifier (UDI)
- Secondary Admin UDI (optional)
- Accept End User License Agreement (EULA)
- End user contact information (if the person registering the license is not the end user)

The UDI information is unique information to the node (whether hardware or software). The information can be displayed on the license page of the node by browsing: Administration → System → Licensing.

Then scrolling to the bottom to see this.

Licensing Details

Administration Node	**ise1**
Product Identifier (PID)	**ISE-VM-K9**
Version Identifier (VID)	**V01**
Serial Number (SN)	**EU6ENSRSIEL**

 Help

The ISE UDI is the combination of the Product ID (PID), Version ID (VID), and Serial Number (SN) of the node. You can also accomplish the same task by issuing the following command on the CLI: show udi.

While technically adding the secondary Admin node's UDI is optional to the creation of license files, because the licenses are tied to nodes, should you have to promote the secondary Admin to primary (in the case of a catastrophic node failure) and you don't want to have to immediately relicense the cluster, adding the secondary UDI during the licensing process is recommended.

---

[9]http://www.cisco.com/go/license.

PATCHING

Before we get deep into the configuration, we think it's crucial to make sure you're running the most recent patch of ISE.

This can be counterintuitive for some old school network guys. When it comes to selecting IOS software, for years it paid off to be a laggard and only use versions of software that had been around for a while and leaving the latest and greatest release for those who have hard feature requirements or were adventurous. Those who wanted stable environments stuck with old code. In our experience with ISE the opposite may be true and the newer versions can provide a lot of stability especially when it comes to deployments with some of the more advanced ISE features. This comes down to the fact that newer mobile devices and third parties you end up integrating into can have a high feature velocity and it's helpful for ISE to be able to keep up with those device's behaviors. We recommend organizations not get beyond a few months back on patches. It's not always critical to be on the latest ISE version, but keeping up with patches buys you a lot.

First download the latest patch from Cisco Connection Online (CCO).

To actually apply patches it's pretty straightforward. In the primary Admin node browse: Administration → System → Maintenance → Patch Management

Click the "Install" button and browse to the file you downloaded. The file will be uploaded to ISE primary Admin node. The cryptographic checksum will be first run by ISE and given to you so that you can validate against what's on CCO so you can be sure that don't have a bad file.

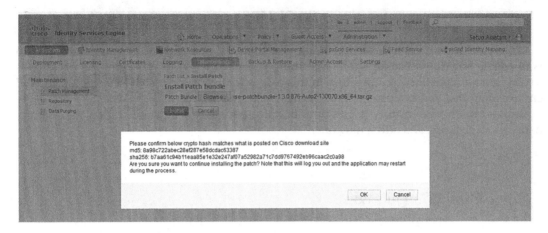

When you click "OK," ISE will first install the patch on the primary Admin node. First, you're going to be logged out. Then the ISE services on this node restart, and depending on what the patch is doing to the server it may even reboot. You won't get any warning either way but don't be surprised if the server does reboot. Once the primary Admin node is patched, ISE will deploy the patch on each node in the cluster in alphabetical order. This would typically be a great time to go get a cup of coffee or take a lunch break depending on the size of your cluster.[10]

After the first one is done you can log back into primary Admin node, browse back to the "Patch Management" page, and select your patch number and "Show Now Status." This will tell you which nodes have the patch installed on them and which ones do not. ISE doesn't have much of a progress indicator so your patience is required here; if a node reboot is not required, it can take about 10 min per node but if a reboot is required, the patch process takes much longer. Monitor the console of your ISE nodes if possible to see the progress of the node booting.

As you deploy patches on your cluster you'll also want to be aware that each patch to a particular version of ISE is cumulative, in that when patch 2 comes out, it has all the fixes that patch 1 had. If you skip a patch, because maybe you went on vacation or none of the caveats fixed interest you, that's not a big deal.

[10]You are probably wondering if there is going to be an outage when an ISE patch is deployed. The short answer is: yes; easy ISE node will have its services restarted so any services bound to those services will go down. The longer answer is: if you're deploying your policy nodes redundantly, you may end up with a very small outage as the NADs declare one ISE node dead and switch over to the other. We wouldn't encourage you to deploy a patch on a live ISE cluster in the middle of business hours, but you also shouldn't make a huge deal about deploying a patch either presuming you've deployed ISE redundantly anyway.

BACKUPS

Once you've patched ISE, the last thing you should do as part of the basic cluster setup is to enable scheduled backups. The first thing you need to do to configure ISE backups is to configure a repository. A repository in this case is a directory typically[11] hosted off the ISE environment that you can use for a few things including backups.[12]

Browse to the Repository Configuration page, which is Administration → Maintenance → Repository, and add a new one.

Repository List > **Add Repository**

Repository Configuration

* Repository Name | backup |

         * Protocol | SFTP ▾ |

Location

     * Server Name | |

              * Path | |

Credentials

      * User Name | |

       * Password | |

[Submit] [Cancel]

Give your repository a name and select the protocol you'd like to use. The protocol is the file transfer method that you're going to use to copy your backup files. These include:

- FTP
- SFTP
- TFTP
- NFS
- HTTP
- HTTPS

Then select the server name, path, and login credentials for your remote server.

I recommend you use SFTP or FTP with my preferred method being SFTP for security. If SFTP is unavailable or inconvenient, an FTP repository will work just fine for you.

---

[11]Could be the ISE local disk, but don't do that; put your backups off your ISE server.

[12]You also use repositories for ISE version upgrades.

If you select SFTP, you need to manually add the SSH server host keys on the CLI of the ISE server before you can use them. You can do that through the following command:

crypto host_key add host 192.0.2.1

where 192.0.2.1 is the IP address of your SFTP server.

Once you have your repository configured, you need to set up the schedule your backups will happen. To do that you need to browse to the backup configuration menu, which is Administration → System → Backup & Restore.

When you get there, you'll notice that there are two options for your backups. These include:

- Configuration Backup
- Operational Backup

The "Configuration Backup" option includes all the configuration of the ISE primary Admin node and the CLI information that is saved. This includes the following:

- All ISE policy
- ISE identity store configuration
- Local ISE identities and profiles
- Certificates issued by ISE
- ISE CA certificate information[13]
- Portal customizations

Without going into extraordinary minutia it includes everything on the primary Admin node but will specifically exclude logging or troubleshooting information you may see in the "Operations" menu.

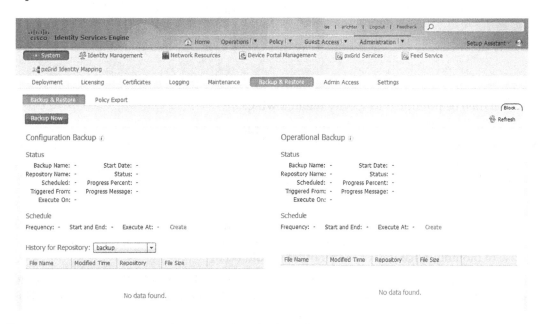

---

[13]This does not include the CA certificate private key. That has to be backed up manually. More to follow on that in Chapters 13 and 17.

To configure the backup schedule click "Create".

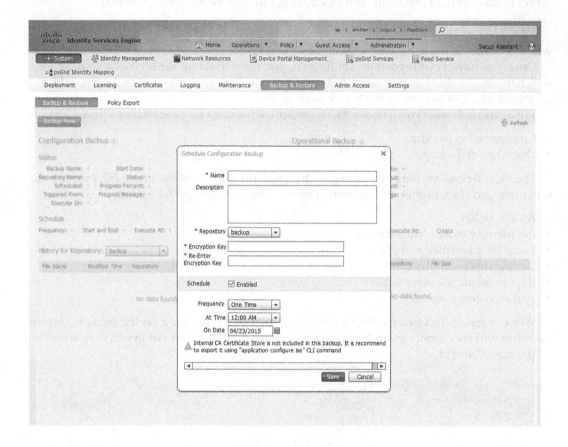

You'll then be prompted to specify the following:

- Name: This becomes the prefix for the backup file
- Description: Optional
- Repository destination
- Encryption key
- Enable/disable schedule
- Frequency (daily, weekly, monthly, one time)
- Time: Time of day on primary Admin node the backup occurs
- Day in the frequency the backup occurs: In case of weekly what day of the week; in the case of monthly, what day of the month it should occur

The "Operational Backup" configuration includes the ISE authorization logs you would see in the Operations menu and any additional troubleshooting data available there. This would include no actual ISE configuration.

So how often should one back up one's ISE cluster? That's a great question and it broadly depends on your specific configuration.

As to "Configuration Backup" weekly or monthly is sufficient depending on how often you change configuration. If you feel that you will rarely change your configuration and your profiling configuration is solid, then monthly ISE configuration backups should be sufficient. If you are often changing your ISE configuration or are often finding high turnover of profiled devices, then weekly ISE backups are probably appropriate.

With "Operational Backup" it's a little more complicated (but the configuration is exactly the same). The first question you may ask when determining how long you should keep your ISE backups is the following: Do I care about losing historical log data? If you don't care about losing historical log data (and you have no regulatory requirement to keep it), then back up the operational data infrequently or not at all. If you need to maintain you operational data with the ISE servers, then you need to determine how often you should back up the information. First examining how large your ISE cluster will scale in terms of endpoints will help you determine how often your logs are rolled on your primary monitor node per how much disk space it has. The ISE hardware installation guide in the VMware section (http://bit.ly/1LVSVdu) describes how many endpoints a cluster may manage and the interval at which the logs are lost.

At the time of this writing with ISE 1.4 if you had 10,000 endpoints and 600 GB of disk space, you may be able to keep your ISE logs for 378 days. This may seem like a really long time but you need to weigh this on the risk of what it may mean to your deployment to lose logs. For example, if you choose to back up only your small ISE deployment yearly running 3415 VMware OVAs (with 600 GB of disk space) because you have no risk of running out of disk space, it's possible that you may lose many months of data if the datastore is lost in the VMware cluster. If you choose to back up the data monthly, the risk of datastore loss is mitigated if you choose to back up your operational data more often.

If you choose to send your ISE operational logs to an external server via syslog, then there may be little reason to back up your ISE operational logs because in that case any ISE authorization logs may be backed up when your syslog server is backed up.[14]

Lastly, if you're working with Cisco TAC and want to quickly send them a copy of your authentication and authorization configurations without having to do a full server configuration backup, you have the option of sending a simple XML file of your AuthC and AuthZ policies. You can do this from the link available on the AuthC and AuthZ policy pages and browsing: Administration → System → Backup & Maintenance → Policy Export.

---

[14]Don't do double duty in deployments—if your Security Information and Event Management (SIEM) is backed up reliably, don't feel obligated to also independently back up your ISE operational logs.

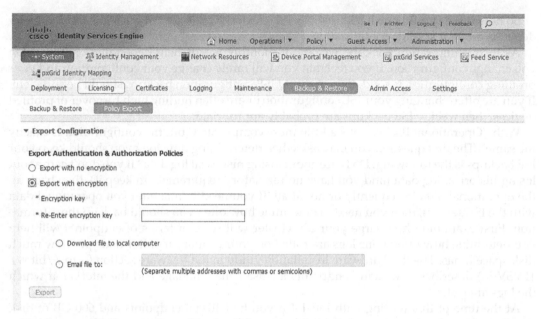

You're prompted to configure the backup with or without an encryption key. Then you'll be asked to either download the file locally or send it directly from the ISE server.

If you are convinced that there is an AuthC or AuthZ issue with the ISE configuration, then you can proactively send this to the TAC; otherwise send it only when a TAC engineer asks for it.

ACTIVE DIRECTORY

The last thing I often do when performing the basic setup tasks while building an ISE cluster is to join the nodes to the AD. Joining AD will be critical later when creating ISE policy where AD authentication or authorization is required, or if you'd like to use a domain account to login and administer ISE.

To start, browse to the AD integration portion of the ISE Admin UI Administration → Identity Management → External Identity Services. Select Active Directory.

Click "Add".

Fill out what you'd like the name of the AD will be in ISE where it says "Join Point Name." This field is cosmetic in that it will be what shows up in the policy menus. The AD domain is the actual domain you wish to join.[15]

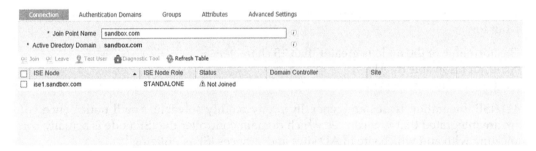

At this point you'll see that you have an AD integration available in ISE, but none of your nodes are joined so the integration isn't actually usable yet. To join ISE to AD you need to select your ISE nodes and click the "Join" button.

Join Domain   ✕

Please specify the credentials required to Join ISE node(s) to the Active Directory Domain.

* AD User Name ⓘ [   ]

* Password [   ]

☐ Specify Organizational Unit ⓘ [   ]

                                              OK   Cancel

---

[15]It's important at this point to remember, if you hadn't done it previously when you were joining your ISE nodes together in a cluster, that the nodes should be in DNS in the AD.

At this point you'll be promoted to provide an AD credential to join the ISE nodes to AD. The credential used here is used to create machine accounts that ISE will use to actually perform authentications. The credential you provide to create these accounts is not saved by ISE once you're done joining the nodes to AD so typically you wouldn't need to use a service account.

If you want to join ISE to a specific Organizational Unit (OU), you would also specify that here. This would typically be because you have policy in place where the default OU would be unacceptable.

Once you put in your credentials, presuming you've set up your cluster as we've directed so far, it should just join AD without substantial issue.

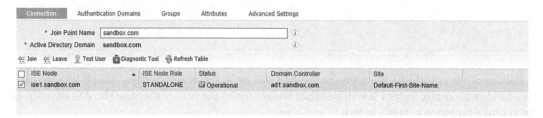

If you have issues joining the ISE nodes to AD, there are a couple of common situations to look out for:

- The hostname of the node is greater than 15 characters.
- ISE is not resolvable by AD.
- The time is offset if not synced.

AD/ISE integration issues are generally pretty readily solvable. You'll notice once your nodes are integrated that you can see which domain controller the ISE node is actually communicating with and which site in AD sites and services ISE is utilizing.[16]

The last thing that we normally do when configuring an AD/ISE integration is to select the security groups that I'm planning on using in the ISE policy.

To do this click the "Groups" menu in your AD integration.

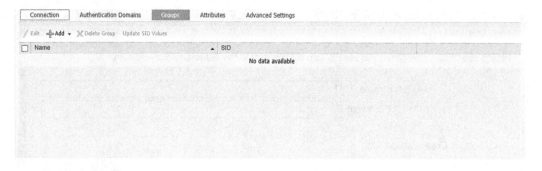

---

[16]If you're using a distributed ISE deployment across geographically dispersed data centers, it's important for speedy and reliable authentications to AD that sites and services are deployed in AD and that ISE is joined to a Domain Controller (DC) that is nearby. If you see that ISE is joined to a DC that is geographically far from the ISE node, this is a great time to call the AD administrator and ask them to double check their site configuration in the domain.

Then click "Add" and "Select from Active Directory." This will bring up a new box where you can search the domain for the groups you'd like to use.

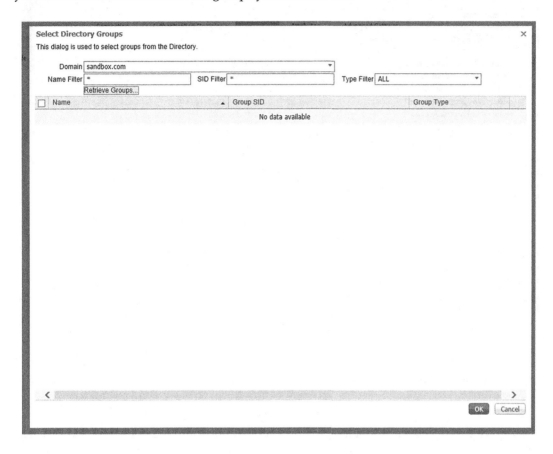

The easiest way I find is to use the "Name Filter" box and search the AD for the group name you'd like to use. The filter does allow for the use of wild card and I'll search for the built-in domain accounts and select "Retrieve Groups".

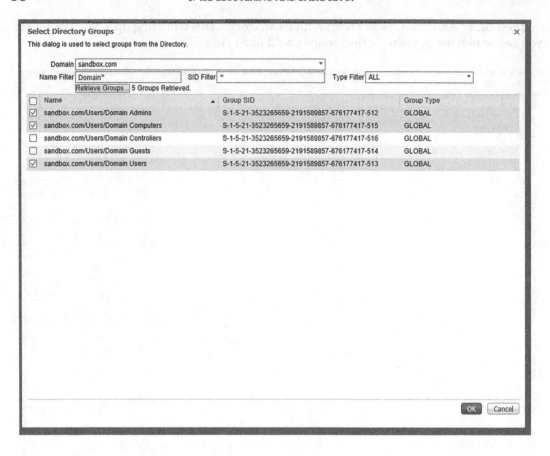

You'll see I've selected a few of the groups there that I may use in policy later and I'll click "OK."

You'll be brought back to the AD integration page and you'll see that the groups are listed there in the group list.

At this point, be sure you save because if you don't, those groups will be lost if you happen to browse away.

If you're wondering why you don't see any AD groups in your policy menus, it's likely because you haven't selected the groups in the AD integration.

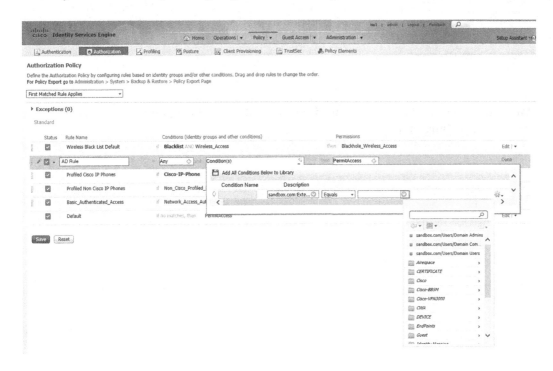

There are a variety of advanced things that you could look to do as in your deployment in the integration to AD. First, it's not uncommon for organizations to have multiple ADs for architectural, security, or historic reasons. If this is the case for your organization, you have a couple of choices:

1. ISE supports integrating directly into multiple ADs at the same time. This is often the preferred way of deploying ISE if you have the ability of joining ISE to the separate directories.[17]
2. ISE supports cross-domain authentication if the multiple ADs support full trusting. In this case you would integrate ISE into a single AD and then search for the other ADs through the domain that you've joined and authenticate and authorize through it.[18]

If you're inclined to use the Machine Access Restrictions (MAR) feature in ISE, the default aging time is 5 h.[19] Under the Advanced Settings tab this can be changed.

---

[17]This requires ISE 1.3 or later.

[18]Take time to ensure that your Cross-Domain trusting configuration is highly available so you don't experience an authentication outage should the domain trusting break.

[19]We do not recommend using MAR unless your design absolutely requires it. We won't be discussing it in detail in the policy portions of this book.

| Connection | Authentication Domains | Groups | Attributes | Advanced Settings |

▼ **Advanced Authentication Settings**

☑ Enable Password Change
☑ Enable Machine Authentication
☑ Enable Machine Access Restrictions
　　Aging Time [48] (hours) ⓘ
☐ Use Kerberos for Plain Text Authentications.

We recommend, in the case you need to use MAR, that the aging time be increased to a more reasonable time-out.

3

Authentication Methods

While configuring and designing your environment it's important to keep in mind that there are a few different authentication methodologies you're going to be using. Each of these methodologies have advantages and disadvantages and are useful in different scenarios depending on the specific functionality you're trying to achieve.

As we go through these please do take note that all of these methodologies are agnostic of the physical media that they could potentially be running on. This means that in these cases they may be either wired or wireless-type authentication methodologies. Also, the authentication communications generally happen between the client and the ISE policy node. The network access device (NAD; e.g. switch or Wireless LAN Controller (WLC) or Adaptive Security Appliance (ASA)) is participating in the communication in that it will transmit data back and forth, but it isn't necessarily an active participant and may have limited knowledge as to what is happening between the client and the server, especially if the traffic is encrypted as part of the security design.

The most basic authentication methodology that is used in ISE is MAC Authentication Bypass (MAB). Before MAB was available, when you wanted to configure your network for 802.1x authentication, you had very limited options in allowing an intelligent way to authenticate devices that did not support 802.1x authentication, like printers, and other noninteractive devices. The most popular and effective method was to not configure authentication on switchports that were connected to devices that didn't support authentication. Sometimes, VLAN access control list (VACL)-type MAC filtering provided some additional security, but it was hardly robust and didn't provide easy centralized logging or authorization.

MAB was a feature originally developed by Cisco in order to provide network administrators the ability to authenticate devices just with their MAC address to resolve this issue. You could then create a list of MAC addresses you'd like to allow on your network without doing 802.1 x authentications, have a consistent edge switchport configuration, and maintain centralized control of your edge.

The authentication process in this case is very simple.

When the switchport learns the MAC address of the device on the port (through a broadcast for Dynamic Host Configuration Protocol (DHCP) and/or Address Resolution Protocol (ARP)), the MAB process may start:

Endpoint	NAD	ISE
Packet to allow NAD to learn MAC→		
	RADIUS Access-Request→ Username: MAC Password: MAC (encrypted)	
		←RADIUS Access-Accept/Access-Reject Authorization results (VLAN, downloadable access control list (dACL))
	RADIUS Accounting-Request→ Start	
		←RADIUS Accounting-Response

It's really that simple. The NAD provides the MAC to the ISE server, and the server accepts or rejects the MAC address.

While MAB is useful, there are very few people who are going to be deploying ISE without 802.1x. Also, configuring and designing 802.1x is much more complicated, partly because the authentication methodologies provided by methodologies are so diverse and flexible. There are three Extensible Authentication Protocol (EAP) methods we're going to go over here because they're by far the most common and useful methodologies in the field. EAP is the protocol that happens over Ethernet between the client and the switch (configured on the client ultimately). The most common methods are as follows:

- Protected EAP (PEAP)/Microsoft version of the Challenge-Handshake Authentication Protocol (MS-CHAPv2)
- EAP Transport Layer Security (EAP-TLS)
- EAP Flexible Authentication via Secure Tunneling (EAP-FAST)

PEAP is a really popular EAP methodology. If asked, we would take a guess and say that PEAP is the most widely deployed EAP method. Almost every deployment uses PEAP for some use even if it's not the primary authentication methodology.

While PEAP specifically provides only an outer method of server authentication with multiple possible inner methods, the most common are the MS-CHAPv2 methods. PEAP also supports inner methods:

- TLS
- EAP Generic Token Card (EAP-GTC)

MS-CHAPv2 is popular because it's well supported with Microsoft Active Directory (AD) as the backend authentication source, and it doesn't require a lot of complicated client configuration or design. Clients simply need to be configured to pass a username/password back up to the RADIUS server.[1]

---

[1]There is a glaring disadvantage of PEAP that is largely the result of supplicant design by device manufacturers. Due to the broad lack of server certificate validation enforcement by mobile devices, it's often easy to attack PEAP-configured clients with rogue wireless networks. If you'd like to know the mechanics of this, we invite you to Google around and you'll surely find examples of how this works. If you're going to securely use PEAP as your authentication method, it's crucial to ensure your clients are properly validating the server certificates.

The PEAP/MS-CHAPv2 flow is summarized like the following:

Endpoint	NAD	ISE
EAP-Start→		
	←EAP-Request/Identity	
EAP-Response/Identity→ (username)		
	RADIUS Access-Request→	
		←RADIUS Access-Challenge Requests authentication methodology
	←EAP Challenge	
EAP-Response→ PEAP TLS Client Hello		
		←EAP-Response TLS Server Hello, server certificate
	←TLS Tunnel Build→	
		←RADIUS Request/Identity
EAP-Response/Identity→ MS-CHAPv2 credential		
		←RADIUS Access-Accept/ Access-Reject Authorization results (VLAN, dACL)
	RADIUS Accounting-Request→ Start	
		←RADIUS Accounting-Response

When working with PEAP, it's important to look at each step in the event of an authentication failure. Common reasons for PEAP authentication to fail include:

- Client cannot validate the server certificate.
  - Client doesn't have the trusted chain to verify that the certificate is valid.
  - Server certificate has expired.
  - Signature check has failed.[2]
- Server rejects the client credential.
  - Client password is incorrect or has expired.
  - Authorization of the user fails.
  - Client does not response to EAP-Identity request.[3]
  - Directory doesn't respond to password lookup in time.[4]

---

[2]The certificate signature check failure could be because the certificate is actually invalid, or the client's configuration is configured in such a way that the CA used to generate the server certificate isn't used.

[3]In wireless 802.1x authentication deployments you'll see lots of error messages where the client doesn't respond, or doesn't respond in time, or has any number of other error conditions. This is normal. Clients can be roaming, have poor supplicant software, or are out of range of Wi-Fi. Just because you're seeing lots of weird dot1x errors accumulating that look like EAP problems doesn't necessarily mean anything is actually wrong.

[4]An issue to keep in mind is that if your directory takes a really long time to authenticate the user's password, the authentication could time out. This happens occasionally to me in the field. Your options in this case are a couple fold: Make AD respond faster or increase your timeouts so AD can respond in time.

EAP-TLS, also a very popular methodology for authentication, is considered the gold standard. It has a very similar authentication flow to PEAP in that the server certificate is validated, but rather than username/password being used as the client credential a certificate is used (some call this mutual certificate authentication).[5]

The EAP-TLS flow is summarized like the following:

Endpoint	NAD	ISE
EAP-Start→		
	←EAP-Request/Identity	
EAP-Response/Identity→ (username)		
	RADIUS Access-Request→	
		←RADIUS Access-Challenge Requests authentication methodology
	←EAP Challenge	
EAP-Response→ EAP-TLS Client Hello		
		←EAP-Response TLS Server Hello, server certificate
	←TLS Tunnel Build→	
		←RADIUS Request/Identity
	←EAP-Request/Identity	
EAP-Response/Identity→ Client Certificate		
	RADIUS Response→	
		←RADIUS Access-Accept/Access-Reject Authorization results (VLAN, dACL)
	RADIUS Accounting-Request→ Start	
		←RADIUS Accounting-Response

When working with EAP-TLS, it's important to look at each step in the event of an authentication failure. Common reasons for EAP-TLS authentication to fail include:

- Client cannot validate the server.
  - Client doesn't have the trusted chain to verify that the certificate is valid.
  - Server certificate has expired.
  - Signature check has failed.
- Server cannot validate the client.
  - Server doesn't have the trusted chain to verify that the client certificate is valid.
  - Client certificate has expired.
  - Signature check has failed.

[5]Because mutual certificate authentication is used, you will negate some of the risk that AD will not respond in time because there isn't necessarily an authentication dependency outside of ISE (no username/password lookup in a directory). For this reason certificate authentication is very efficient.

- Client certificate has wrong key usages.
- Authorization of client fails.

The wrong key usage issue mentioned is an important one to consider. If a client (laptop, phone, etc.) has multiple certificates it could potentially select for use for EAP-TLS authentication, it's the responsibility of the supplicant to choose which certificate to utilize. If the client selects a certificate that cannot be properly processed by your ISE policy, this will cause an AuthC or AuthZ failure. We highly recommend reducing the number of certificates that are installed on clients where possible. Some supplicants make this easier. For example, the Apple iOS supplicant can have the certificate installed on the profile. Android allows for specific certificates to be selected on a wireless local area network (WLAN) configuration. Also the AnyConnect Network Access Manager (NAM) can help in the selection of certificates on Windows PCs.

EAP-FAST is a methodology that is not dissimilar to PEAP in its deployment, but the mechanics of how it works are different. EAP-FAST intrudes cryptographic files that provide additional functionality and flexibility to authentications; these files are called Protected Access Credentials (PACs).

The history of EAP-FAST is that it was developed by Cisco after Lightweight Extensible Authentication Protocol (LEAP) was determined to be too insecure to be feasible to many customers' implementations and at the time PEAP authentication wasn't widely available. The idea was to make an authentication methodology as simple to deploy as LEAP and as secure as PEAP. In reality when you look at the protocol, it's possible to make EAP-FAST as insecure as LEAP if you're not careful.[6]

The deployment of EAP-FAST can be a daunting protocol for the uninitiated because of its use of PACs. PACs have to be provisioned by the RADIUS server (ISE) to the clients to utilize EAP-FAST. There are three methods of PAC provisioning:

- Manually:
  - PAC files are specifically and manually installed on a client.
- Without authentication (anonymous in-band):
  - PAC files are provisioned by the server without validating the server certificate.
- With authentication (authenticated in-band):
  - Server identity is validated and a TLS tunnel is created before any PAC provisioning occurs.

It's possible to use the first two without issues if your deployment will tolerate limitations, but there are deployment issues:

- Manual: It can be labor intensive to manually provision certificates to create individual PAC files for each machine/user you wish to authenticate and then install those everywhere they need to go. This is nuts; no one really does this.

---

[6]LEAP is a depreciated authentication methodology. We're not going to go over it. If you have it out there, it's time to move on to something else.

- Anonymous in-band: It's possible, since PAC provisioning occurs without TLS server authentication. This provides an attack vector for attackers to harvest client credentials similar to PEAP authentication attacks. This may be mitigated to some extent on wired deployments because in-band snooping may be physically challenging, but, regardless, anonymous in-band provisioning is not generally recommended.

For these reasons, we highly recommend authenticated in-band PAC provisioning as the only suitable methodology wirelessly. On wired networks where snooping is less of a risk anonymous in-band provisioning is plausible but you'd want to design your authentication conditions and results to ensure that anonymous in-band provisioning would not occur over wireless medium.

Without going into an incredible amount of detail into how the cryptography works, which for most IT guys isn't relevant, let's go over how PACs are created and their purpose. PACs are simply secrets generated by ISE used to generate a TLS tunnel between the client and the ISE in order to facilitate security for the inner method of client authentication. ISE generates a master PAC at the time of installation and periodically through the life of the deployment (by default once a week). ISE will provision an authenticated user or computer a PAC file generated from the master PAC. When the master PAC outlives its Time to Live (TTL), a user is provisioned a new PAC on its next successful authentication.[7]

In the provisioning and establishment of that mutual cryptographic authentication, the same inner methodologies that PEAP provides can be utilized by EAP-FAST. What is the point of EAP-FAST in modern deployments? Great question.

In our world deploying ISE, Cisco has extended EAP-FAST to allow multiple tunneled authentication inner credentials (EAP-Chaining) to allow both the user and the computer authentication to happen in one single authentication transaction. We'll go over EAP-Chaining in Chapter 12.

Here is an overview of an EAP-FAST exchange with authenticated in-band PAC provisioning:

Endpoint	NAD	ISE
EAP-Start→		
	←EAP-Request/Identity	
EAP-Response/Identity→ (username)		
	RADIUS Access-Request→	
		←RADIUS Access-Challenge Requests authentication methodology
	←EAP Challenge	
EAP-Response→ EAP-FAST TLS Client Hello		
		←EAP-Response TLS Server Hello, server certificate

[7]A specific point here must be noted that the identity provided by the PAC must match the identity provided by the inner method; otherwise authentication will fail.

	←TLS Tunnel Build→	
		←RADIUS Request/EAP Payload TLV/EAP Inner Method Challenge
EAP-Response→ Inner Method Response (response with both username and password)		
		← EAP-Request/EAP-FAST-MS-CHAPv2 (success)
EAP-Response→ EAP-FAST-MS-CHAPv2 (success)		
	←PAC provision→	
		←EAP-Success
	RADIUS Accounting-Request→ Start	
		←RADIUS Accounting-Response

Once a PAC has been provisioned, subsequent authentications can reuse the previously provisioned PACs making authentication more efficient. Here is a summary of that flow:

Endpoint	NAD	ISE
EAP-Start→		
	←EAP-Request/Identity	
EAP-Response/Identity→ (username)		
	RADIUS Access-Request→	
		←RADIUS Access-Challenge Requests authentication methodology
	←EAP Challenge	
EAP-Response→ EAP-FAST TLS Client Hello (client sends PAC)		
		←EAP-Response TLS Server Hello, Server PAC
	←TLS Tunnel Build→	
		←RADIUS Request/Identity
EAP-Response/Identity→ MS-CHAPv2 credential		
		←RADIUS Access-Accept/ Access-Reject Authorization results (VLAN, dACL)
	RADIUS Accounting-Request→ Start	
		←RADIUS Accounting-Response

When working with EAP-FAST, because username/password-type authentication is what is in use, common failure types are very similar to PEAP. Common reasons for EAP-FAST authentication to fail include:

- Client cannot validate the server certificate.
  - Client doesn't have the trusted chain to verify that the certificate is valid.
  - Server certificate has expired.
  - Signature check has failed.
- Server rejects the client credential.
  - Client password is incorrect or has expired.
  - Authorization of the user fails.
  - Client does not response to EAP-Identity request.
  - Directory doesn't respond to password lookup in time.

ISE also provides for robust client authentication via web authentication. The most common and robust functionality provided by ISE is called central web authentication (CWA). The "central" part of the authentication refers to the fact that ISE is providing the website for the authentication and that part of the functionality is centralized. A legacy feature called local web authentication ("LWA") refers to local in that the web authentication occurred on the NAD (switch or WLC).[8]

In CWA a MAB operation is actually used, but rather than the station being directly authorized, a web page is presented to the client for authentication. The client is required to pop up a browser and enter a username/password. If that authentication is successful, the ISE policy node will issue a CoA[9] to the NAD to remove the requirement for web authentication redirection, and then allowing the client network access. It's important to note that while other methodologies don't require direct IP communication between the client and the ISE policy node, CWA does require the client to authenticate directly through the web browser and as such all other network requirements for that browser to work must be met. The client has to have an IP address, it has to resolve the ISE node, and it has to have a functioning web browser. Presuming those requirements are met, here is a summary of CWA authentication:

Endpoint	NAD	ISE
Packet to allow NAD to learn MAC→		
	RADIUS Access-Request→ Username: MAC Password: MAC (encrypted)	
		←RADIUS Access-Accept/ Access-Reject Authorization results: web authentication URL (ISE policy node), redirect access control list (ACL), dACL (if IOS)

[8]LWA is generally depreciated in most modern deployments and we won't be directly addressing it.

[9]CoA is really a lot of the magic behind many of the advanced ISE features available to us. It's discussed in RFC 5176 for reference. Get used to seeing and using CoA.

	RADIUS Accounting-Request→ Start	
		←RADIUS Accounting-Response
	NAD applies ACL and redirects URL to switchport in case of wired authentication, or client association in the case of WLC	
Web browser open: request web page→		
	←Web redirect packet changing URL to ISE Policy Services Node (PSN)	
Client browser to ISE PSN→		
		←ISE PSN web page response
Client authenticates with username/password in browser→		
		←RADIUS CoA Request: reauthenticate
	RADIUS CoA-ACK→ RADIUS Access-Request→ Username: MAC Password: MAC (encrypted)	
		←RADIUS Access-Accept/ Access-Reject Authorization results (dACL)

You'll notice that the CoA type requested is reauthentication. This is because when ISE reauthenticates this endpoint, it knows that the web authentication was just successful and it's changing that endpoint's authorization and no longer requires it to have the web authentication redirect in place.

When you're having difficulty with configuring CWA, there are a few different common issues to look at:

- Client cannot validate the server certificate.
  - Client doesn't have the trusted chain to verify that the certificate is valid.
  - Server certificate has expired.
  - Signature check has failed.
- The client cannot connect to the ISE policy node.
  - Client doesn't have an IP.
  - Client is unable to resolve the ISE PSN hostname used for authentication.
  - Access control prevents access to the ISE policy node (dACL, firewall policy, or airspace ACL are all possible issues).
- Server rejects the client credential.
  - Client password is incorrect or has expired.
  - Authorization of the user fails.

CHAPTER

4

Policy Elements

What are policy elements? If we were to think of rules within ISE (be it AuthC, AuthZ, Profiling, Posture, etc.) as recipes, then policy elements are all the ingredients that go into the dish.

Let's start off with the first area of the policy elements section: dictionaries. Dictionaries are the area you will use the least (but are the most basic elements so it's important to understand them); they are used to define attributes that will be used within conditions you build. Out-of-the-box ISE provides a huge number of attributes for all of the supported devices and chances are you won't need to customize this section at all.

To navigate to policy element dictionaries you need to browse: Policy → Policy Elements → Dictionaries.

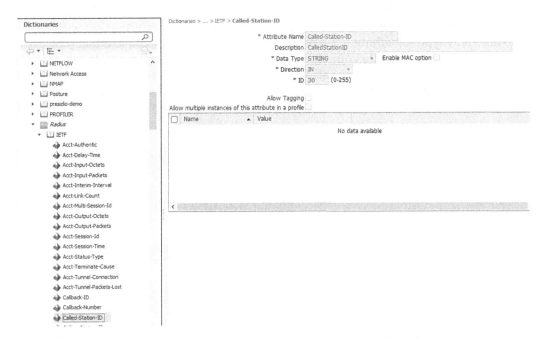

Looking at the existing attributes you will see the Dictionary files provide four: a name, an attribute number, direction, and the data type. Name and description are pretty straightforward. The attribute number is how ISE will identify what to take out of the RA-DIUS request/response it gets from the NAD. The direction is used if you want to pull out an attribute that is being sent only in a certain direction, like if the incoming value is what you want because the outgoing value gets changed, but if you are dealing with that then typically you will already know. Most of the time setting the direction to "BOTH" is the easiest way to get an attribute and probably is what you want to do. Data type tells ISE the format of the data the attribute contains; is it a string, is it just a number, or is it an IPv4 address? Setting this value correctly will help ISE use the data so make sure that you get it correct or you could have conditions you make based off of it not work how you expect.

Now that we've got our dictionary attributes covered (or just attributes for short), let's get into some of the real meat of policy elements with conditions. Conditions take a single or set of attributes and define what they should or shouldn't be. There are six categories that conditions can fall into and they are the general areas of ISE that makes use of them: Authentication, Authorization, Profiling, Posture, Guest, and Common. As the name would indicate, Common is the only one that has conditions that can be used across all of the other five major areas. Right now the only common attributes are Date/Time ones.

Authentication, Authorization, and Guest conditions are all very similar so we'll cover them at the same time.[1] Under each you will be able to select either a simple or a compound condition. Simple conditions are just that: simple! They contain the name of the condition, the attribute you are checking, the operator (equals, not equals, contains, greater than, less than, etc.) which will depend on the attribute you pick, and then the value. Like the operator, the value field can also change depending on the attribute you select; picking an attribute that has selectable options such as the Session:PostureStatus[2] attribute will allow you to pick values from a drop down but selecting Network Access Server (NAS)-Port will require you to manually type something in.[3] A compound condition allows you to either pick existing simple conditions or create your own on the fly in order to check multiple attributes at one time instead of just one. You can also quickly add conditions you create under the compound area as a simple condition if you find yourself using it a number of times or feel you might use it again in the future without having to get out of the compound condition area.

[1]By default there are very few simple conditions available since you would most typically build them in your rules from dictionaries. When you go to look at the default simple conditions, don't be surprised when there aren't many there.
[2]For the uninitiated here, posture status can be compliant, noncompliant, or unknown.
[3]This would be like selecting the specific interface an authentication is coming from: IE gigabitEthernet 0/1.

The normal view permits you to only check multiple conditions so that they all match or any of them can match and for some of the sections, such as Authentication, that is the only option. However, Authorization and Guest conditions let you go into an advanced mode that allows you to create complex conditions that include parenthesis/and/or/not conditions. You can access the advanced mode by creating a new compound condition, clicking either of the attribute addition options, and then clicking the Advanced View Grid button in the top right of the condition building area. Using this mode gives you an extremely flexible way to check conditions and is limited to only what you can think of in terms of what to check. For advanced Authorization conditions there is also a feature to validate the expressions you build so you know they will work, at least if the raw logic checks out anyway—your conditions could still never match if you don't build them right.

The Profiling and Posture conditions sections are much different since they each focus on their own special/specific conditions. The Profiling conditions let you pick from a prebuilt (read: not customizable) list of attributes that can be used during Profiling to determine what a device is. Looking over the extensive list you can see some of the included attributes and how they are used; OUI, hostname, and User-Agent are big ones. The Posture conditions have nine subtypes that are mainly used for creating the different types of checks that are used in the posture process. You also have the option of having access to some limited (compared to the full list) dictionary conditions that can be used to check things such as AD group, service set identifier (SSID), location, agent type, OS, EAP method, etc., to target Posture a bit more. Both of these areas have their own sections in the book and are covered in much more detail there.

The last policy elements area is Results. Results are things that happen after a condition matches (or doesn't) and tell either a NAD or ISE how to handle that event. Since the types of results for each section vary greatly we'll cover them one at a time.

Authentication results are probably the simplest ones of the group; they define what authentication protocols are allowed for a client when their request comes into ISE. Out-of-the-box ISE gives us the "Default Network Access" result that is used in the prebuilt AuthC policies. This result gives you a basic set of allowed protocols, allows both MAB and 802.1x to work in most environments, and is generally a good place to start for all deployments. If you have some special use cases or you decide to build a very granular AuthC policy, you might also want to limit the protocols that can be used. For example, you might want to set a preferred EAP type of PEAP for clients in one location and EAP-TLS in another or maybe tweak PAC TTLs differently per identity store. You can also obviously edit the existing default and disable some methods if you don't use them; it's a good security practice to disable things you aren't using anyway!

Authorization results have three subtypes: Authorization Profiles, Downloadable ACLs, and Inline Posture Node (IPN) Profiles.[4] The Downloadable ACL results contain dACLs that you will select within your Authorization Profiles so it's a good idea to define them first since it will save you time and prevent you from having to switch back and forth while building results. dACLs are formatted like named ACLs (not numbered ACLs!) and accept the same format, including remarks. When you save the dACL, ISE will validate it to ensure it will correctly apply and warn you otherwise. If it doesn't validate, you can use the "Check DACL

---

[4]The latter we won't bother with; the support of CoA within newer ASA-OS versions removes any need for IPNs so discussing them isn't really worth it.

Syntax" area to see which line isn't correctly formatted as well as get the acceptable options that can be used. Finally, Authorization Profiles get passed to the NAD authenticating the client after they successfully match an AuthZ rule. Defined in here you have a list of common tasks (dACL to use, VLAN, Web Redirection, Reauthentication Timeout, etc.) as well as the ability to define custom attributes that will also be passed as part of the profile. Most of the time the common tasks will cover everything you need to do, but if you ever want to do a custom URL redirection profile you would need to manually define the attributes for it.

Profiling results have two types and only one is really relevant: Exception Actions and Network Scan (NMAP) Actions. NMAP Actions are basically all predefined for you and the only possible condition you could create would be one that triggers all the scan types if NMAP is run against an endpoint; chances are the actions that are there will work for your needs. Exception Actions have three prebuilt results there already so that ISE can take actions when endpoints are deleted, profiled, or change profiles. These options will be fine for almost all deployments but if you are doing some more advanced Profiling then you can define custom results to force devices to have specific Profiling policy assignments which allows you to take further corrective actions (different AuthZ rule maybe).

Posture and Client Provisioning results are fairly complicated, and, like previously stated for the conditions section, are covered extensively in Chapter 14.

BREAKDOWN OF COMPOUND CONDITION

By default ISE ships with a couple of compound conditions you will make extensive use of and those are the wired/wireless dot1x/MAB conditions. You will use these in AuthC in order to target Identity Source Sequences (ISSs) or in AuthZ to target different permissions for different access types, but what's behind these rules? Honestly, nothing too complicated. They each contain two RADIUS checks that check the Service-Type and NAS-Port-Type of the incoming RADIUS sessions. If you go to Policy → Policy Elements → Conditions → Authentication → Compound Conditions and then click "Wired_802.1x," you should see something similar to Figure 1.

Authentication Compound Condition List > **Wired_802.1X**

Authentication Compound Conditions

* Name | Wired_802.1X

Description | A condition to match an 802.1X based authentication requests from Cisco Catalyst Switches

Condition Name	Expression			AND
◇	Radius:Service-Type	Equals	Framed	AND
◇	Radius:NAS-Port-...	Equals	Ethernet	

We can see that this rule is checking for a Service-Type of "Framed" which indicated that it's an 802.1x authentication and also checks the NAS-Port-Type to make sure it's of type "Ethernet" which then indicates it's a wired connection. If we take a look at the "Wireless_MAB" condition in Figure 2, we'll see a similar layout just with different checks.

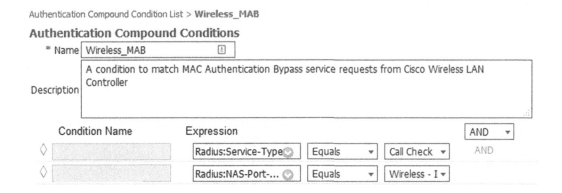

Here we are checking the same Service-Type and NAS-Port-Type RADIUS attributes but we're looking for "Call Check" (to indicate MAB) and "Wireless—IEEE802.11" (to indicate wireless, obviously) instead. The "Wireless_802.1x" and "Wired_MAB" are similar but just check for their respective media and service types instead.

CHAPTER

5

Authentication

Remembering that ISE is a RADIUS server it's important to remember that we're going to go through the AAA steps: authentication, authorization, and accounting.

To start the AAA process the first thing you have to do is steer the RADIUS authentication (AuthC for short) to the correct identity store or stores. Good ISE design calls for AuthC rules to be as short as is plausible so don't try to get too fancy.

The idea is not to try to decide what to do with the user (what kind of access they should have); that's the role of the authorization ruleset later. Rather the purpose of the authentication is to establish who is asking for network access. Different methods of authentication require us to look in different identity stores for the correct type of authentications.

Anatomy of authentication policy includes the following items:

- Conditions
- Network Access Service
- Identity store

    Conditions would be the network access methodology or specific authentication types:

- Dot1x, wired or wireless
- MAB, wired or wireless
- VPN
- Web authentication
- Certificate authentication
- MS-CHAPv2 authentication

    Network Access Service can be one of two things:

- Allowed Protocols
- RADIUS proxy

Most typically it's "Allowed Protocols" where there is a list of allowed RADIUS authentication methodologies. This is important because it allows you to specify which authentication methodologies are allowed in your RADIUS authentication in ISE. Examples of these include (but are not limited to):

- Password Authentication Protocol (PAP)
- CHAP

- EAP-TLS
- PEAP:
  - EAP-MS-CHAPv2
  - EAP-GTC
- EAP-FAST:
  - EAP-Chaining

To configure an authentication result, or allowed protocol, you need to browse to the authentication policy element: Policy → Policy Elements → Results → Authentication → Allowed Protocols.

A lot of deployments don't require a lot of customization here. There are a few nondefault customizations that you should consider when you're designing ISE authentication.

When deploying EAP-Chaining, this method is not enabled by default so if you want to use it you will need to enable it under EAP-FAST.

▾ ☑ Allow EAP-FAST

    EAP-FAST Inner Methods
    ☑ Allow EAP-MS-CHAPv2
      ☑ Allow Password Change Retries [3] (Valid Range 0 to 3)
    ☑ Allow EAP-GTC
      ☑ Allow Password Change Retries [3] (Valid Range 0 to 3)
    ☑ Allow EAP-TLS
      ☐ Allow Authentication of expired certificates to allow certificate renewal in Authorization Policy
       ⓘ
    ◉ Use PACs   ◯ Don't Use PACs
    Tunnel PAC Time To Live   [90]   [Days ▾]
    Proactive PAC update will occur after [90]   % of PAC Time To Live has expired
    ☑ Allow Anonymous In-Band PAC Provisioning
    ☑ Allow Authenticated In-Band PAC Provisioning
      ☑ Server Returns Access Accept After Authenticated Provisioning
      ☐ Accept Client Certificate For Provisioning
    ☑ Allow Machine Authentication
      Machine PAC Time To Live   [1]   [Weeks ▾]
    ☑ Enable Stateless Session Resume
      Authorization PAC Time To Live   [1]   [Hours ▾] ⓘ
  ☑ Enable EAP Chaining
☐ Preferred EAP Protocol [LEAP   ▾]

If you are implementing a feature that requires anonymous in-band PAC provisioning, it is not recommended to allow this kind of provisioning wirelessly. You can restrict this by configuring multiple allowed protocols where anonymous PAC provisioning is allowed over wired media where session snooping is unlikely, and disallowed wirelessly.

Lastly, the preferred EAP Protocol field is an option that is used when you need to propose an EAP method to a client that is authenticating to a network. In operations of a well-designed enterprise network, nearly all clients will have their supplicant configured with a specific EAP method (EAP-TLS or PEAP). In some cases, where a client is connecting to a network for the first time, it's helpful to propose a specific EAP method for them to use.[1]

If your authentication store is actually in another RADIUS platform, you would need to configure the authentication policy to use an external RADIUS service as your Network Access Service. This is a less common, but not an uncommon deployment.

The last piece of an ISE AuthC rule are the identity stores (presuming you're not using a RADIUS proxy); this is where one should actually look for the credential to determine if the identity is to be validated.

---

[1]If you have LEAP enabled for a specific design reason, LEAP will be the default preferred EAP protocol. In that case, we'd recommend picking a more secure EAP method like PEAP as your preferred method so you don't accidentally get gratuitous LEAP authentication.

These stores include the following:

- Internal endpoints
- AD
- LDAP
- Certificate authentication profile
- Identity source sequence (ISS)

Let's look into some examples of what ISE policy most typically looks like.

Typically the foundation ISE authentication policy rule starts with MAC authentication by-pass rules. In all common cases, the policy will look like this where all MAB authentications will be authenticated with the internal ISE endpoint database.[2]

When you go to design and deploy ISE, it's important to keep in mind how your users/devices are going to supply credentials for authentication. This is going to guide how you design your ISE rules. For example, if you expect the majority or all of your dot1x authentications to require AD credentials, then you need to create AuthC rules to steer those dot1x authentications to look for username/password credentials in AD. This is really typical in a deployment that uses PEAP.

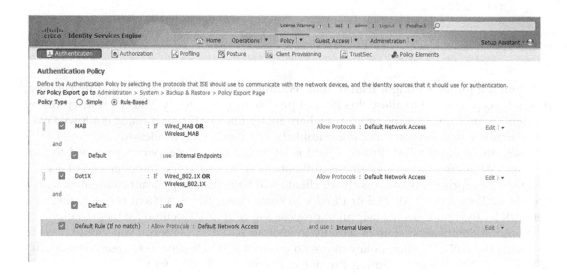

In some designs authentications will largely be certificate authentications and in that case the specific certificate authentication profiles become important to differentiate between both mechanisms used to issue the certificate (AD enrollment vs. Simple Certificate Enrollment

---

[2]Endpoints for MAB may be stored in an LDAP database. This is not a common deployment so we're not covering it but it could be practical for your specific environment.

Protocol (SCEP)). In that case a certificate authentication profile needs to be referenced. What's the easiest way to do that? Making a subrule inside the dot1x authentication ruleset is often the best way.

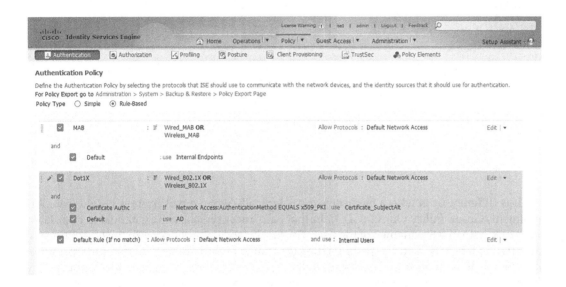

The rule flow allows for multiple results in this case. Inside the dot1x ruleset, if the authentication method is x509, the authentication is steered toward our certificate authentication profile. If it's not, authentication is then directed toward AD. This technique gets useful when you have to worry about multiple different authentication types and getting them to the right place at the right time.[3]

Let's take a look at this in a little more detail.

When a certificate is issued via the ISE BYOD process or through another SCEP service, the Common Name (CN) of the certificate contains the username of the end user who requested the certificate. The Subject Alternative Name (SAN) and OU fields can be filled with various other pieces of useful information depending on the exact issuer. In ISE's case the SAN is populated by the calling station ID, which is the MAC address of the device requesting the certificate. In the case of the certificate issued by ISE then, the AuthC policy should be configured such that those certificate authentications are directed to a certificate authentication profile that specifies the CN as the principal x509 username.

---

[3]Obviously, you'll also have to be sure that the trusted chain of the client certificate is installed for client authentication in the trusted certificate store in ISE. Otherwise ISE will not be able to successfully trust the client certificate.

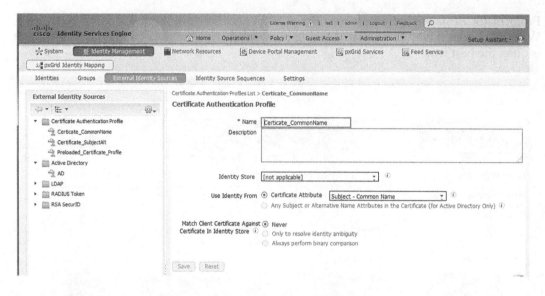

This is different from where the username is typically when a certificate is issued from AD enrollment/Group Policy Object (GPO). In that case, most typically the CN field is populated with the "$firstname $lastname" of the user. The SAN is then populated with the User Principal Name (UPN) which is the fully qualified directory name of the user (e.g., mmaroney@presidio-labs.local for domain presidio-labs.local). In this case, it's important to create the AuthC policy where a certificate authentication profile specifies the SAN field as the principal x509 username.

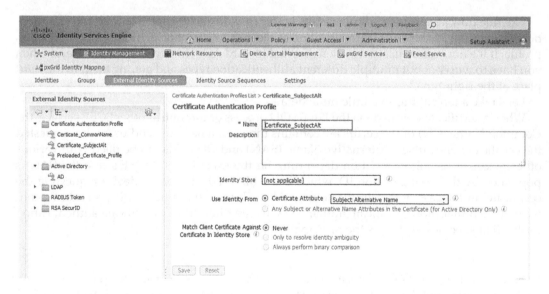

How is this best way to set the certificate authentication profile to accomplish this differentiation you ask? Well, that's a great question; you need to understand exactly how your certificates are deployed. In our example the UPN will be used in the SAN field for the AD certificate enrolled devices. That means each SAN will contain "presidio-labs.com." I can then construct a rule with the "CONTAINS" operator for the contents of the certificate SAN name.

Then, any other certificates issued from other places (e.g., SCEP) would typically have the username in the CN and that can be referenced pretty reliably.

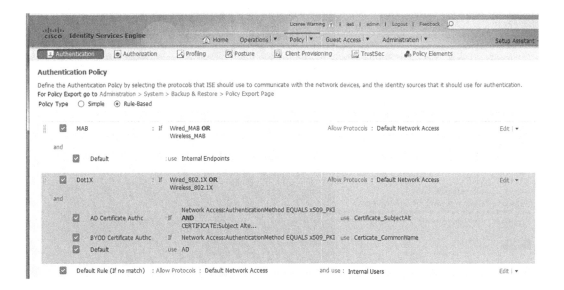

Your deployment may be wildly different than this depending on your requirements. If you prefer to identify which certificate has been issued by the CA, that's entirely possible just by modifying the conditions. You can use a variety of mythologies to match the correct authentication methodology you're looking to use. We've used regular expressions very effectively looking for the correct style of string in different certificate attributes. It's important though to understand the contents of the certificates you're deploying to be able to properly authenticate devices with them.

Now that we've hammered on certificate authentication for a while, what if you wanted to authenticate the default dot1x rule to multiple places potentially? Presuming you're looking to authenticate usernames and passwords to multiple identify stores, the easiest way to do that is through an ISS. In the case that you may look in multiple different identity stores you can use an ISS. The ISS is literally a list of identity stores you can use to chain together.

Let's look at a specific example; if you're doing wireless dot1x authentication and you know that most of your users will be in AD, but you want to use some users locally configured in the ISE user identity database and you want to keep your authentication rules simple, you can have your AuthC rules reference the ISS where the dot1x authentications first look in AD, and if the user is not found, internal ISE user identities is checked second.

To configure this you're simply creating yourself an ISS with the relevant identity sources, and giving it a reasonably intelligible name. This ISS is then referable in your identity store configuration of your authentication rule.

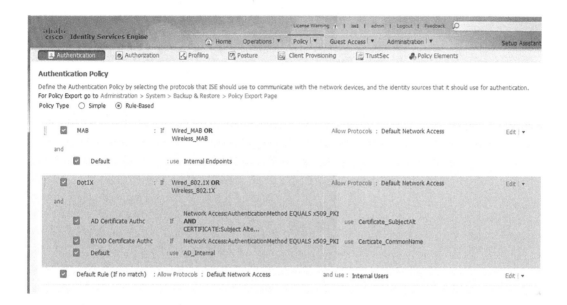

This configuration gives you a fair amount of flexibility. The bulk of your dot1x username/ password authentications will be properly steered toward AD, but should you then need to reference users who are not in AD, you would have to add users to the internal ISE user database.[4]

As you can see, authentication policy isn't about applying policy to live users, rather just identifying where we should figure out who they are. Now that we've done that, we can move on in our policy and look at what kind of access we may permit them.

---

[4]While this configuration is great as an example, if you have a really large AD to search, it may not be plausible to use local authentication second to AD in reality if the time it takes to search AD exceeds a RADIUS or EAP timeout. If you have a large AD environment in your enterprise, then you should have your ISS utilize the smaller identity source before you ask it search AD.

Authorization

Authorization (AuthZ) policies are the core of ISE functionality. The purpose of the authorization ruleset is to establish what kind of network permissions are assigned to a user or device. Permissions in terms of network permissions can take the form of a variety of things.

The anatomy of an authorization rule is very simple. Typically we recommend that you utilize conditions identifying some basic parameters about the connectivity being used including:

- Connectivity medium:
  - Wired
  - Wireless
  - VPN
- 802.1x:
  - Password-based AuthC
  - Certificate-based AuthC
- Does the device match a profiling policy (printer, phone)?
- Is the MAC address a member of a static group (security badge reader, custom device)?
- Does the authentication have RADIUS attributes we care about?
  - Calling station ID
  - Called station ID
- What network device is the session originating from?
- What directory security group does the user belong to?
- What user identity group does the user belong to?
- What kind of information from the client certificate is available (if they're authenticating with X509 credentials)?
  - Certificate issuer
  - Subject attributes (O, OU, State, City, Country)
  - Subject Alternative
  - Certificate expiration

Conditions come in two flavors when you're configuring them in the authorization policy.

- Existing conditions
- New conditions

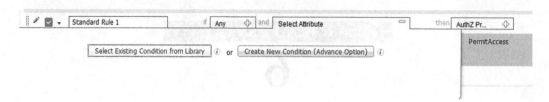

Let's start with the new condition. The new condition option is where you select a single attribute you'd like to match, things like what you see in the above list of possible attributes. To start with, let's match PEAP in our authentication.

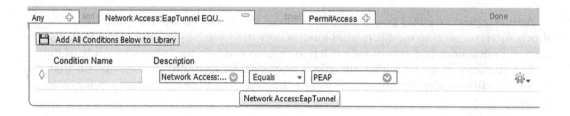

You're thinking you want to be more specific in your authorization rule and you want to add a second condition to the rule. If you select the gear, and select Add Attribute/Value, this is exactly like selecting "Create New Condition" from a new rule .

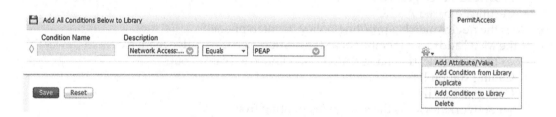

In this case we select "Domain User" membership in AD.[1]

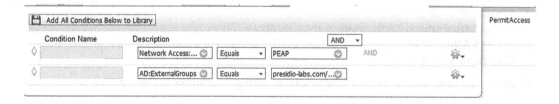

[1]Notice that there is a Boolean operator available there. The conditions by default have an "AND" operator on them all, but it's possible to use the "OR" operator, but it is not on by default (you won't use OR operators very often).

This would be really typical of a wireless authentication deployment for simple AD username/password authentication to ISE but to add a convenient way to specify that this was in fact a wireless authentication, and that it was done via 802.1x, we can use some of the ISE built in compound conditions. On the same gear icon select "Add Condition from Library"; this is exactly the same as clicking "Select Existing Condition from Library".

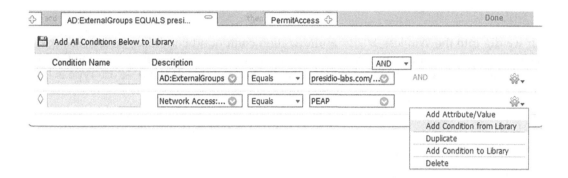

There are a few options when you go with library conditions. They include:

- Simple conditions
- Compound conditions
- Time and date conditions

If you want to see what is available by default, or configure additional simple or compound conditions, you can browse to them via: Policy → Policy Elements → Conditions → Authorization.

Time and date conditions are available in: Policy → Policy Elements → Conditions → Common.

Simple conditions are the same types of conditions you're selecting in Attribute/Value. They are just preconfigured in the policy library and given names the administrator may find useful.

Compound conditions are commonly used in authorization rules as they provide a nice short way of making authorization rules specific. They have multiple simple conditions in them to allow us to shorten our authorization rules.[2]

In our case here, we want to specify that the authorization rule is used for wireless 802.1x sessions by using the "Wireless_802.1x" compound condition. There are also a couple of other conditions added to handle AD group matching and EAP type.

---

[2]Nearly all of the authorization rules we have/will write include a compound condition specifying what media is being used to authenticate (wired vs. wireless) and what authentication methodology they're using (MAB vs. dot1x). We highly recommend using these compound conditions heavily in your deployments.

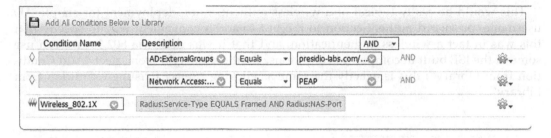

If we dig into the Wireless_802.1x authorization compound condition, we can see that it has its own two subconditions. One is that its used RADIUS Service-Type is framed, which is typical for 802.1x authentication. We can also see that the RADIUS NAS-Port-Type is IEEE 802.11.

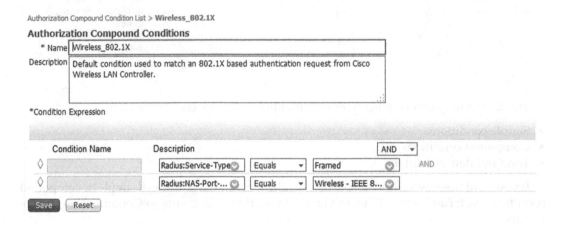

This allows us to be more specific quickly and easily in our AuthZ rules without as many specific lines of conditions in each rule we write.

After selecting those conditions our rule looks like this.

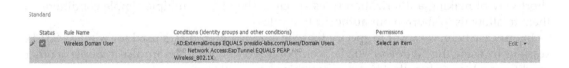

But we're not done yet since we've configured some conditions in a rule; we still need the "then" side of an AuthZ rule. In our basic policy, let's start out by permitting the wireless domain users to get on the network on the default VLAN the WLC WLAN is configured for and select "PermitAccess" under the "Standard" profiles menu.

This will return a simple Access-Accept RADIUS message to the WLC. With this policy we're validating that the users are using 802.1x, wireless networking, they're using PEAP as their EAP type, and they're members of domain users. To conform to best practices we also added a "domain computers" policy in case the endpoints are configured for machine authentication. The end result of the policy is the following.

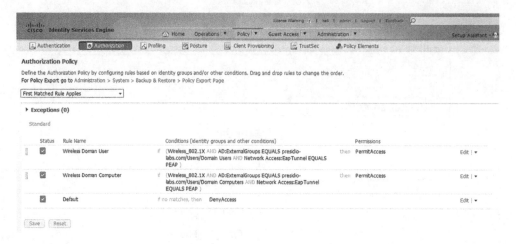

Like we said earlier, it is critical to identify the media with which a device is connecting because that media will have different options in what kind of permissions you're applying to that user session. As you can see, wireless, wired, and VPN have a variety of different options. You want to be sure you're applying the correct result to the correct media so that the user gets the correct permissions you're looking to apply.

Permissions in our case are found: Policy → Policy Elements → Results → Authorization → Standard Profiles.

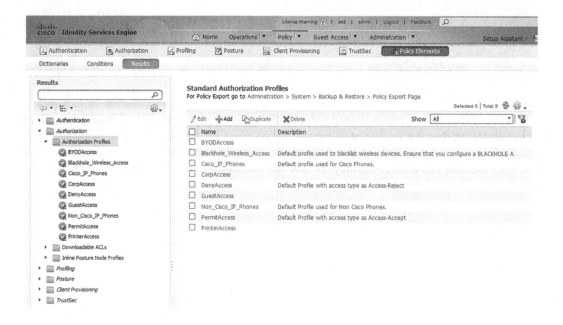

Each profile allows you to set what results are to be passed back from ISE to the NAD. You can set a variety of permissions per authorization profile, not just one. An example of that may be that you want to override both the VLAN *and* the ACL, and that is definitely allowed. When you go into an authorization profile, you can see that there are four sections:

- The top has Name, Description, Type (accept or reject), and service template.[3]
- Common tasks: These are check boxes for various settings you may push.
- Advanced Attitudes Settings: These are menu-driven override settings determined by Cisco to not be "Common."[4]
- Attributes details: This is a list of the exact RADIUS attributes and variables being sent to the NAD.

For wired implementations the most commonly deployed overrides are as follows:

- Downloadable ACL
- VLAN
- Voice domain
- Session timeout
- Web authentication (central web authentication (CWA))

Downloadable ACLs are a pretty sweet feature ISE provides to us. A downloadable ACL is an ACL configured in ISE that is sent down the specific switchport that the user is on. This means if you don't have to configure this ACL on all your switches, and when you want to make an update to the ACL, you only have to update it in ISE.[5]

dACLs are configured in the menu: Policy → Policy Elements → Results → Authorization → Downloadable ACLs.

When you configure them for wired access, there are a few things to think about:

- They support extended named ACL IOS syntax, including source port, destination port, and IP host/subnet.
- The source address of the ACL must be "any."
- They do not support some operators including the following: time range and log.

This leaves you loads of flexibility; if you want to send a result down to a client that prevents a client from getting to a specific subnet, the ACL configuration is really straightforward. Let's take a look at a really common dACL we use.

---

[3]We're not going to go over service templates. Nothing against them *per se* but they're not commonly used.
[4]Don't be afraid of using these. If you feel like one works for you deployment, you should definitely give it a shot.
[5]Remember that a dACL is applied only when a user is authorized. If you update a dACL in ISE, the update will not be pushed down. You will have to wait for clients to reauthenticate, have to disconnect them at the NAD (shut/no shut), or need to issue them a CoA to force them to reauthenticate.

Downloadable ACL List > Deny_Internal

Downloadable ACL

    * Name | Deny_Internal |

  Description [   ]

* DACL Content
```
 1 permit udp any eq bootpc any eq bootps
 2 permit udp any any eq 53
 3 deny ip any 10.0.0.0 0.255.255.255
 4 deny ip any 172.16.0.0 0.15.255.255
 5 deny ip any 192.168.0.0 0.0.255.255
 6 permit ip any any
 7
 8
 9
10
```

▸ Check DACL Syntax

[Save]   [Reset]

The ACL, when applied to a client session, does the following:

- Permits Bootstrap Protocol (BOOTP)/DHCP to function so the client can get an IP address
- Permits DNS so the client can look up DNS names
- Denies all access to RFC1918 networks
- Permits anything else

For users who don't have public IP space in their local area network (LAN) (which is frankly still pretty common) this restricts the device with this ACL from connecting to anything internally other than DHCP and DNS and allows them to access the internet.

Another popular dACL looks like this.

Downloadable ACL List > High_Impact

Downloadable ACL

    * Name | High_Impact |

  Description [   ]

* DACL Content
```
 1 permit udp any eq bootpc any eq bootps
 2 deny ip any any
 3
 4
 5
 6
 7
 8
 9
10
```

▸ Check DACL Syntax

[Save]   [Reset]

Here the dACL is doing the following:

- Permits the client to obtain an IP address
- Denies all other traffic

In the case where you want to deny access to devices on the wired network, but still obtain profiling information about a device I find this to be a really useful dACL. Obtaining DHCP information provides you information about the device's operating system (OS) and potentially its manufacturer and this could be useful in applying appropriate policy. I often use this ACL instead of simply denying network access to a device that otherwise doesn't match our policy.[6]

Using them in an AuthZ rule is as simple as referencing the dACL you created in a standard authorization profile.

Authorization Profiles > **New Authorization Profile**
Authorization Profile

    * Name `Wired_Deny_Internal`

    Description `                                        `

    * Access Type `ACCESS_ACCEPT`

    Service Template ☐

▼ **Common Tasks**

☑ DACL Name   `Deny_Internal`

Frankly, as you create dACLs in your environment we encourage you to get creative as appropriate. Use of dACLs provides you a boatload of flexibility and functionality in wired enforcement.[7]

[6]One thing that makes some people crazy is that while we're denying the device from basically any network resource and typically I'd call this a failed authentication, from ISE's perspective the authentication will be successful and we're just giving it a result that denies it almost complete network access and the log entry in ISE will be green, rather than red, for a truly failed AuthC or AuthZ.
[7]dACLs are applied on the switchport in hardware generally so the length of the dACL is dependent on the hardware resources available on the switch platform and some platforms such as the Cat3750 allow you to adjust how ternary content-addressable memory (TCAM) resources are allocated. In those cases it's recommended you allocate more resources to security where possible (run "sdm prefer access" from config mode).

You'll also notice that there is a dACL syntax checker; we highly recommend you use this every time before you click Save on your dACL. If you have a syntax error in your dACL, the authentication on the port will fail when a bad ACL is downloaded by the switch. This can be very difficult to troubleshoot.[8]

If dACLs don't work for you and you have specific VLANs you need specific users or devices on, you can absolutely override the VLAN and set the VLAN of these sessions. There are a few things to note about doing VLAN overrides:

- You can override the VLAN ID (number) or the VLAN name. This is really important because you have a specific VLAN, say for printers, you specify that you want printers on the VLAN named "Printer" and the specific number could be different for every switch or site.[9]
- You cannot override the VLAN to the VLAN that is configured on the port as the voice VLAN. This is not supported.
- When you perform a VLAN override, the running configuration will show the original VLAN configured. This is because the configuration is not changed but the switch functionality is. If you execute "show interface gig 1/0/1 switchport" or "show authentication session interface gig 1/0/1," you will see the VLAN ISE has configured while the running configuration has not changed.
- You need to take care when performing VLAN overrides as a device is profiled that it's given a chance to get the IP on the VLAN it's assigned. Let's take the example of a policy where printers are assigned to a specific printer VLAN while everything else is left on the port's default VLAN. When you plug in a new DHCP printer to the network before ISE has a chance to establish any profiling details on the device, it will be assigned to the default VLAN. Once ISE processes the device's profiling information, ISE will send a CoA to the switch and ask the device to reauthenticate the MAC address (presumably with MAB). The switchport will reauthenticate and be assigned a different VLAN but the printer won't know that it needs to obtain a new IP address because it's on a different subnet. The printer will either have to have its port disconnected and reconnected or need to be rebooted so that it requests a new IP on the correct subnet.

Configuring a VLAN override is also done in an authorization profile.

---

[8]If you do have to troubleshoot this, we recommend starting with "debug radius" on the switch command-line interface (CLI) and the culprit should show itself quickly.
[9]If you're doing VLAN override, it's highly recommended you standardize on overriding the name rather than the ID.

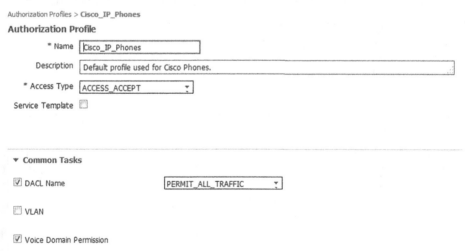

When this authorization result is applied to an AuthZ rule, the device is set on the VLAN named "Printer."[10]

The next common wired result is the "voice domain permission." This permission is set so that the MAC address of the phone that is assigned the AuthZ result is put on the voice VLAN. In this configuration you'll notice that ISE does not set the specific VLAN ID or name that should be used for voice. In this case the switch allows the phone on the VLAN the switchport has configured for voice. This is important to remember because in configurations where voice VLAN is used for E911 or the like, ISE remains independent from any of that functionality. Have the voice guys set the voice VLAN they'd like and we can just allow their phones on that VLAN they'd like. The default Cisco IP Phone rule looks like this.

---

[10]While VLAN override is a popular feature and many users find it to be a compelling enforcement mechanism, using it does not in itself actually change resulting security design. This is because overriding a device's VLAN does not inherently change their network access permissions. To change network access permissions with VLAN override you have to either have an ACL on an upstream router or use firewall policy based on the source subnet to apply access policy. If you're going to be applying policy with either of those methods, then definitely VLAN override is a good choice; if you're not otherwise applying security policy based on VLAN membership, VLAN override may not be a worthwhile effort.

Session timeout is a fairly popular option that needs to be used carefully.[11] It is used to determine how long a device may remain authenticated on a switchport before it must perform authentication again. The default is that session does not time out and once a device is authorized it may remain there until the device disconnects, switch reboots, or a CoA is issued for the device.

▼ **Common Tasks**

☑ Reauthentication

                             Timer| 1800   (Enter value in seconds)

Maintain Connectivity During Reauthentication | RADIUS-Request   ▼ |

☐ MACSec Policy

Session timeout is configured in seconds and the default value when timeout is enabled is 1800 s. If you wish to allow the device to remain connected during the reauthentication, then select "RADIUS-Request." If you would prefer the device to be disconnected while reauthentication is occurring, select "Default."

Lastly on wired AuthZ results, a popular and common result is CWA. There are a few different types of web authentication that provide for a few different functions:

- CWA: Standard web authentication user login
- Device Registration: Registering the MAC to an identity group
- Native Supplicant Provisioning: NSP BYOD
- Posture Discovery: Provisioning of posture agent and discovering an endpoint's posture state
- MDM: Mobile device management onboarding

In our example we'll be focused on the standard CWA. Applying a CWA result for a session has a few requirements:

- You must configure a dACL to restrict what a device may access before authentication completes. This typically restricts access of the endpoint to only resources required to actually connect to the website to do the login.
- You must configure the web portal they will use to log in.
- You must configure a redirect ACL on the switch that governs the traffic that is redirected to the ISE node. Typically this is only HTTP or HTTPS traffic not destined to the ISE PSN.

---

[11]We recommend using session timeout on wireless sparingly because typically once a session is authorized, we normally want to leave it there and not mess with the user/device. Occasionally we'll use session timeout in a monitor mode deployment to limit the amount of time a device may stay in the monitor mode result but we rarely find session timeout on wired dot1x sessions to be really useful.

Let's look at the dACL first. The device needs to be able to do the following to perform a web authentication:

1. Obtain an IP address via DHCP.
2. Resolve hostnames via DNS (specifically the hostname of the ISE policy nodes they will be using to log in).
3. Connect to the web server on the ISE policy nodes that hosts the web authentication pages. This web server runs on port 8443. In the case of our example our PSNs are 192.168.254.133 and 134.

Downloadable ACL List > **WebAuth**

Downloadable ACL

* Name   `WebAuth`

Description

* DACL Content

```
 1 permit udp any eq bootpc any eq bootps
 2 permit udp any any eq 53
 3 permit tcp any host 192.168.254.133 eq 8443
 4 permit tcp any host 192.168.254.134 eq 8443
 5 deny ip any any
 6
 7
 8
 9
10
```

▶ Check DACL Syntax

Authorization Profiles > **Webauth**

Authorization Profile

* Name   `Webauth`

Description

* Access Type   `ACCESS_ACCEPT`

Service Template ☐

▼ **Common Tasks**

☑ DACL Name   `WebAuth`

☐ VLAN

☐ Voice Domain Permission

☑ Web Redirection (CWA, MDM, NSP, CPP)

Next we'll select the web page that we'll be assigning to the client. In our case we'll be using the default sponsored guest Webauth page. If you wanted a customized page, you'd select it in the Value drop down.

Authorization Profiles > **Webauth**
Authorization Profile

* Name	Webauth
Description	
* Access Type	ACCESS_ACCEPT
Service Template	☐

▼ **Common Tasks**

☐ Voice Domain Permission

☑ Web Redirection (CWA, MDM, NSP, CPP)

| Centralized Web Auth ▼ | ACL | WEBAUTH-REDIRECT | Value | Sponsored Guest Portal (defa ▼ |

☐ Display Certificates Renewal Message
☐ Static IP/Host name

Lastly for CWA, you need to have the redirect ACL set correctly. That is the "ACL" setting in the Web Redirection setting in the AuthZ profile. The redirect ACL is an extended named ACL configured in the switch that governs what traffic is redirected to the web authentication website. The ACL in our case works in reverse of what we're used to. A deny statement will prevent a packet from being redirected, and a permit statement will allow the switch to redirect a session to the ISE server.

```
ip access-list extended WEBAUTH-REDIRECT
 deny udp any eq bootpc any eq bootps
 deny udp any any eq domain
 deny tcp any host 192.168.254.133 eq 8443
 deny tcp any host 192.168.254.134 eq 8443
 permit ip any any
```

Looking at the webauth ACL, we are excluding all traffic we need for web authentication to occur properly, and with a permit any at the end, any other traffic may be subject to web authentication redirection.

For wireless access we can easily provide similar functionality as wire sessions on Cisco AirOS but with slightly different syntax. The different syntax is required simply because wireless controllers running the Cisco AirOS run differently than Cisco IOS switches.[12] The following are common authorization policy results used on wireless infrastructure:

- Airspace ACL
- Airspace interface
- Quality of Service (QoS) profile
- Web authentication (CWA)
- Session timeout

Airspace ACL is an ACL configured on the WLC. The ACL is configured statically on the WLC and simply referenced by the ISE policy.

---

[12]We're not going to cover converged access because it is not currently broadly deployed but its syntax is comparable to the wired syntax described in this chapter.

Without getting into the details of the functions of the airspace ACL there are a few things that are important to remember about them:

1. They are stateless.
2. They impact traffic bi-directionally.
3. They have scalability limits to 64 rules.

Applying the airspace ACL via ISE to a user session applies the ACL to just that user session. It does not affect other user sessions on the same VLAN.

Setting this attribute is simple. Select the Airspace ACL Name common task, and type on the name of the ACL. Keep in mind that if you misspell the ACL name, the user authentication will fail.

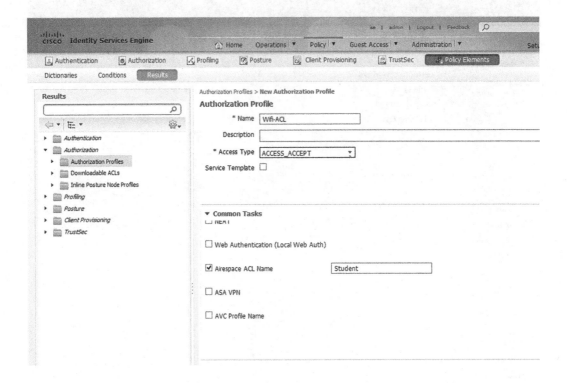

Like overriding a VLAN on a wired LAN, the same functionality is available for override on a Cisco WLC but instead of overriding the VLAN ID you will be using the airspace interface override feature. Like using a VLAN name rather than ID in case the VLAN ID is different between switches, if you have multiple WLCs, you may have multiple VLANs associated the different controllers. If you have configured the airspace interface the same between your different WLCs, you can have different VLANs associated to each WLC potentially.

On the WLC here is where you may configure each airspace interface.

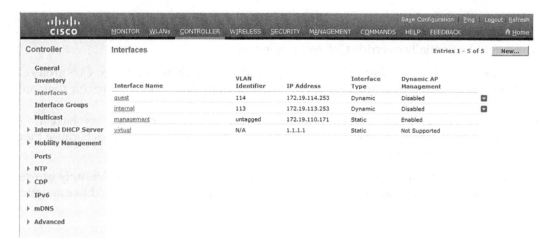

Inside ISE the override is actually configured as an advanced task. You need to browse the tasks Airspace → Airspace Interface Name. Then you may manually input the name of the airspace interface you'd like assigned to the session.

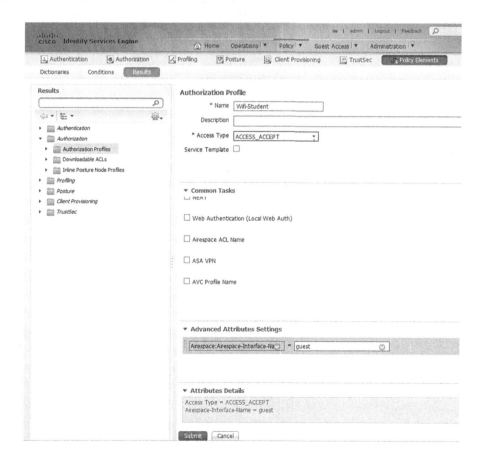

While typically on wired networks there are very limited use cases for differentiated QoS functionality, on wireless differentiated QoS configuration is much more common. Use cases where you'd potentially override QoS features include:

- Wishing to limit the number of WLANs deployed and configure per device QoS profiles. Giving wireless phones Platinum QoS while maintaining Silver QoS profiles for standard PCs.
- Configuring lower QoS profile levels for nonbusiness critical users. When you have a WLAN with mix of users, some users may be provided Bronze QoS profiles because they are less critical for business.

Like airspace interfaces, airspace QoS level is also an advanced attribute. Simply browse through Airspace → Airspace-QoS-Level and then assign the QoS profile you'd like assigned to the session.

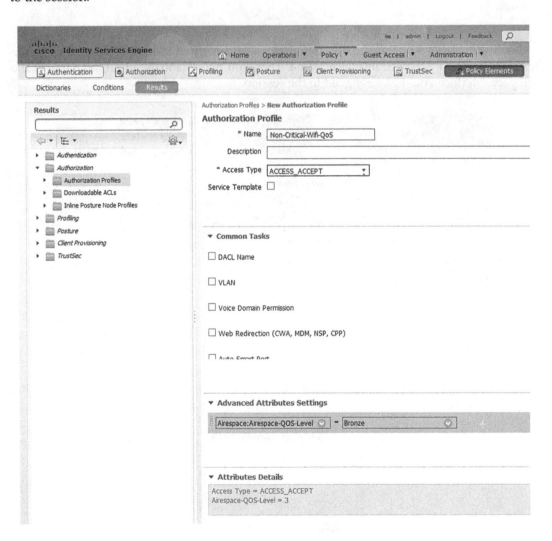

Wireless CWA is a really common implementation configuration when you're configuring ISE services because CWA is used in almost every guest or BYOD or posture deployment. It's configured very similar to how it's configured in a wired switch environment with the difference being how the ACLs are implemented. First, because we're implementing this on a WLC there is no dACL to configure. You only need to configure an airspace ACL that will both provide redirect functionality and also restrict network access while prior to CWA authentication.

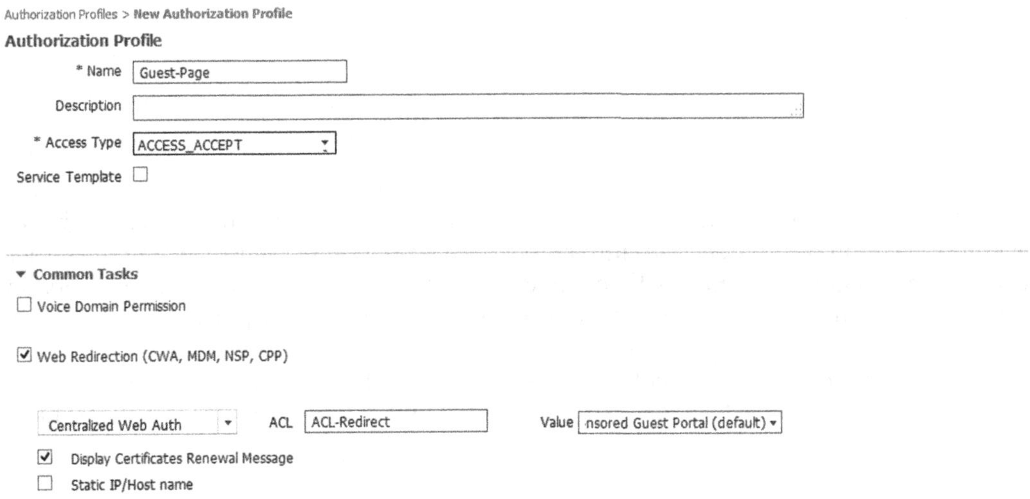

Authorization Profiles > **New Authorization Profile**
Authorization Profile

* Name   Guest-Page

Description

* Access Type   ACCESS_ACCEPT

Service Template ☐

▼ **Common Tasks**

☐ Voice Domain Permission

☑ Web Redirection (CWA, MDM, NSP, CPP)

    Centralized Web Auth ▼   ACL ACL-Redirect   Value nsored Guest Portal (default) ▼
    ☑ Display Certificates Renewal Message
    ☐ Static IP/Host name

In this case we've specified "ACL-Redirect" as the ACL governing this CWA page and because it's a guest CWA redirect we need to allow only the ports and protocols that will enable a client to connect to the ISE PSN (172.19.110.164): DHCP, DNS, and the port the ISE web server servers CWA guest pages (8443).[13]

[13]When you're performing other kinds of CWA redirect actions such as NSP or posture client provisioning, you'll need to enable other TCP and User Datagram Protocol (UDP) ports (8905 and 8909) but the fundamental configuration is the same whatever you happen to be using CWA for.

Access Control Lists > Edit   `< Back`   `Add Ne`

General

Access List Name   ACL-REDIRECT

Deny Counters   0

Seq	Action	Source IP/Mask	Destination IP/Mask	Protocol	Source Port	Dest Port	DSCP	Direction	Number of Hits	
1	Permit	0.0.0.0 / 0.0.0.0	0.0.0.0 / 0.0.0.0	UDP	DHCP Client	DHCP Server	Any	Inbound	0	☑
2	Permit	0.0.0.0 / 0.0.0.0	0.0.0.0 / 0.0.0.0	UDP	DHCP Server	DHCP Client	Any	Outbound	0	☑
3	Permit	0.0.0.0 / 0.0.0.0	0.0.0.0 / 0.0.0.0	UDP	DNS	Any	Any	Outbound	0	☑
4	Permit	0.0.0.0 / 0.0.0.0	0.0.0.0 / 0.0.0.0	UDP	Any	DNS	Any	Inbound	0	☑
5	Permit	0.0.0.0 / 0.0.0.0	172.19.110.164 / 255.255.255.255	TCP	Any	8443	Any	Inbound	0	☑
6	Permit	172.19.110.164 / 255.255.255.255	0.0.0.0 / 0.0.0.0	TCP	8443	Any	Any	Outbound	0	☑

Lastly on the wireless common authorization results is session timeout. Even though we'll cover this we don't recommend you implement it because mobile clients naturally reauthenticate with much greater frequency than wired clients; forcing them to authenticate every few hours is often pointless since their sessions don't last that long anyway. If you have a specific use case where you require sessions to not last more than X seconds, select the reauthenticate button under common tasks and enter a value in seconds. If you are going to select a session timeout, then you should set a value that is longer than the period you believe a client should be working.[14]

▼ **Common Tasks**

☑ Reauthentication

Timer `1800`   (Enter value in seconds)

Maintain Connectivity During Reauthentication `RADIUS-Request      ▼`

☐ MACSec Policy

[14]Setting this value on wireless deployments can additionally be problematic for the scalability of your ISE cluster. If you're forcing clients to reauthenticate at a high interval, you will be forcing ISE to consume more resources for more authentications for the same number of clients. Do use this feature sparingly.

Last, but certainly not the least, important medium for authorization results is VPN. With ASA VPN there are a few common results we use to enforce network access policy:

- Downloadable ACL
- Group policy

Downloadable ACL is really popular because it works very similar to the wired dACL results we talked about a few pages ago. These allow you to apply an ACL directly to the user's VPN session without having to necessarily have the ACL configured on the ASA. The main difference in configuring the ACL for ASA implementation versus IOS is that ASA by default don't use wild card masks; standard netmasks are used. For those who have trouble with wildcard syntax this is often a welcome reprieve. In the next example we permit DNS, deny access to 10.0.0.0/8, and then permit all traffic.

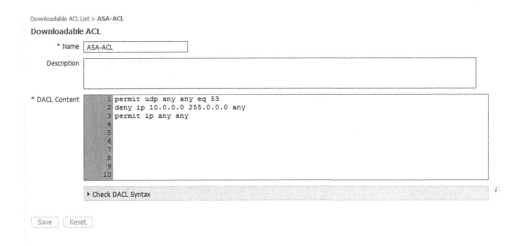

If you are inclined to use wildcard network masks in your dACLs with an ASA, the ASA will allow wild card masks but they have to be explicitly permitted with the following command:

```
hostname(config)# aaa-server ISE protocol radius
hostname(config-aaa-server-group)# aaa-server ISE host 172.19.110.164
hostname(config-aaa-server-host)# acl-netmask-convert wildcard
```

Without that the ASA will attempt to auto-detect when a wildcard is used, but this may not be effective depending on what mask is used specifically.

The other common authorization result in ASA is the group policy. When you're looking for maximum flexibility in manipulating your VPN users, the group policy is the gold standard in customization. With group policy you can manipulate the following:

- Split tunneling
- Split DNS
- Static VPN filters
- Statically assigning a VLAN ID
- Possible allowed VPN tunnel protocols
- Session timeouts
- Proxy settings

And more.[15] To configure some of these features the first thing you need is to create a group policy on your ASA:

```
group-policy VPN-Users internal
group-policy VPN-Users attributes
 dns-server value 8.8.8.8
 vpn-tunnel-protocol svc
 default-domain value presidio.com
```

Then specify the group policy in the "ASA VPN" field under common tasks as shown in the screen shot.

Authorization Profiles > **New Authorization Profile**
Authorization Profile

* Name   ASA-Group-Policy

Description

* Access Type   ACCESS_ACCEPT

Service Template ☐

▼ **Common Tasks**
☐ NEAT

☐ Web Authentication (Local Web Auth)

☐ Airespace ACL Name

☑ ASA VPN   VPN-Users

☐ AVC Profile Name

▼ **Advanced Attributes Settings**
Select an item =

[15]Typically we use group policy when there is a need to specify the tunnel configuration (full or split) or we need to override webvpn-type settings between groups of users. Other configurations are totally fine in your group policy but some of them are less useful in actual network access enforcement. Your mileage may vary.

This result will assign that group policy to your VPN user who is authenticating through your ISE.

So that is the mechanics of writing basic ISE AuthZ rules. The real challenge of creating an AuthZ policy is not just the simple rules, but how to create a ruleset that works cohesively without having incorrectly matching rules.

For a new user of ISE, authentication rules pose a design challenge that we hope to help with over the course of the next few pages. There is a huge amount of flexibility offed by ISE in deploying network authorization. That's nice when you get used to it, but during initial deployments the level of flexibility can be overwhelming. As we break down writing AuthZ rules, we need to think about what we really care about in a user session, identify the major components of what matter to our policy, and apply them in a sensible order.

Well-written ISE AuthZ rules have a few components. They identify what media was used to authenticate (wired/wireless/VPN), what authentication method was used (dot1x, MAB, PAP for VPN), and the directory group membership for a user that you're looking to authorize. Additionally, you'd want to specify any other pertinent information that can be useful in differentiating a specific authentication from another. That would be things like EAP method or perhaps a specific location:

- Corp
- BYOD
- Guest
- Profiling
- Phones

By default ISE AuthZ rules are read and applied in a first match manner. Meaning that when a request comes in, each rule is evaluated top down. Once an AuthZ rule is found that contains conditions that exist in the authorization request, processing is stopped and the result is sent to the NAD, a log entry is created, and accounting is started. For this reason it's important that when you create your authorization profiles, you ensure that they are specific enough that you're confident you won't be applying incorrect results to an authorization request.

A few common examples of these and strategies to avoid them include:

- It's possible to accidentally match the results for domain users when a guest username overlapped with a username that exists in AD. This is more common when you're using common names such as "msmith" that could match any number of people in a large environment. Looking at the AuthZ policy below, if a guest user happens to have the same username as a domain user, the AuthZ rule for corporate access would be matched.

Standard

Status	Rule Name	Conditions (identity groups and other conditions)	Permissions	
✓	Wireless Corp User	if AD:ExternalGroups EQUALS presidio-labs.com/Users/Domain Users	then CorpAccess	Edit | ▼
✓	Wireless Guest	if GuestType_Daily (default)	then GuestAccess	Edit | ▼
✓	Default	if no matches, then DenyAccess		Edit | ▼

- Solution: Use the RADIUS called station ID to match the SSID name for guest user authorizations along with specific compound conditions around how authentication should happen, or derive the guest username from their email. The example below validates the methodologies of the corporate user auth, and the guest user, and what SSID the guest user is using. More on this in Chapter 9.

Status	Rule Name	Conditions (identity groups and other conditions)		Permissions	
☑	Wireless Corp User	if (Wireless_802.1X AND AD:ExternalGroups EQUALS presidio-labs.com/Users/Domain Users AND Network Access:EapTunnel EQUALS PEAP)	then	CorpAccess	Edit | ▾
☑	Wireless Guest	**GuestType_Daily (default)** AND (Wireless_MAB AND Radius:Called-Station-ID CONTAINS GuestSSID)	then	GuestAccess	Edit | ▾
☑	Default	if no matches, then DenyAccess			Edit | ▾

- Matching a domain PC authorization rule with a nondomain mobile device. This is very common when you neglect to specify the authentication methodology required to determine if the device is corporate owned. In our example here we have AuthZ rules that would cause our EAP-TLS authenticated corporate users to also match the BYODAccess permission because we have nothing that specifically would exclude them from matching that rule. More on this in Chapters 12 and 13.

Standard

Status	Rule Name	Conditions (identity groups and other conditions)		Permissions	
☑	Wireless BYOD	if (Wireless_802.1X AND AD:ExternalGroups EQUALS presidio-labs.com/Users/Domain Users)	then	BYODAccess	Edit | ▾
☑	Wireless Corp PC	if (Wireless_802.1X AND AD:ExternalGroups EQUALS presidio-labs.com/Users/Domain Users AND Network Access:EapAuthentication EQUALS EAP-TLS)	then	CorpAccess	Edit | ▾
☑	Default	if no matches, then DenyAccess			Edit | ▾

- Solution: Ensure you're specifying the authentication methodology as specifically as you can. For example, corporate PCs should be authenticating with certificates while mobile phones should be authenticating with username/passwords; you should specify the authentication method as x509 for corporate devices. If BYOD devices also use certificates, be sure to identify which CA was used to issue the certificate to ensure you're identifying the device correctly. In our case below, we're specifying which CA is issuing our certificates and this allows us to determine the correct authorization profile to use per device type. More on this later in Chapters 12 and 13.

Standard

Status	Rule Name	Conditions (identity groups and other conditions)		Permissions	
☑	Wireless BYOD	if (Wireless_802.1X AND AD:ExternalGroups EQUALS presidio-labs.com/Users/Domain Users AND Network Access:AuthenticationMethod EQUALS x509_PKI AND CERTIFICATE:Issuer - Common Name CONTAINS Intermediate CA - ise1)	then	BYODAccess	Edit | ▾
☑	Wireless Corp PC	if (Wireless_802.1X AND AD:ExternalGroups EQUALS presidio-labs.com/Users/Domain Users AND Network Access:EapAuthentication EQUALS EAP-TLS AND CERTIFICATE:Issuer - Common Name NOT_ENDS_WITH Corp Issuing CA)	then	CorpAccess	Edit | ▾
☑	Default	if no matches, then DenyAccess			Edit | ▾

- Using a profile that matches only on OUI instead of matching another authorization profile later on. Some profiles, for better or worse, may be matched only via OUI. These are useful for things like printers (HP or Xerox) and may be required to use if DHCP or Simple Network Management Protocol (SNMP) can't be assured for higher profiling fidelity. So you're using these profiles to set your HP printers on the correct printer VLAN. If you're not careful, it may be possible for HP corporate laptops to match this profile if you fail to specify MAB as required for printer/profiling policy. In the example below, if a PC has an HP OUI, it's possible to match the printer profile even if it authenticates with dot1x because the HP device profile rule is above the dot1x ruleset.

Standard

Status	Rule Name	Conditions (identity groups and other conditions)		Permissions	
☑	Printer	if HP-Device	then	PrinterAccess	Edit | ▾
☑	Wireless Corp PC	if (Wired_802.1X AND AD:ExternalGroups EQUALS presidio-labs.com/Users/Domain Users)	then	CorpAccess	Edit | ▾
☑	Default	if no matches, then DenyAccess			Edit | ▾

- Solution: Ensure you have robust profiling information available including DHCP. Profiling policies should typically be below corporate dot1x authorization policies as the dot1x policies may be more specific and more easily matched. Also because each media provides for different methodologies for enforcement, you should create authorization rules and results for each potential use case you're looking to apply. Looking at the policy below, this issue would not be encountered because both the printer rule is below the dot1x rule and the printer rule requires MAB as part of its conditions.[16]

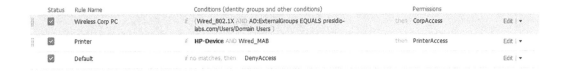

Status	Rule Name	Conditions (identity groups and other conditions)		Permissions	
☑	Wireless Corp PC	if (Wired_802.1X AND AD:ExternalGroups EQUALS presidio-labs.com/Users/Domain Users)	then	CorpAccess	Edit | ▾
☑	Printer	if HP-Device AND Wired_MAB	then	PrinterAccess	Edit | ▾
☑	Default	if no matches, then DenyAccess			Edit | ▾

[16]If you run into this problem in the wild, your options may be limited in dealing with it at times. Depending on the device type and amount of unique information ISE can get from it using a static endpoint identity group with MAB might make things slightly easier.

7

Network Access Device Configuration

Now that you have ISE basically set up, it's time to get into the actual configuration of your network devices to work with ISE. It's really important to keep in mind that different platforms, wired and wireless, support different features and that while ISE may support specific functionality, if the NAD you're using does not support that feature, you'll be out of luck. Most modern (2008 and forward) Cisco switch platforms have really great feature support for ISE but as you design your ISE deployment, take a look at the ISE compatibility matrix in the platform section to verify that what you're looking to configure has platform support (http://bit.ly/1OVXDXi).

There is also an important point that is frequently talked about when starting to discuss implementing ISE: "Does it support X model switch/wireless access point (AP)/firewall?" That question is the wrong one to ask because the vast majority of what ISE does is RADIUS authentication and thus is standards compliant or broadly compatible with modern Cisco code. The better question is: "Does my infrastructure support ISE?" The answer most often is: yeah, mostly. ISE has loads of features that may not exist on each and every platform, particularly non-Cisco infrastructure or older infrastructure.

Just a couple of examples. Look at the Cisco 2950 switch, a platform lots of us dealt with over the years. It is capable of being integrated into ISE but it has a variety of feature limitations. First, it does not support MAC Authentication Bypass (MAB) and it doesn't support downloadable ACLs (dACLs) which are an extremely popular and effective ISE feature. For enforcement on that platform, it's only real feature is VLAN override, or changing VLANs based on who the user is. In this way, you can say that you can deploy ISE on a network of 2950 switches, but you will be limited in the features and functionality of the edge switches.

Other platforms that are newer but not very modern will have less dramatic feature deficiencies. One of the more common ones is the 3560 switch that has 100-Mb copper Ethernet ports. These model switches support only 12.x IOS and as such they won't support a feature called device sensor that makes profiling of endpoints (determining what they are) really easy and efficient. The switch still supports many the other major functions required to deploy ISE policy (MAB, dot1x, dACL, HTTP redirect). In the case of this situation ISE provides a workaround to the device sensor feature where you may integrate the switch into ISE via SNMP which provides nearly identical functionality, albeit less efficiently.

In any case, when you go into deploy ISE, it's important to spend some time assessing what the features and functionality are that you need to be successful and make sure each of those are available for each of the edge platforms you are looking to deploy policy on.

If you've deployed your network with Cisco hardware in the past few years, you're going to find that you have very few feature gaps to contend with. We're going to focus on IOS 15.x later and provide you syntax on that specific feature set.

WIRED

The switch integration into ISE is primarily RADIUS. When you're configuring the switch into ISE, the first part is to configure the RADIUS servers, attributes, and AAA. It's important as you start creating your configuration scripts that different model Cisco switches can and do have slightly different syntaxes. Traditionally you'd start by configuring your RADIUS servers and AAA groups something like the following:

```
aaa new-model
radius-server host 192.168.254.133 auth-port 1812 acct-port 1813\
key 0 RADIUS-KEY
radius-server host 192.168.254.134 auth-port 1812 acct-port 1813\
key 0 RADIUS-KEY
aaa group server radius ISE
  server 192.168.254.133
  server 192.168.254.134
  deadtime 15
```

This syntax while easy to configure is not actually supported in newer platforms and is frowned upon on older platforms running more modern IOS. Everything else you define RADIUS servers like the following:

```
aaa new-model
radius server ISE1 address ipv4 192.168.254.133 auth-port 1812 acct-
port 1813 key 0 RADIUS-KEY
radius server ISE2 address ipv4 192.168.254.134 auth-port 1812 acct-
port 1813 key 0 RADIUS-KEY
aaa group server radius ISE
  server name ISE1
  server name ISE2
  deadtime 15
```

Obviously this syntax is longer in line, but it allows for the configuration of readable names and more flexibility in the configuration in general.

Once you have the ISE servers defined as RADIUS servers, we'll want to configure AAA policy on the switch. For this, we're going to need to configure each of the A's in AAA plus a few other things:

```
aaa authentication dot1x default group ISE
aaa authorization network default group ISE
aaa authorization auth-proxy default group ISE
aaa accounting dot1x default start-stop group ISE
aaa session-id common
aaa accounting update periodic 5
aaa accounting dot1x default start-stop group ISE
aaa server radius dynamic-author
 client 192.168.254.133 server-key RADIUS-KEY
 client 192.168.254.134 server-key RADIUS-KEY
```

Let's break those commands down one at a time. For clarity:

- Set default dot1x authentication to go toward ISE.
- Enable network authorization by default to come from the ISE servers.
- Enable ISE to perform authentication proxy for web authentication transactions.
- Enable dot1x accounting to communicate with ISE.
- Ensure that the same session ID is used for RADIUS transactions.
- Update accounting messages to the RADIUS server every 5 min.
- Enable dot1x accounting to by default be sent to ISE.
- Configure the ISE nodes as dynamic-authors, which then allows ISE to send CoA messages to the switch.

Once you have AAA set up, the general RADIUS configuration in IOS needs to be updated to support ISE-specific functions:

```
radius-server attribute 6 on-for-login-auth
radius-server attribute 8 include-in-access-req
radius-server attribute 25 access-request include
radius-server dead-criteria time 5 tries 3
radius-server retry method reorder
radius-server vsa send accounting
radius-server vsa send authentication
ip radius source-interface <replaceme>
dot1x system-auth-control
dot1x critical eapol
authentication critical recovery delay 1000
lldp enable
epm logging
```

Let's break down these commands down one at a time:

- Send RADIUS attribute 6 which defines a significant amount of information that can be used by ISE conditions. These would include if the service type is "login" for dot1x or "call-check" which would identify MAB. There are other call-check types, but those are the common ones for ISE.

- Send attribute 8, the IP address of the endpoint device if it's known.
- Send attribute 25; include the class attribute in the access request so that it's available for conditions in policy.
- This is the dead criterion where a RADIUS server is determined to be dead. We typically set a 5-s RADIUS timeout and there are three tries before a RADIUS server is declared dead. If ISE or your directory can't respond within 5 s, you'll have to increase that to a time that your directory can reasonably respond.
- When a RADIUS server is declared dead, reorder their priority so that the newly declared dead server is lower in the priority.
- Enable the switch to utilize Vendor Specific Attributes (VSAs) in accounting packets.
- Enable the switch to utilize VSAs in authentication packets.
- Specify the source of all RADIUS packets from the device. This is critical if there are multiple potential source interfaces from which RADIUS packets could be sourced from. We recommend using a loopback interface, or an interface which if it went down would result in you having big problems anyway.
- Enable dot1x globally.
- Send an EAP success message to the client in the event of a critical authorization event.
- Delay recovery for 1000 s in the event of a critical authorization event. In this case if critical authorization occurs, it will wait 1000 s before it attempts to recover the port.
- Enable LLDP neighbor discovery for non-Cisco-embedded device discovery. This is extremely important for profiling of non-Cisco phones (if, God forbid, you don't use Cisco phones).
- Enable enterprise policy management logging so you can watch what is actually happening.

If you're looking for basic ISE port authorization, or perhaps VLAN override, that's all you actually need. If you're looking to set up dACL or web authentication, there are some additional commands that are required.

For dACLs to function device tracking is required:

```
ip device tracking
ip device tracking probe delay 10
```

Let's break down these commands down one at a time:

- Enable device tracking globally. The switch will track what IP address is used on what port by snooping ARP information.
- Second, we want to delay device tracking by 10 s in order to avoid duplicate IP errors on platforms that utilize RFC 5227. If you don't include this, it's likely you'll encounter Windows PCs exhibiting duplicate IP address errors due to the way device tracking interacts with ARP messages when it does address discovery.

If you need to configure web authentication, we need to enable a few more features and also create some ACLs to govern our web authentication redirects. First, you need to ensure that device tracking is enabled for dACLs (as they are always used in conjunction with ISE web authentication). Next you'll need two more things. You'll need to enable the HTTP and HTTPS servers on your switch and you'll need redirect ACLs to govern the redirection:

```
ip http server
ip http secure-server
ip http active-session-modules none
ip http secure-active-session-modules none
!
ip access-list extended WEBAUTH-REDIRECT
 deny udp any eq bootpc any eq bootps
 deny udp any any eq domain
 deny tcp any host 192.168.254.133 eq 8443
 deny tcp any host 192.168.254.134 eq 8443
 permit ip any any
!
ip access-list extended POSTURE-REDIRECT
deny udp any eq bootpc any eq bootps
deny udp any any eq domain
deny udp any host 192.168.254.133  eq 8905
deny udp any host 192.168.254.134 eq 8905
deny tcp any host 192.168.254.133  eq 8905
deny tcp any host 192.168.254.134 eq 8905
deny tcp any host 192.168.254.133  eq 8909
deny tcp any host 192.168.254.134  eq 8909
deny udp any host 192.168.254.134 eq 8909
deny udp any host 192.168.254.133  eq 8909
deny tcp any host 192.168.254.133 eq 8443
deny tcp any host 192.168.254.134 eq 8443
permit ip any any
```

Configuring these features for some companies can be challenging because for a decade, organizations have standardized on leaving the HTTP server disabled. In our case, HTTP redirection does require packets to originate from the HTTP or HTTPS server on the switch. To alleviate the pain that organizations feel for enabling the HTTP and HTTPS servers, we can ensure that no management modules are enabled. This leaves the HTTP and HTTPS servers as open ports on the IPs of the switch, but that's all they are, open ports.

The ACLs in the case of web authentication on IOS configuration here aren't actually designed specifically to deny or permit traffic. We are simply trying to identify traffic we would attempt to redirect to the ISE servers. When we say "deny," this is traffic we don't wish to deny. For the "WEBAUTH-REDIRECT" ACL, we don't want to redirect the following:

- DHCP
- DNS
- Traffic destined to the web server on the ISE server for guest authentication

Then the permit any at the end of that ACL provides for redirects for everything else toward ISE.

For the POSTURE-REDIRECT ACL the configuration has the same philosophy, but we need to allow for more protocols to be permitted to our ISE nodes without redirection:

- DHCP.
- DNS.
- TCP/UDP 8905 allows for posture SWISS communications.
- TCP/UDP 8909 allows for client provisioning.
- TCP 8443 is for posture discovery.

In your specific configuration having both ACLs may not be required at the outset of your deployment. Having said that, we would recommend that where plausible include both ACLs so that you don't have to revisit IOS configuration on switches should you wish to enable web authentication or posture features on your switches at a later date.

To enable profiling, we're going to need to enable a few additional integrations. Most commonly wired profiling requires ISE to learn the following information about endpoints from the switch:

- OUI/MAC of the endpoint
- DHCP information
- CDP/LLDP neighbor information about the clients

To obtain DHCP, CDP, and LLDP information the most efficient way of accomplishing that is to integrate the switch into ISE via device sensor[1]:

```
device-sensor filter-list dhcp list dhcp_list
 option name host-name
 option name domain-name
 option name default-ip-ttl
 option name requested-address
 option name parameter-request-list
 option name class-identifier
 option name client-identifier
!
device-sensor filter-list lldp list lldp_list
 tlv name system-name
 tlv name system-description
 tlv name system-capabilities
!
device-sensor filter-list cdp list cdp_list
 tlv name device-name
 tlv name address-type
 tlv name capabilities-type
 tlv name platform-type
device-sensor filter-spec dhcp include list dhcp_list
device-sensor filter-spec lldp include list lldp_list
device-sensor filter-spec cdp include list cdp_list
device-sensor accounting
device-sensor notify all-changes
```

[1]When configuring device sensor, it's important to remember that this feature is limited to more modern IOS and generally only 15.x IOS versions will support device sensor. If you are deploying ISE on older switches and you need to obtain CDP/LLDP information, you'll need to include SNMP integration with to ISE. This is less efficient than device sensor but will provide similar functionality. Also if you're using IOS XE version 3.3 or earlier, device sensor requires IP base licensing. In 3.6 or later it's included in LAN base.

These commands are broken down to a couple of sections.

You create filter lists that are lists of information that you would like to specifically include (or potentially exclude depending on your situation). The information would include information derived from CDP or LLDP Type–Length–Values (TLVs) or information derived from DHCP options. The example above includes my typical options; if you want to add or remove some, don't be shy about it.

Once you've created your lists, you need to actually apply those to device sensor to include those in the accounting messages that are sent to the RADIUS server.

An additional step you should take when configuring wired ISE for profiling is to set a DHCP helper address on the default gateway of any client access VLAN pointing to one of the policy nodes (in the example below, 192.168.254.133). While this does provide redundant DHCP information to ISE on clients that have been profiled via device sensor, it will simultaneously capture profiling information about endpoints that are not connected to ISE-enabled switches. This gives you some additional network viability and can help expand ISE control at a later date. It's important to remember that ISE is not a DHCP server and will not respond to any DHCP requests; rather it will just monitor the DHCP requests as they come in and update the endpoint database with relevant information. The configuration looks something like the following:

```
interface VLAN 100
 description ACCESS
 ip address 192.0.2.1 255.255.255.0
 ip helper-address 192.168.254.133
 ip helper-address <DHCP server>
```

```
interface Gig 1/0/1 - 48
description ISE Access
switchport host
authentication open[1]
authentication host-mode multi-auth
authentication periodic
authentication timer reauthenticate server
authentication event fail action next-method
authentication event server dead action authorize
authentication event server dead action authorize voice
authentication event server alive action reinitialize
authentication order dot1x mab
authentication priority dot1x mab
authentication port-control auto
authentication violation restrict
mab
dot1x pae authenticator
dot1x timeout tx-period 10
```

At this point you should be ready to configure your edge switchports for ISE integration. The configuration here may be summarized as follows:

- Ensure that the port is mode access.
- Authentication open provides some limited network access functionality while dot1x is running on the port.

- Host-mode multi-auth allows for multiple authenticated sessions on the switchport.[2]
- Periodic authentication provides for authentication timeouts to be set.
- Timer reauthenticate server allows ISE to set the session timeout where the default action is for the timeout to be set on the switch.
- Authentication event fail action next-method allows for the switchport to move from one authentication method to another. For example, if dot1x either fails or time outs, the switchport can try to authenticate the endpoint via MAB.
- Both event server dead action commands provide for what is called critical authorization. When all RADIUS servers are unavailable (due to catastrophic DC failure, or other network outage), the switchport can be set to fail open entirely authorizing both the data domain (access VLAN) and the voice domain should a phone be present.
- Event server alive action reinitialize provides that if critical authorization is used, when the RADIUS servers come back alive, the switchport is reauthenticated.
- Authentication order configuration provides for dot1x to occur before MAB occurs.[3]
- Authentication priority says that dot1x is more important than MAB. Don't change this.
- Port-control auto enables authentication on the port.
- Violation restrict logs when a new MAC is associated to the port over the maximum limit and restricts the MAC from sending/receiving traffic.[4]
- MAB enables MAC Authentication Bypass as an available authentication method on the port.
- PAE authenticator sets the port as an authenticator. In some configurations it's possible to configure a switchport to try to authenticate to what it's connected to (this is called supplicant mode), but in this case we want to authenticate the device that is connecting to us.
- Dot1x timeout is how long to attempt to do dot1x authentication before moving on. The best practice timeout is 10 s. After this timer expires the authentication process will attempt to perform MAB. It's possible to make this timer slightly faster, but be wary if dot1x misbehaves and change it back to 10.

Now is as good a time as any to talk about "critical authorization" in a wired ISE implementation. Critical authorization is functionally where, if all ISE policy nodes are unavailable to the switch, the switch will then allow the endpoint device access to the local LAN. Some people call this "fail open," which is not an unreasonable characterization.

First, it's not unreasonable to make sure people understand that you're *only* going to be using critical authorization in a true emergency and this functionality should not be relied on day to day—which means, as you begin testing its functionality, don't be surprised when

---

[2]Take some time getting to know the host-mode options in your deployment. I prefer multi-auth in general, but depending on security requirements single-host and/or multidomain can be really effective options. Single-host works well when you need to not centrally authorize your phones and multidomain works when you know you will have only a single data host and a single voice host per port max.

[3]This is a really critical design element. Devices that rely on MAB/profiling or CWA will have network access much faster if you order MAB first, but if you order dot1x first the switch will send an EAP-start which will cause dot1x to work much more efficiently. If you're doing more dot1x, order dot1x first; if you're doing more MAB and CWA, order MAB first.

[4]There are a few options here but typically restrict is the best practice. Packets are dropped and a log message is generated.

going into or recovering from a critical authorization isn't exactly instantaneous. If you're on a production network and utilizing critical authorization, we can be pretty well assured that you're not having a good day.

To start, for critical authorization to work, all RADIUS servers need to be declared dead. In the configuration I have described above, the dead criteria have to be met for each one of your ISE PSN nodes. That is, a RADIUS server is tried three times with a 5-s timeout on each of them. If an ISE PSN does not respond in 15 s, it is declared dead. That declaration of a dead RADIUS server stays for the length of time configured in the "deadtime" configuration. In the previous example that deadtime is 15 min, which is the interval we nearly universally put in production systems. That means that for the next 15 min the switch will not try to contact that RADIUS server. If all the RADIUS servers are declared dead and an edge switchport, configured for authentication, comes up, a critical authorization event for that switchport occurs. That may mean that the endpoint device is just authorized on the default VLAN (as is in our configuration example), or that device is given a specific critical VLAN to join.[5]

If your ISE nodes recover before those 15 min are up, that's great but the switch won't actually try to contact a RADIUS server until the deadtime has expired. If you have an extended outage where ISE is down (presumably because your WAN is down) every time that deadtime expires, the switch will attempt to contact the RADIUS server again and have a 15-s time where it attempts to authenticate a client.

Frankly the result of the behavior is that in the case of a total ISE failure the user experience isn't great. Every 15 min (or whatever your deadtime interval is) the switch will try to reconnect to ISE and during that time clients will have to wait for a time while the switch times out. In the case of having two ISE nodes (presuming in our scenario that they're both unavailable), that means after every 15-min timeout an endpoint client will have to wait 30 s to obtain network access while both ISE nodes time out. In the case of a catastrophic WAN failure, this may be acceptable because presumably all DC resources are also unavailable to your users and they may not be able to do work anyway.[6]

WIRELESS

AirOS WLC ISE integration requires several steps and while the mechanics of doing the integration is totally different than switch integration, the resulting functionality is broadly the same.[7] First thing you'll want to do is configure your ISE servers as RADIUS authentication servers and accounting servers.

---

[5]Critical authorization for the voice VLAN is a separate command and requires 15.x or SXJ trains of IOS.

[6]When you're thinking about how to design your ISE cluster, it's prudent to deploy your ISE nodes wherever you would have critical business servers and/or AD domain controllers. That is because if you are unable to perform business tasks anyway, network authorization would not be quite as critical as it would be if the business application servers were otherwise available. If you're thinking about installing an ISE node at a large site, please do be sure that a domain controller is also there because if there is not one there and the WAN goes down, ISE will also not be able to perform AD authentications.

[7]It is important for some features that require CWA redirection that you are on at least WLC version 7.2.110 or later. If you're on an earlier version, you will be greatly restricted in what you can accomplish.

Under RADIUS authentication servers you'll need to include the following:

- IP
- Pre-shared Key (PSK)
- Server Status (Enable)
- RFC 3576 support (Enable CoA)[8]
- Server Timeout[9]
- Enable Network User
- Disable Management User
- Disable Tunnel Proxy
- Disable IPSec

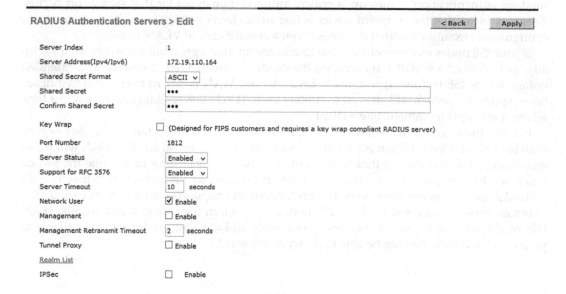

Next configure ISE as a RADIUS accounting server, with similar functionality to the RADIUS authentication server:

- Server IP
- PSK
- Server Status (enabled)
- Server Timeout (match authentication server timeout)
- Enable Network User

---

[8]If you find that CoA is not working with ISE, 9 out of 10 times you'll find that you forgot to enable RFC 3576 support. Be sure you have this enabled.

[9]Typically the default is too short especially if you're integrating to a large or slow AD which may take longer than 2 s to respond back to a request. Depending on the deployment I prefer to increase this to between 5 and 10 s.

- Disable Tunnel Proxy
- Disable IPSec

Next we'll want to create some WLANs that will utilize ISE to authenticate. First, let's create a dot1x-enabled SSID. This SSID would be good for the following common use cases:

- Standard 802.1x authentication
- 802.1x coupled with posture assessment
- 802.1x coupled with single SSID NSP
- 802.1x coupled with MDM on boarding

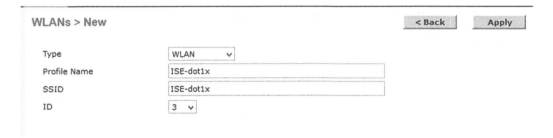

On the General page, you want to enable the SSID, assign it to an airspace interface (which is not management because this is a best practice), and enable broadcasting.[10]

---

[10]We've encountered many customers who insist that not broadcasting their SSID is a security requirement or that it is part of their corporate policy. This is extraordinarily misguided. If you are considering disabling SSID broadcasting, please Google "microsoft broadcast ssid" and read why it is not a good security practice to disable WLAN broadcasting.

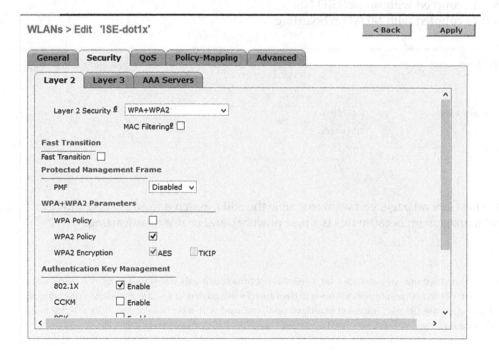

Under Security → Layer 2 be sure that you have WPA2 AES and 802.1x enabled.

Make sure you have "None" specified under Layer 3.

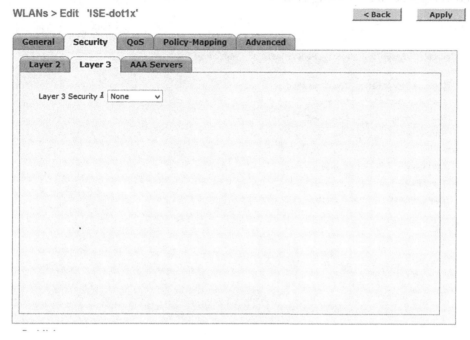

Under AAA specify the ISE servers you're looking to use and enable Interim Update with an interval of 3600 s.

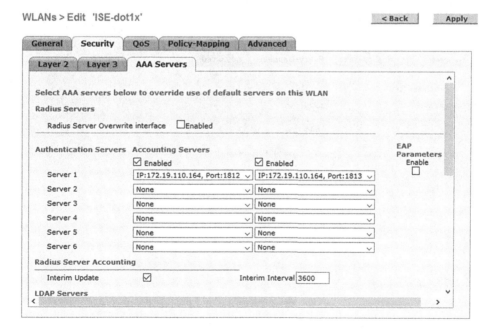

Under Quality of Service (QoS) it doesn't matter much what you configure. We recommend enabling AVC and allowing WMM.

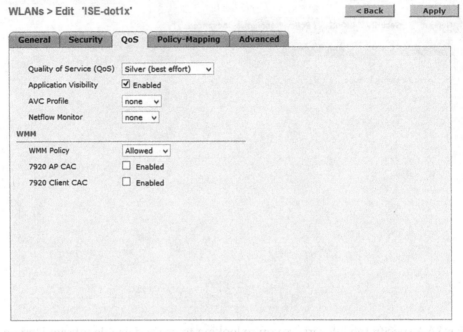

Under Policy-Mapping we highly recommend you not configure anything. The same functionality can be accomplished from ISE centrally.

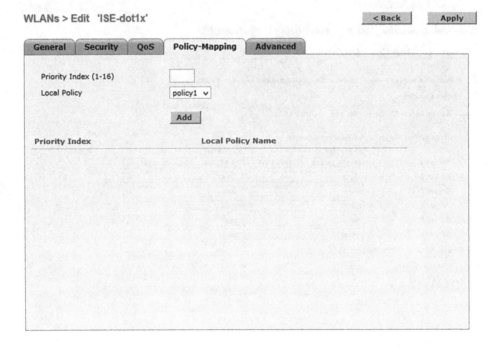

Under the Advanced tab is where most of the magic happens here. Let's list out the features that are commonly enabled and disabled often when we configure an ISE-enabled SSID:

- Enable AAA Override.
- Ensure Coverage Hole Detection is enabled.
- Disable Session Timeout.
- Disable Aironet IE.
- Disable Client Exclusion.
- Enable DHCP Addr. Assignment.
- Set NAC State to Radius NAC.
- Enable Client Band Select.
- Enable DHCP Profiling.
- Enable HTTP Profiling.

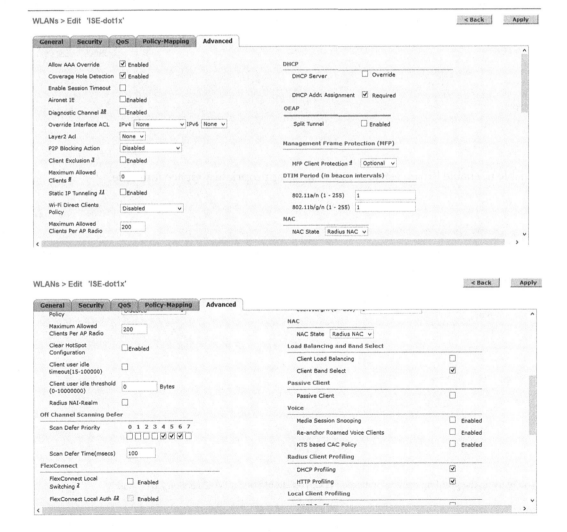

The options that may cause me to deviate in how you configure the WLAN for ISE integration is typically only whether FlexConnect is enabled, which we'll get into later.

You're probably asking yourself at this point: What do those "Radius Client Profiling" check boxes do? When the APs are in "local mode," all traffic is forwarded through the WLC; the WLC is able to capture traffic and forward it to ISE to be analyzed. In this case, when you enable DHCP profiling, any DHCP_REQUEST-type packet sent by a wireless client is sent to ISE via RADIUS Accounting packets to be analyzed. When you enable HTTP profiling, the first HTTP packet a client sends is intercepted by the WLC and also forwarded to ISE via RADIUS accounting packets for profiling analysis. This is both effective in that it provides ISE a wealth of information about wireless clients and efficient in that you don't need to rely on Switched Port Analyzers (SPANs) or redirects or anything else to obtain all that profiling information.[11]

Next if you're looking to configure a guest SSID and you need to configure the SSID without encryption or 802.1x authentication, you'll want to configure an SSID with the following characteristics.

First, create your SSID.

WLANs > New   < Back   Apply

Type	WLAN ⌄
Profile Name	ISE-Open
SSID	ISE-Open
ID	4 ⌄

Enable it, enable Broadcast, and put it on an appropriate airspace interface.

WLANs > Edit 'ISE-Open'   < Back   Apply

General Security QoS Policy-Mapping Advanced

Profile Name	ISE-Open
Type	WLAN
SSID	ISE-Open
Status	☑ Enabled
Security Policies	[WPA2][Auth(802.1X)] (Modifications done under security tab will appear after applying the changes.)
Radio Policy	All ⌄
Interface/Interface Group(G)	guest ⌄
Multicast Vlan Feature	☐ Enabled
Broadcast SSID	☑ Enabled
NAS-ID	WLC

[11]If you're using the profiling features with the WLC, you should be on WLC version 7.6 or later.

Set Layer 2 Security to "None" and enable MAC Filtering.

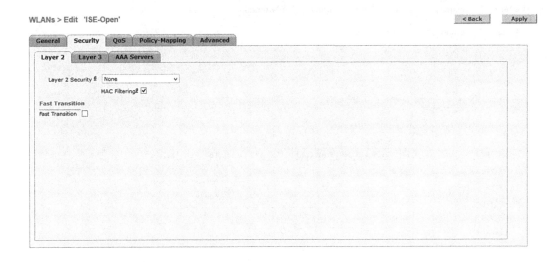

Select "None" under Layer 3 Security.

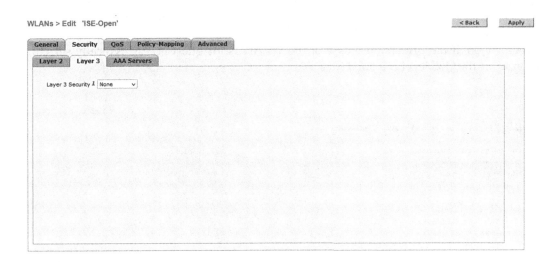

Under AAA servers, select your ISE servers for authentication and accounting and enable Interim Update with an interval of 3600 s.

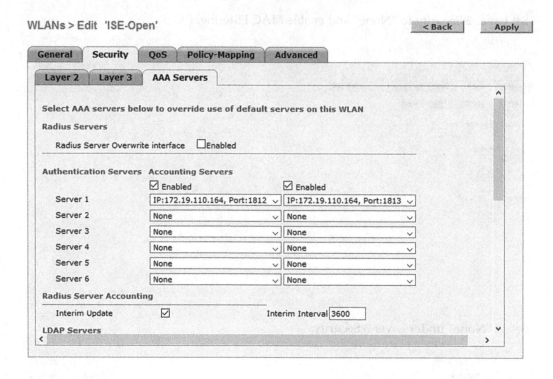

As for QoS, if the primary use case of the WLAN is for guest access, typically selecting "Bronze" as the QoS level is a good idea.

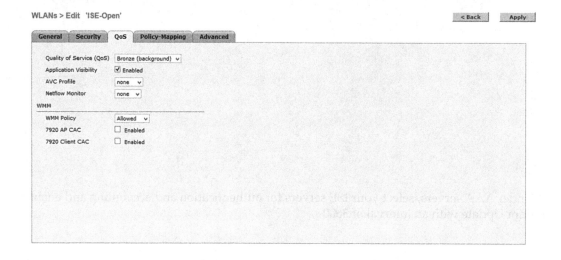

Like previously, we recommend that you don't configure any Policy-Mapping when the SSID is to be ISE enabled.

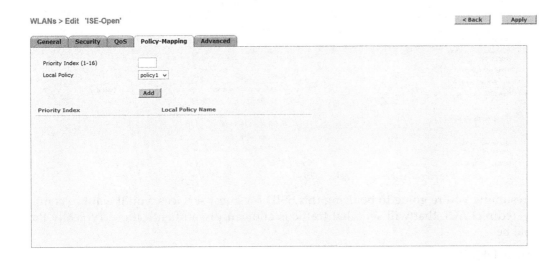

On the Advanced tab, configure the fields similarly to an 802.1x-enabled SSID. You typically disable HTTP profiling on this SSID because the HTTP profiling information is obtained when the client is redirected to the client portal for login.

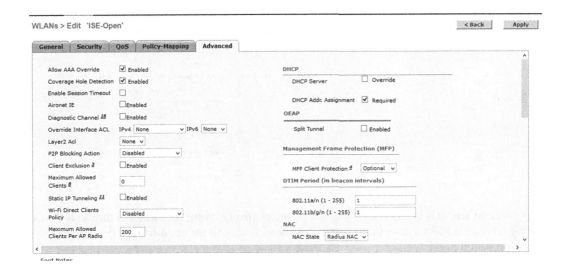

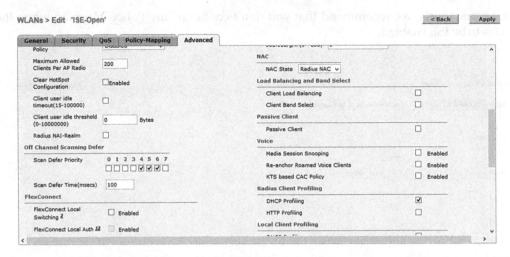

Presuming you're going to be using this SSID for guest services, you'll want to configure a redirect ACL that will set what traffic is allowed pre-authentication. Typically that would be:

- Allow DHCP.
- Allow DNS.
- Allow access to the ISE CWA portal.[12]

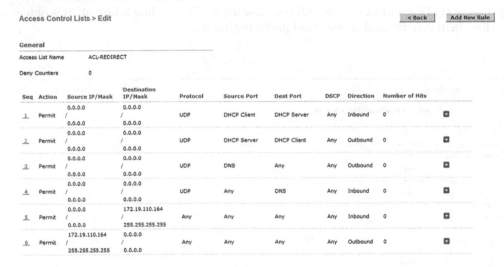

As you can see, this is all really simple as long as you're using APs in local mode. If you're looking to enable FlexConnect on your WLANs and APs, there are additional pieces of configuration you'll need.

---

[12]ISE web authentication ports are on port 8443 by default. If you're going to require posture assessment or BYOD, you'll need to include other ports and protocols, TCP and UDP 8905–8909.

To enable FlexConnect on your WLAN you need to configure the WLAN to enable FlexConnect under the Advanced tab.

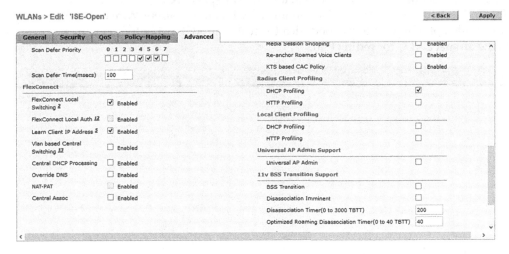

You'll also want to configure your AP in FlexConnect mode.[13]

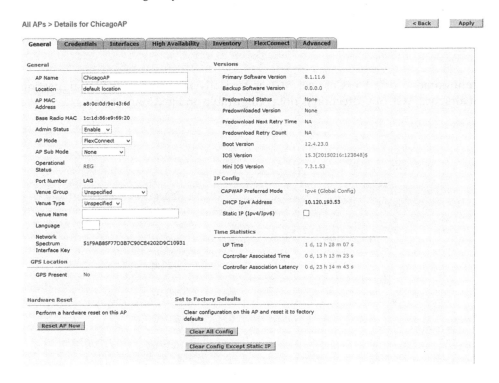

[13]Remember that changing AP modes causes the AP to reboot.

The first thing is when you're looking to configure a web authentication redirect on a WLAN that is switched locally at a FlexConnect AP, you'll need to configure an ACL for redirection in a FlexConnect ACL rather than a simple airspace ACL.

To do this you browse to the FlexConnect ACL configuration: Wireless → FlexConnect ACLs. While not required, it's a good idea to create the ACL using the same name you used with the airspace ALC for redirection.

The configuration of a FlexConnect ACL is basically the same as the configuration of a standard airspace ACL but direction is not configurable on FlexConnect ACLs.

Access Control Lists > Edit   < Back   Add New Rule

General

Access List Name   ACL-REDIRECT

Seq	Action	Source IP/Mask	Destination IP/Mask	Protocol	Source Port	Dest Port	DSCP	
1	Permit	0.0.0.0 / 0.0.0.0	0.0.0.0 / 0.0.0.0	UDP	DHCP Client	DHCP Server	Any	▼
2	Permit	0.0.0.0 / 0.0.0.0	0.0.0.0 / 0.0.0.0	UDP	DHCP Server	DHCP Client	Any	▼
3	Permit	0.0.0.0 / 0.0.0.0	0.0.0.0 / 0.0.0.0	UDP	DNS	Any	Any	▼
4	Permit	0.0.0.0 / 0.0.0.0	0.0.0.0 / 0.0.0.0	UDP	Any	DNS	Any	▼
5	Permit	172.16.110.164 / 255.255.255.255	0.0.0.0 / 0.0.0.0	TCP	8443	Any	Any	▼
6	Permit	0.0.0.0 / 0.0.0.0	172.16.110.164 / 255.255.255.255	TCP	Any	8443	Any	▼
7	Deny	0.0.0.0 / 0.0.0.0	0.0.0.0 / 0.0.0.0	Any	Any	Any	Any	▼

Next you'll need to configure the AP to utilize this ACL as a redirect ACL. When using FlexConnect ACLs with ISE for either policy enforcement or redirection, enable the ACL for use on the AP. The reason this is required is that when the WLAN is locally switched at the remote AP, the ACL is actually applied at the AP and the AP has to download the ACL into its configuration before it's available for use by the AP.

To push down the ACL to a group of APs (presumably you have more than one AP deployed), you enable the ACL on a FlexConnect Group.[14] To configure a FlexConnect Group browse: Wireless → FlexConnect Groups.

Select New; then give your FlexConnect group a name.

Go into the FlexConnect group you created and there are two things you'll want to do. First, add the relevant APs to your group under the General tab of the FlexConnect group configuration.

---

[14]There are other advantages to using FlexConnect groups beyond ISE configuration. Things like fast roaming are enabled by FlexConnect groups, same with image upgrade optimizations. In short, please always use FlexConnect groups when you have a site with more than one FlexConnect AP.

Next you need to configure your ACL as a policy ACL to be used on the FlexConnect group. To do that you want to browse in the FlexConnect group configuration → ACL Mapping → Policy; then add your ACL to the list of Policy Access Control Lists.

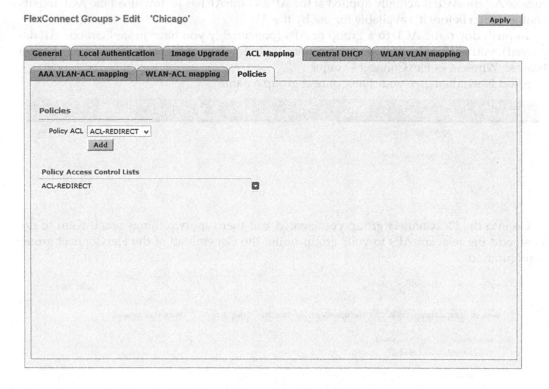

Once this is in place, you can configure your AuthZ policy just like you had configured policy for an AP in local mode for your FlexConnect APs.[15]

---

[15]There were requirements that you had to have FlexConnect ACLs configured with the same name as standard local mode AirOS ACLs but in more recent version of code (7.6 and later) this requirement has been relaxed.

ISE Profiling

INTRODUCTION

Profiling is the process of taking one or more attributes known about a device, such as MAC OUI or HTTP User-Agent, and using those attributes to determine what that device is (printer, access point, workstation, phone, etc.). Once ISE knows, or has a rough idea, AuthZ policies can be used to determine the level of network access a device should have. Authorization rules could use MAB and a known profile to support devices like printers that might not support 802.1x but still need to be network connected. They could also be used along with 802.1x to steer specific clients to a different location, that is, moving employee mobile devices to a specific mobile device VLAN.

In any deployment, moving toward a fully automated wired access layer is going to rely on some form of profiling in order to determine how devices (especially ones without dot1x support) should be treated. Lucky for us, ISE ships with a lot of profiles out of the box and has the ability to update them via the Profiler Feed Service provided by Cisco. New profiles will be downloaded when they are available and merged into your rules. There are some caveats that are important to make note of though:

1. Unless you take them into account, new rules from the Feed Service will generally take precedence over rules you create. This can result in devices reprofiling and not gaining network access.
2. When creating custom profiling rules, do your best to avoid editing anything that is Cisco provided. Once edited, feed profiler updates can't be merged into the changed rule.

Previously you would have needed to edit rules to change the value of "Create an Identity Group for the Policy" in order to create an Identity Group that can be used in AuthZ rules. With the introduction of logical profiles, however, you can add groups into these profiles without breaking their ability to be updated by the Feed Service.

When creating your own rules, be sure to either prepend or append something unique to your site to the rules. It makes it easy to identify which rules you have made and reduces any issues that may surface if Cisco ever introduces new rules through the Feed Service that use the same name.

SETTING UP PROFILING

The first thing to do to get ISE profiling your endpoints is to verify that the service is turned on and assigned to the proper node (more about that in Chapter 2). Go to Administration → Deployment → Choose Your PSN → Profiler Configuration tab. The table given in the following has the basic recommended settings depending on your access layer switches. If you have a mixed environment containing more than one category, enable all relevant sensors.

	3560X/3750X/3650/3850/4500	2960/6500/6800ia	AirOS (WLC)
NetFlow*	Off	Off	Off
DHCP	Off	On	Off
DHCPSPAN	Off	Off	Off
HTTP	On	On	Off
RADIUS	On	On	On
NMAP	Off	On	Off
DNS	Off	Off	Off
SNMPQUERY	Off	On	Off
SNMPTRAP	Off	Off	Off

It's our view that profiling with NetFlow is a great way to DoS your policy nodes and you should generally avoid this unless you have extraordinary reasons.

There are differences between these switch models because of the support (or lack thereof) for a feature called "Device Sensor." Switches/WLCs that support this feature are able to glean CDP/LLDP/DHCP (and in the case of a WLC, HTTP User-Agent) about clients and then send that information to ISE and send that data back in RADIUS packets. Without Device Sensor, ISE must use SNMP to poll devices and gather information about clients before it is able to accurately profile a device.

Obviously the configuration of profiling is a critical part and while not complex there are multiple technologies that get used and they all provide important info. One technology not working correctly might be the difference between a smooth deployment and one with lots of end-user/executive complaints. If you haven't already, now is the time to check out Chapter 7 and verify that your devices are properly configured with the settings outlined there. Those configurations have been tested in numerous real-world environments and provide the optimal settings for profiling.

PROFILING BASICS

Profiling rules basically work by matching a "minimum certainty factor." This factor is a relatively arbitrary number that determines how certain we are that conditions are met, and that this is in fact the correct profile to match for the physical device. Conditions include the following:

- OUI
- CDP characteristics

- LLDP characteristics
- DHCP characteristics
- Browser User-Agent
- Information gathered via SNMP gets
- NMAP information
- NetFlow ports used

When conditions are met, one of two things may happen. Either the certainty factor is matched or an NMAP scan is executed. If NMAP shows that SNMP is open, an SNMP get may be executed on the device with the SNMP strings configured globally for profiling. The global default is "public" but you can add additional strings under Administration → System → Settings → Profiling.

Profiling rules are also hierarchical in that some profiles will not be matched if others are not matched first. If you look at the Apple device profile at the time of this writing, if the OUI of the device shows that it was manufactured by Apple, then the device is determined to be an Apple device. There are then subprofiles that can further determine if it's an iPad, iPhone, iPod, or Apple TV (for those who like Netflix™). The subprofiles will match to determine if the iPad is an iPad by looking for DHCP or HTTP information to identify the DHCP host-name or the HTTP User-Agent as an iPad physical device.

In the case two possible profiling policies are matched, the one with the higher certainty factor that is matched is selected. If certainty factors are the same, the lower alphabetical order is selected. Keep in mind that a subpolicy match can occur only if the device has been matched into the parent policy. Assuming the following structure:

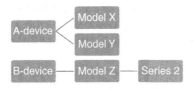

If a device has been profiled into the Model Y group but should be in the Series 2 group, it will never move over if it wouldn't match both the B-Device and Model Z parent groups.

It is possible to get into a chicken-and-the-egg scenario with profiling and it is something you should watch out for when creating your own rules or creating authorization (AuthZ) policies using Cisco-provided rules. Let's assume that you have created a new profiler condition for WidgetGroup-Device using the attribute check "dhcp-class-identifier CONTAINS 'Widget Group' and based a new Identity Group + AuthZ rule off of that profile. When you plug one of these devices into your network, it will just sit there. See the problem? Your rule depends on info gleaned from DHCP but that info can be obtained only by authorizing that device for network access, which ISE will not do because the device is still unknown. There are a couple of fixes here, but the best one is to add another condition to your profiling rule that checks for the OUI of "WIDGETGROUP, INC" and increments the certainty factor enough to allow the device to match that rule and thus be allowed onto the network.

You will want to build your profile policies so that they generally start off matching generic attributes (matching things like OUI that ISE will always have) and then moving to more exact attributes such as CDP, LLDP, and HTTP User-Agent. Cisco's own "Cisco-Device" profile demonstrates this quite well.

After any device has its profile change, either because of a Feed Service update or because a manual update and that change would impact the authorization level, ISE will issue a CoA for the device so that its network access can be updated. There is a global CoA type defined under Administration → System → Settings → Profiling and by default it is set to No CoA, which means that ISE will do nothing if device's profile changes. What you have this set to in your environment will largely depend on how you use profiling, device churn, impact of a possible profiling change, and how much time you wish to spend managing profile policies. In an environment with lots of devices being brought on daily and a low business impact if something were to incorrectly profile, then you could set this to "Reauth" so that ISE will tell the device on the edge to reauthenticate and have new policy apply to it. In a very static environment and/or one where a device having its network access changed could be business impacting, you may want to leave the default setting to none. You also have the option of overriding the global setting in each profile, permitting you to do CoAs or not do CoAs for a subset of devices without having that setting impact your entire deployment. Changing this setting will not impact the "Cisco Provided" status of the rule, so you can safely do it without worrying you won't get new changes from the Feed Service.

A common use case for profile-specific CoA settings might be for devices that aren't 802.1x aware and authenticated via MAB. In an environment with a lot of consumer electronics this could be things such as game consoles, smart TVs, and Blu-Ray players, and these devices might initially end up in a dead-end or guest VLAN that wouldn't permit them access to anything until they are profiled. Changing the CoA type in their profiles to "Port Bounce" can allow those devices to detect network changes and smoothly move over without any effort on the user's part.

In the global settings for profiling there is another option that will be important to understand and possibly critical to your environment's performance/success: Endpoint Attribute Filtering (EAF). When EAF is enabled in ISE, only attributes actively used in profiling or for internal reasons are kept in the database and all others are discarded. The advantage is that there is less information that needs to be synced to PSNs—an important factor to consider if you have PSNs that are across any WAN or other high-latency links. Keeping EAF has its own advantages and that is because all attributes ISE learns about (and supports) are kept, because it is easier to find unique values that can be used to initially/further profile a device type.

A more advanced profiling function within ISE is the use of "exception actions" to take some action on a device if a condition is met within the profile policy. Simply put, it's an "exception" to the current set of rules within its current policy. These actions are rarely used and typically rely on information gleaned from NetFlow data (which if you will remember from above is also rarely used and should be used cautiously) to identify actions that are not normal to a device group and move the device into a different VLAN or apply different policy to it. For example, a hospital has developed a profile policy for some of their medical devices that they know to communicate only to two different IP addresses. They could create a condition and policy rule that check for any communication to different addresses and immediately quarantine the device since it is doing something it shouldn't. Similarly, using a game console as an example, exception actions could be used to move a device from a profile that would use MAB to authenticate to one that would require 802.1x if traffic outside the normal of a game console was detected (TOR, SSH, Torrents, etc.). In both cases exception actions can be used to quickly isolate, and potentially correct, devices that are a possible threat to the network.

The final important feature in profiling is the concept of "logical" profiles. Logical profiles allow you to take any existing profiling policies and join them together into a single container which can then be referenced in AuthZ rules. From a purely management perspective this is nice because it lets us take something like Figure 1.

And turn it into this (Figure 2).

Now this may not seem like a huge change but taking that change over just a handful of AuthZ rules will result in a much easier-to-read policy. The second advantage is an important one because it relates to your ability to get updated profiles from Cisco. In order to add identity profiles to AuthZ rules like Figure 1 the profile must be configured to create a matching Identity Group. This is fine for profiles you create or for Cisco-provided ones that come with that enabled by default but it's a problem for provided profiles that do not have that set. Once you change the "Create an Identity Group for the Policy" setting in a Cisco-provided policy, the policy is considered "Administrator Modified" and will no longer get updates from Cisco. This might not be an issue for a seldom-changing policy but for something like the "Microsoft-Workstation" or "Apple-Device" policies it could prevent you from getting important updates. You can still get those updates but it would require you to deploy a fresh ISE instance and then manually compare your profiling rules, not exactly a sustainable change. Logical profiles would let us pick any of those policies, without impacting their ability to update, and still use them in AuthZ rules. Basically we get the best of both worlds.

PROFILING CUSTOM DEVICES

So where does that leave us? Well, let's write our own policy! Each policy is composed of two parts: conditions and actions taken based on those conditions. Continuing on our WidgetGroup example from before, we're going to use the information in the following tables to construct our own profiling policy and then two child policies:

Widget Group Phone

Attribute	Value
OUI	WIDGETGROUP, INC
dhcp-class-identifier	Widget Group
LLDP Attributes	T
CDP Attributes	P

Widget Group Workstation

Attribute	Value
OUI	WIDGETGROUP, INC
dhcp-class-identifier	Widget Group
User-Agent	WG-Internet-Browser

The first thing we want to do is create the conditions under Policy → Policy Elements → Conditions → Profiling that we will use in our parent and child policies. Click "Add" and begin going through the attributes above and creating rules for them. Your final set should look something like Figure 3:

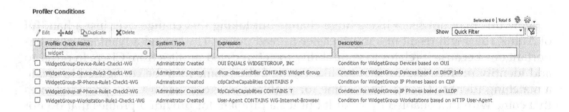

As you can see, we've followed the standard naming convention that Cisco uses out of the box for rules but we've added our own "_WG" to the end of each rule like we talked about at the beginning of this chapter.

Next we want to create the first profiling policy that we will use. Go to Policy → Profiling and click Add. We'll name our first policy simply "WidgetGroup-Devices-WG," leaving the default certainty factor of 10 alone, not creating an Identity Group, no parent policy (since we are a new parent), and leaving the CoA settings to use the global defaults. In the rules area we are going to want to add the OUI and DHCP rules we created previously (select from library) and have each of them increase the certainty factor by 10. This covers new devices by letting us profile them solely off their OUI and also increases their certainty if we have DHCP info.

Once that is done, you are going to go through the process two more times, one for each of the other device policies we will create. The minimum certainty factors for both child policies will be 40; we'll create Identity Groups for both and make sure that the parent policy is set to the first rule we created above. Follow the previously established naming conventions and add the relevant rules we created (each increasing the certainty factor by 40) to each policy. When you are completed, you should have three policies that look like Figure 4:

Profiling Policies

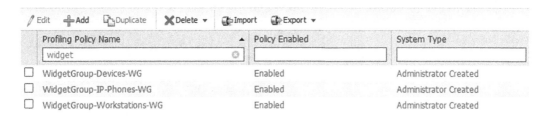

If you scroll down to the bottom of the menu on the left, you should also see your "WidgetGroup-Devices-WG" policy and expanding it will show you the two child policies.

EXAMPLE AuthZ

Using profiling information in AuthZ rules is extremely easy; profiles are added via the Identity Group's area or as logical profiles in the other conditions section. As discussed previously, the first is useful only if you have identity profiles created for your profiling policies but it's quick and simple. The second takes a little bit more work but logical profiles are the recommended method since they provide more flexibility, are easier to read, and prevent you from needing to make changes to Cisco-provided profiling policies. Figure 5 shows both examples, the top being the default Cisco IP Phones AuthZ and the bottom being the Non Cisco IP Phones rule but modified slightly to show that a logical profile is in use.

DEVICE EXAMPLE—iPHONE

Let's look at some real-world devices and see what they look like to ISE and which attributes are used to profile them correctly.

The iPhone policy is a child policy of Apple-Device and thus before we can worry about iPhone-specific conditions we need to match the generic Apple ones first. Figure 6 shows us what that Apple policy looks like OOTB.

Profiler Policy List > **Apple-Device**

Profiler Policy

* Name	Apple-Device	Description: Generic policy for all Apple devices
Policy Enabled	☑	
* Minimum Certainty Factor	10	(Valid Range 1 to 65535)
* Exception Action	NONE ▼	
* Network Scan (NMAP) Action	OS-scan ▼	
Create an Identity Group for the policy	◉ Yes, create matching Identity Group	
	○ No, use existing Identity Group hierarchy	
Parent Policy	***NONE***	
* Associated CoA Type	Global Settings ▼	
System Type	Cisco Provided	

Rules

If Condition	Apple-Device-Rule2-Check1 ✛	Then	Certainty Factor Increases ▼	10	⚙ ▼
If Condition	Apple-DeviceRule1-SCAN ✛	Then	Take Network Scan Action ▼		⚙ ▼
If Condition	Apple-DeviceRule1Check1 ✛	Then	Certainty Factor Increases ▼	10	⚙ ▼

We can see here that this policy has a minimum certainty factor of 10 and that either "Apple-DeviceRule1Check1" or "Apple-Device-Rule2-Check1," if matched, will increase the certainty to that minimum threshold so our device would be tagged as an Apple-Device. The former condition checks the OUI of the device and if it contains the word "Apple," then bumps us up 10 while the latter condition uses AnyConnect attributes sent during VPN authentication[1] to do the same. The middle option tells ISE to also then run a NMAP scan on the device (assuming you have that profiler turned on) that was profiled just as an Apple-Device so that some additional information can be gleaned from it and used to place it correctly into the subpolicies.

---

[1]This is important for VPN profiling because the machine is using a pseudo-adaptor for the VPN connection; its real MAC addresses are not sent across and thus can't be used to accurately profile the device.

Now that our hypothetical device is tagged as an Apple-Device we'll start looking at the Apple-iPhone conditions in Figure 7.

Profiler Policy List > **Apple-iPhone**

Profiler Policy

* Name | Apple-iPhone   Description | Policy for Apple iPhones

Policy Enabled ☑

* Minimum Certainty Factor | 20   (Valid Range 1 to 65535)

* Exception Action | NONE

* Network Scan (NMAP) Action | NONE

Create an Identity Group for the policy ⦿ Yes, create matching Identity Group
○ No, use existing Identity Group hierarchy

* Parent Policy | Apple-Device

* Associated CoA Type | Global Settings

System Type Cisco Provided

Rules

If Condition | Apple-iPhoneRule2Check1 ⟡ | Then | Certainty Factor Increases ▾ | 20

If Condition | Apple-iPhoneRule1Check1 ⟡ | Then | Certainty Factor Increases ▾ | 20

Other than bumping our certainty factor to 20 and having a parent policy, the Apple-iPhone policy is very similar to the more generic one. Our two conditions will check both the DHCP hostname and the HTTP User-Agent to see if they contain "iPhone" and if so bumping the certainty factor up 20 which, since we already matched a 10 from the Apple-Device policy, pushes our "Total Certainty Factor" to 30 and our device is now correctly classified.

If we look at a (slightly condensed/edited) screenshot of a sample iPhones attribute (Figure 8), we should be able to see what was used to determine the device's profile policy.

Attribute List

BYODRegistration	No
Calling-Station-ID	ec-85-2f-
DeviceRegistrationStatus	NotRegistered
EndPointPolicy	Apple-iPhone
EndPointSource	FeedService
IdentityGroup	Apple-iPhone
LastNmapScanTime	2012-Jul-28 01:22:10 EDT
MACAddress	EC:85:2F
MatchedPolicy	Apple-iPhone
NAS-IP-Address	10.141.253.18
NAS-Port-Type	Wireless - IEEE 802.11
NmapScanCount	1
OUI	Apple
PolicyVersion	231
PostureApplicable	Yes
StaticAssignment	false
StaticGroupAssignment	false
Total Certainty Factor	30
User-Agent	Mozilla/5.0 (iPhone; CPU iPhone OS 5_1_1 like Mac OS X) AppleWebKit/534.46 (KHTML, like Gecko) Mobile/9B206

We can see here that the device's OUI variable contained the word "Apple" and that HTTP User-Agent information contained the word "iPhone" "which, in total," correctly bumped our Total Certainty Factor to 30.

ISE Portals and Guest Access

INTRODUCTION

You've got your authentication rules done, and you've got your authorization rules laid out and maybe some profiling configured—but how do your users complete all of those steps? Sure a properly configured 802.1x supplicant will take care of it but you are almost always going to have some type of user who isn't going to reliably have a supplicant configured that you don't want to need one or that you need to get do more actions with. In those cases some sort of web portal is going to be what solves your problem. Portals in ISE 1.3 and later are all built very similarly and from the same location but each one can offer different configurations and work for different use cases so you will want to match your use up with the proper types in order to provide your users with the best experience.

PORTAL OVERVIEW

The portal sections of ISE are located in two places: under the Guest Access mega menu and under the Administration → Device Portal Management; the former obviously can be a little misleading since there are more than just guest portals there. The portals are highly customizable, allowing beginners/basic requirements to use the defaults without many changes being needed but still allowing advanced users the ability to customize almost all aspects of the portals to fit their business needs.[1]

Going to the "Configure" section of the Guest Access menu you will be shown an overview of the general process used to set up guest access for a network using ISE. It will show you that you need to prepare certificates, identity sources, Simple Mail Transfer Protocol (SMTP), SMS, etc., and then follow those up with types of portals, types of guests, and sponsor settings—all of which is probably a bit daunting to swallow if you just want to get guests onto your network. The truth is basic guest access isn't that hard to accomplish but highly customized guest access can be. We'll start with the former and work our way to the latter.

---

[1]Anyone coming from version of ISE earlier than 1.3 take note: *all* guest portal configuration is now done in this area. Settings are not spread out like they used to be prior to 1.3 and at the time of this writing custom HTML portals are not supported.

GUEST PORTAL TYPES

First thing you see when looking at the guest portals is that out of the box three default portal types are created and preconfigured for you—Hotspot, Self-Registered, and Sponsored. These are the three main types of portals that you will be creating for your guest needs and each one has its own pros/cons:

- Hotspot: This is just an "I accept," the AUP button.
  - Pro: Very simple and quick guest access, no registration required but you can still display them a welcome message and AUP.
  - Con: No actual user identity tracking of your guests/who they are. Anyone in range of your wireless network can get on.
- Self-Registered: Lets users create their own accounts.
  - Pro: Second simplest way to get on for guests and little to no Helpdesk overhead. Users register themselves based on criteria you set and are then given access.
  - Con: There are always bad apples. In our experience lots of guests will correctly fill out the required information but the rest will put fake information in to some effect. Expect to see lots of users named "a a" with emails of a@gmail.com.
- Sponsored: Requires credential to be created for the guest.
  - Pro: You will know who your guests are and who approved them. This ensures that only approved guests are on your network.
  - Con: Your user's interaction with the community; they will need to authorize/create users who want access to the network.

All portal configurations start with a similar layout; you have two sections you can work from—Portal Behavior/Flow Settings and Portal Page Customization. The Behavior/Flow Settings let you define how the portal is going to work, the interfaces/ports/certificates it will use, languages, etc. On the right-hand side of the page there is a flow that describes the steps guests can pass through as they gain network access. As you add/remove components you will see this area change to reflect the new login flow; it's a good way to verify and understand how your changes will impact guests. At the top of the page there is a "Portal Test URL" link that will open up an example of your saved portal configuration that allows you to test the functionality without needing to actually connect to the portal. Some of the simpler portals might not benefit as much from this but when you start adding employee BYOD support, AUPs, and pre/post access banners, it can be helpful to step through everything to make sure it's working the way you want it too. Each portal also has an option of including a "support information page" that guests can view that will show them information used to diagnose any problems they might run into. You might want to enable this when you first roll out guest access so that it's easier to iron out any issues you run into.

Moving over to the Portal Customization area, you have control in the UI over the images/color scheme used as well as some prebuilt themes to choose from. This is also where you will customize the text for each page of the guest flow you are working on.[2] Choosing a specific

---

[2]If you are really motivated, you can export the default themes as CSS templates or build completely new themes using the JQuery Mobile ThemeRoller tool. If your custom templates don't work well, always retest with the built-in themes.

page from the left-hand side will bring up all the text areas and let you put in straight text or HTML for each area. The right-hand side of the page will display a constantly updating view of what the page looks like on a phone-form factor mobile device giving you instant feedback to your changes. There is also the option to make some quick settings changes without needing to switch back to the Behavior/Flow Settings area. Right at the top of the preview, select Settings and you will see a listing of settings that apply for that page you are working on, another quick way to make changes if you need to. Lastly, as with the Behavior/Flow page, there is a link at the top to launch a test of the portal if you want to see how the complete product looks.

Hotspot Portal

The Hotspot portal is the simplest of all three types, which makes sense since the type of access is simple. OOTB there is a basic AUP configured and guests only need to accept or decline it. Clicking the portal test link should give you something like this.

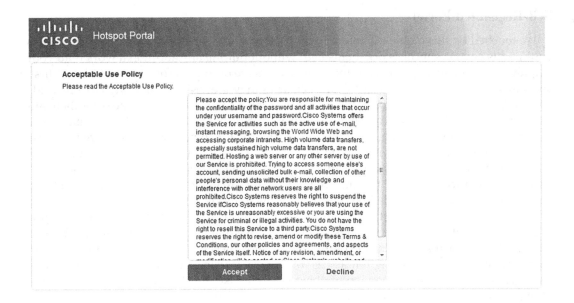

Should you use this the way it is, the only change you really need to make is edit the AUP so that it no longer says "Cisco Systems" (unless, you know, you *are* Cisco—hey guys!) and instead is your company name. If you have a standard AUP, you can put it here as well. In terms of configuration there isn't much you can select here other than requiring an access code and requiring that guests scroll to the end of the AUP. The latter might be required by your legal team but it's good to enable anyway so that clicking the Accept button isn't just an automatic option.

▼ Acceptable Use Policy (AUP) Page Settings

☑ Include an AUP page

☐ Require an access code: [_____]

☐ Require scrolling to end of AUP

The access code option lets you specify a code that users have to put in to gain access, preventing someone from sitting in a parking lot or just driving by from using your network. You can have the code printed out inside meeting rooms or your employees could give it out to guests. It can offer a little bit of protection to a typically "open" type of guest access.

Self-Registered Portal

We touched on this a little bit before but let's dive a bit deeper into it. Self-Registered lets your guests get onto the network themselves without putting any additional work onto your employees to help them get an account setup. Guests are prompted for some basic info—first, last, email, phone, company, reason for visit, who they are visiting, and any custom fields you create—and once they submit that info a username/password is generated for them automatically. Any of the fields can be marked as required so if you want first/last/email to be required because everyone will have those but don't want company to be required because you have individual guests, you can do that. Well, unless you have a minimum number of guests and they are very trustworthy, there will be people who fake the registration information to create an account. Now that may not be a big deal to you but it also could be something that completely throws this method out the window in terms of viability.

Option wise, the Self-Registration portal has a lot more options than Hotspot does. Starting out on the Behavior/Flow Settings page we can see that not only is the flow much more complicated (it's actually the most complex portal flow because of the registration part) but we're also going to start seeing references to employees using this portal. If you are purely doing guest access, then you can ignore these options. Like the Hotspot you have the option of requiring an access code when guests log in but you also have the option of using a registration code when guests create their accounts—you could even turn both of them on. Considering the use case though the registration code is probably more lined up with how guests will use the portal. You can have multiple AUPs as well, one for login and another during registration which can come in handy if you want to remind guests about who should be getting accounts as well as what they can/can't do. Splitting up the AUPs can make them easier to read and might make it less likely people will just skip through them but we all know that will still happen.

During account creation besides the normal options, guests will be able to pick a SMS provider where their credentials can be sent after successfully signing up. This is more helpful when dealing with a pure sponsor setup but it can be helpful here as well, sending the credentials to another place to make it easier for guests to remember and it can provide fidelity as to who the guest is. Until ISE 1.3 the only option was integration with an outside service to send the messages to guests but with 1.3 we can now send emails to HTTP gateways that providers offer—for free. Most major providers (AT&T™, Verizon™, Sprint™, T-Mobile™) offer these gateways and are built into ISE but you can easily add more if you have providers in your area that you want to support.

We have some options here to filter emails used during registration but using these will be not that common. The email addresses used during registration aren't actually verified at all so you could say you want only well-known webmail providers such as Yahoo™ or Gmail™; then someone just has to pick fakeemail24592@gmail.com to be able to register with that address. Blacklisting would have a similar effect where emails @baddomain9713.com aren't permitted but someone could just use somethingcleverise@gmail.com and register.

The recommended option rather than whitelisting/blacklisting, abet one that introduces some lag time from sign-up to availability, is to require that guests that self-register get approved by either a designated group of people or the person that the guest claims they are visiting. Both give some verification that someone is who they say they are or at least that they have (seemingly) correctly filled out the form. The group approach might be less likely to approve "bad" info that a person approving access for their friend would allow through but on the flip side the group could take time to respond where the person being visited by the guest is more likely to be with them and can quickly approve the guest account.

There are two features here that we want to call out specifically because unless you have an extremely specific reason, you should probably not enable them—Guest Device Compliance and VLAN DHCP Release. Device compliance enables posture assessment for guest devices and is generally not something you will normally want to make your guests do. Guest access is typically limited anyway (internet only in most cases, sometimes less) and while it makes sense to ensure machines attaching to your network are properly secured it results in a difficult flow for guest to go through. If you are concerned about the machines your guests are connecting with, it is probably easier to use one or more path isolation techniques (guest anchor WLCs, virtual routing and forwarding (VRFs), multipoint Generic Routing Encapsulation (mGRE), multiprotocol label switching (MPLS) VPN, etc.) and then not worry about the state of the machines. VLAN Release implies that your guests would be required to move between VLANs during their access and like your normal clients that is a nondesirable configuration. Using the normal ISE functionality of dACLs and URL redirects is a much better option. Further, you're going to rely on a guest client to cooperate in the DHCP release/renew action and that simply isn't possible.

Moving over to the customization side of the portal settings we see a lot of the same things we saw in the Hotspot portal. The left-hand side lists the different pages that can be customized while the center will show you the different text areas that can be customized to fit your needs. The only areas that are different from the hotpot portal are the Notification sections; under the Settings header of the right-side preview you can send test emails/SMS and preview the printed credentials. Instead of repeatedly registering test accounts you can see what your guests will see for notifications right from the portal where you are customizing them.

The customization area also includes a WYSIWYG editor[3] when applicable to the areas you are editing, that is, you won't see it for titles or labels but you would see it for the content they refer to.

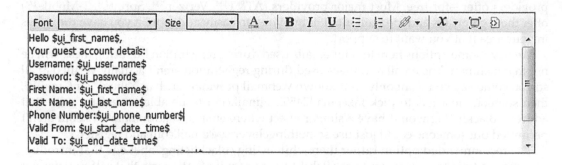

The editor has all the standard features in it such as font, size, color, lists, and links but the one important button to take note of it is the variables one (*x*, third in from the right). Clicking this will let you select variables from a substantial list that contains nearly anything you could want to put into your portal. Most important is that the variables you insert need to be relevant to the area you use them; if you use the "Client Provisioning Install Agent Minutes" in the Sponsor page login, then you aren't going to get anything but the variable string name on your login page.

Sponsored Guest Portal

This is going to be a short description because the last portal type is almost the same configuration wise as the self-registered guest. The only differences here are that the guest flow is simpler because there is no registration taking place and less customization sections.

GUEST TYPES

During creation of guests you have the ability to pick a type of guest account that will be created. OOTB you have three options to pick from—Daily, Weekly, and Contractor. The names give away the difference between each one and that's how long the account is good for: 5 days for the Daily type, 14 days for the Weekly type, and 365 days for a Contractor.

Besides the maximum time an account is valid each account type also lets you customize other options such as time of day limits, maximum number of logins, maximum number of devices, account expiration notification, and the sponsor groups that are allowed to create each account type.

---

[3]Remember that you can use both normal text and HTML to customize the portal.

One of the more interesting options here is the "Allow Guests to Bypass Guest Portal" option. ISE users prior to 1.3 will remember an "Activated Guest" type that would let users authenticate using 802.1x to the corporate SSID without needing to go through the web portal, a handy feature for long-lived guests. That feature is implemented in this portal bypass option. If you use this option, make sure that your AuthZ rules are correctly configured to match guests coming in using PEAP or they could match rules you wouldn't want them too.

SPONSOR SETUP

For use cases with sponsors either approving self-registered guests or creating accounts directly for guests, the sponsor area will be taking care of that. Sponsor functions are broken down into two areas, portals and groups. The sponsor portal is where users will go to perform their designated actions while the groups define the access they have within the portal(s). We'll go into this in detail because there are some gotcha's when it comes to how sponsor permissions and access line up; an incorrect setting can have you chasing your tail if you don't know where to look.

It's also worth noting that you can have multiple sponsor portals if you want. If your company has multiple departments that want different branding and/or different guest permissions, you could accomplish that this way.

Sponsor Groups

Before we configure the portal for sponsors we need to create/configure the sponsor groups so that ISE knows what permissions to give them when they log in. OOTB ISE creates three groups for us:

- All Accounts
- Group Accounts
- Own Accounts

As the names imply, by default the only differentiation in the default groups is who can see what. "All Accounts" is typically given to administrators or Helpdesk personnel since they would need to assist guests that had been created by other sponsors as well as themselves. "Group Accounts" could be used if you have front office people creating accounts and you want them to all be able to assist guests even if someone has gone home for the day but you also don't want to have to wait for/bother the Helpdesk. Lastly, the "Own Accounts" group would be where your typical sponsors go; they are able to log in and perform sponsor functions only to the accounts they have created themselves but obviously still have the Helpdesk to back them up if the guests need it.

Out of the box ISE also creates three local groups whose names match the sponsor groups so that you can easily just add local users to these groups and get your users access to the default sponsor functions. The downside to this is that it works only if you are using local users plus you would really want to tie this to something like AD so that your users don't have to deal with another password.

Sponsor group name:* | ALL_ACCOUNTS (default)

Description: | Sponsors assigned to this group can manage all guest user accounts. By default, users in the ALL_ACCOUNTS user identity group are members of this sponsor group

Members...

Sponsor Group Members

Search

Name ▴

ALL_ACCOUNTS (default)

LAB-AD:lab.local/LAB/Employee/Groups/Helpdesk

In the above figure we can see that we've added a custom group (our example Helpdesk) to the ALL_ACCOUNTS sponsor group. Clicking the "Members..." button will bring up a list of compatible groups, including those from external identity sources that can be used.[4]

Once we grant access to our sponsors, we'll want to determine the types of accounts they can create. The guest types we looked at earlier get assigned to the sponsor groups and permit sponsors to create those types of groups. You may want your normal sponsors that are part of the OWN_ACCOUNTS and GROUP_ACCOUNTS groups to only be able to create "Daily" users but the ALL_ACCOUNTS should be able to create all account types. Or maybe ALL_ACCOUNTS can create only Daily and Weekly accounts and you create another special group that is allowed to create the year-long validity Contractor accounts. You can configure guest locations as well, although this is mainly an accounting feature if you aren't writing specific AuthZ rules for guests in different locations. If you have a single campus and unified guest access, then the location won't matter.

The last part of the sponsor group setup is the configuration of what the sponsors can actually do once they have logged in. All sponsors can create single accounts so that isn't an option but the ability to import guests from a CSV file[5] or generate random guest accounts is something you can grant to your sponsors if it's something they will need to do.

Sponsor Can

- ☑ View guests' passwords
  - ☑ Reset guests' account passwords
- ☑ Extend guest accounts
- ☐ Send SMS notifications with guests' credentials
- ☑ Delete guests' accounts
- ☑ Suspend guests' accounts
  - ☐ Require sponsor to provide a reason
- ☑ Reinstate suspended guests' accounts
- ☑ Approve requests from self-registering guests
- ☐ Access Cisco ISE guest accounts using the programmatic interface (Guest REST API)

[4]Sponsor group permissions are cumulative! If a user is a member of both group A and group B that map to specific sponsor groups, they get the permissions equivalent to both groups.
[5]Seems like a really slick feature but we've never actually seen someone use this in real life.

You can control if sponsors have access to a guest's credentials, if they can send SMS notifications, deleting/suspending/extending accounts and even REST API access. In most situations you are probably going to want to check off all the boxes except for the last one. If you are using the REST API for guest account tasks, you should create a separate sponsor group and assign just that API user/group, which ensures your external application works but you also don't expose more than you need too. You might want to watch the SMS feature as well. If you have configured ISE to use the carrier-provided gateways, then you don't have to really worry about unknown charges, although they might block you for abuse if you have someone creating thousands of guest accounts in bulk. If you set up a service like Click-a-Tell where you have purchased a fixed number of SMS messages, you may not want sponsors to waste those notifications if they don't need to and if not you can disable that feature for them.

DEVICE PORTALS

Guest portals are used to mainly manage and deal with users with a little bit of device registration sprinkled in. On the other hand, device portals focus on use cases where devices are what you will be dealing with such as blacklisted devices, BYOD, and MDM. These portals and their configuration (if any) are the same as the guest versions with the only difference being that they are very basic, even more so than the Hotspot portal. Customizations revolve mainly around theming, ensuring all portals have a similar feel to them, and any wording that is used. Since most of the functionality has already been covered in the guest portal area we won't dive too deep but here is a quick description of the five device portals you could make use of within ISE:

- Blacklist: The most basic device portal, users see this when the device they use has been marked as lost/stolen by the owner or an administrator.
- BYOD: Seen by users registering a personal device for use on the company network. Chapter 13 covers this in more detail.
- Client Provisioning: Portal seen by users when posture is required and NAC or AnyConnect needs to be installed.
- MDM: Portal used to onboard devices into the company MDM platform, covered in more detail in Chapter 12.
- My Devices: This portal lets users manage the devices they have registered or add new ones.

GLOBAL GUEST SETTINGS

There are some settings for guests that can't be configured per type or per portal and those settings are contained in Guest Access → Settings. Here we have settings for usernames, passwords, purge policies, custom fields, etc. The only option listed here that takes you somewhere else is the SMS Gateway settings which take you into the System Settings area.

The first setting covers how often guest accounts are purged from ISE and when that purge occurs. If you hear a muffled cheer, that is anyone who has used ISE prior to 1.3 and had to deal with manually deleting guest accounts or letting them just accrue forever. There are no settings that define how long an expired account will stay around, how often the task runs to remove those expired accounts. That means that if you use the default period of 15 days, then it's possible an account could be expired and still be around for 15 days; likewise, an account could expire and then be immediately deleted if this purge task runs right afterwards. Neither of those cases are generally an issue but if they are it might be helpful to set up the schedule to purge accounts over the weekend or whenever you might have less requirement to reactivate an account. There is also a setting here to purge cached portal information for AD/LDAP users.

The next option is for custom fields which are where you would set up any additional information you want guests to fill out before they can gain network access. You can select the data type for the field as well, allowing some basic verification of the data being entered (if it's a date, phone number, email). Even though you can provide a "tip" to users for the field, be cautious when using this feature as it can lead to frustration if your guests aren't reading the directions provided. Simple use cases work well with Self-Registration but more complicated fields should probably be reserved for sponsor-type guests.

Guest Email Settings let you define if notifications go out to guests and if so who they are sent from. Notifications by default would be an email containing their username, password, and start/end time but if you enabled the expiration notifications in a guest type then these settings apply as well. You can either send notifications from a specified email address or have notifications be sent with the "from" address being the person who sponsored the guest account. This simple setting actually has a big gotcha and it's applicable to one other notification as well (CCing a sponsor when sending guest credentials): Unless you are using locally created sponsors ISE will not know what the email address should be and will always send from the default email address or in the case of CCing the sponsor the sponsor won't get any email. Please reference the administration section for more information about creating users.

The Guest Locations and SSID section might be the most confusing section of the global settings because looking at it initially you would think that it defines the locations that guests can use their credentials and which SSIDs they can use. The reality is that these settings are basically cosmetic and will probably play little role in your guest process. The location option is there to make it easier for you and your sponsors to map a proper time zone so that any time-based restrictions set on a guest type will work correctly for the location the guest currently is at. The SSID is a cosmetic feature that is shown in a notification that goes to the guest (print/email/SMS) so that if you have multiple SSIDs, and maybe they aren't obvious, there is something to help your guests connect. Now technically guest time zone information can be used in AuthZ rules as a condition but we haven't found a good case for it to be used for typical environments. Should you want to use either of these features, remember SSIDs that can be selected by sponsors are configured in the sponsor portal settings and the locations that can be picked are configured under the sponsor groups.

Guest Username/Password policy sections do exactly what their name implies: configure what valid guest usernames and passwords are. The username policies let you select either using the format of "firstname.lastname" or the guests' email address as their username. Unless you decide not to require an email address it's highly recommended to set the username of the guest as their email address. Assuming the email address is correct, it is almost a guaranteed unique value that the guest already easily knows. That may seem like a silly thing to suggest but when using "firstname.lastname" and running into users with the same names ISE will start appending incrementing numbers to the end of the username but guests tend to not always look at the username completely. Instead of logging in with "jon.snow001" they will try to log in with "jon.snow"; the credential given to them won't work; they will lock out their IP/ account and they will complain they can't get online. Picking good password requirements can be equally important; a common issue is that when passwords are sent to guests, some of the characters can start to look the same: l1O0i l all have the possibility to make it more difficult to log in if they get used in a guest's password. The solution to that would be to use customized alphabets that remove those characters so that when ISE generates the password it won't contain anything that's hard to read. These include the characters 0 and O or 1 and l and I.

▼ **Guest Password Policy**   Specify the policy settings that will apply to guest passwords.

Specify the password requirements that will be enforced for all guest passwords. Passwords are case sensitive.

Password Length

         Minimum password   `8`   (1-127 characters)
                length:*

Allowed Characters and Minimums

    Alphabetic lowercase: `Custom ▼`   `abcdefghjk`
      Minimum lowercase: `1`   (0-64)

    Alphabetic uppercase: `Custom ▼`   `ABCDEFGH`
      Minimum uppercase: `1`   (0-64)

            Numeric: `Custom ▼`   `23456789`
      Minimum numeric: `1`   (0-64)

            Special: `All supported ▼`
      Minimum special: `0`   (0-64)

Password Expiration

   ○ Password must be changed every `10`   days (count starts at first login)
   ◉ Password never expires

However, if you do customize the allowed characters, you need to ensure that you don't check off any of the password expiration/change on first login options. Guests would then have to also not use a password that contains any of those characters you removed and your guests won't understand why the password they use everywhere else doesn't work on your network. If you want guests to rotate or set their own passwords, it's a better option to shorten the random passwords that are generated initially so that it's easier to log in and then the guest will set their own password.

MAKING PORTAL MODIFICATIONS

When talking about portal modifications, one of the main reasons for going beyond just the typical settings is that a company wants to make guest portals more "seamless" with other sites guests could see/have seen. Perhaps you even want to expand the languages that are shipped with ISE so that you can better support a more diverse group of guests—happier guests are happier customers after all.

We touched briefly on customization before but it warrants a closer look since it will probably be one of the more desired/requested changes. We'll use the default self-service portal as our example here so let's take a look at what's there by default.

The default theme is called "Default Blue theme" but there are three other provided ones that you can pick from if you think they look better or closer to what you want—Default Olive, Default Fresh Blue, and Default High Contrast. The latter gives you a color scheme that makes it easier for anyone with trouble seeing to view the page on their laptop/mobile device.[6]

Image wise you can customize the mobile/desktop page logos that show in the upper left corner as well as the banner that spans the top of the page or even delete both by clicking the "X" next to them if you don't want the images there at all. Images you do upload will be automatically scaled to the size ISE requires and you can't pick how that is done so take that into account when choosing images; you may have to edit the images a little before uploading to get them to look the way you want. Take the following two images for example; the first shows the use of a new logo and banner but the banner was resized in such a way that we only got the blue top while the second shows how using a slightly cropped version of that image results in the display of the "ice"-like background.

Sponsored Guest Portal

Sign On
Welcome to the Guest Portal. Sign on with the username and password provided to you.

Username:

[   ] *

[6]Other than the High Contrast theme, all the other default themes will look the same when you pick them unless you delete the default banner image first.

Other page values can be changed from the "Tweaks" button next to where you pick the theme. Options here let you adjust the banner color, banner text color, page background color, and page text color; there is however a catch to them. While using a banner image the banner color choice isn't actually used and the page text color impacts only the footer text which isn't there by default but can be entered into the Footer Elements text box. The center portion of the page will, unless using the default high contrast theme, always use a white background with black text and if you want to change that you need to use the tools mentioned previously in this chapter to edit an exported copy of the theme and then import your changes.

Language additions/updates/removals can be handled two ways, the easy way and the hard way. The hard way is to change the language that you are viewing the customization page in and then go to each area of the portal and change the language to what you want it to be. This is really useful only for tiny edits for one or two languages, for example, if you are going to worry only about the English sections, then this might be a bit more feasible but doing that for 15 languages isn't very practical. The easy way is to export the entire Language File, make your edits/additions in bulk, and then reimport the file.

When exported, the files come down in a ZIP file that contains each language's .properties file with the relevant text in each one. If large changes are being made, the whole ZIP can be sent off to a company for translation and then you can import it when they send it back to you without having to worry about error-prone manual methods.

Chances are you will make use of more than one portal type as your network evolves or if you want to have multiple "types" of guests. Perhaps you have a Hotspot or Self-Registered guest network that gives people basic or low-performance internet access so they can quickly get on if needed but a Sponsored portal for guests that need more liberal internet access. This method gives you the best of both worlds; the majority of guests will be able to quickly get on and access their resources but those that need elevated access get verified by a sponsor first.

SCENARIOS

We've gone over the descriptions of the different portals and their most popular settings but let's look at some specific scenarios that you might run into during your ISE deployment. We'll cover a simple Hotspot portal configuration with an access code, configurations of a sponsor portal, and finally the AuthZ rules that support the guest portal.

Hotspot Portal

For this scenario we're going to start with a fresh Hotspot portal but the default OOTB one will work too if you haven't made any changes:

1. To create that portal go to Guest Access → Configure → Guest Portals → click "Create" → Select "Hotspot Guest Portal" and then click "Continue...."
2. Name your new portal and add a description of what the portal will do/be used for.

Portal Name: *	Description:	
Guest Hotspot	Hotspot portal with access code and AUP	Portal test URL

3. Specify which identity group you'd like guest endpoints added to. After they accept the AUP, their MAC address will be added to a group that may be referenced in the AuthZ ruleset. The default is "GuestEndpoints" but in the case where you have multiple portals different endpoint identity groups may be used.

Endpoint identity group: * GuestEndpoints ▾

Configure endpoint identity groups at:
Administration > Identity Management > Groups > Endpoint Identity Groups

4. Leave everything under the "Portal Settings" section the way it is.
5. Under "Acceptable Use Policy (AUP) Page Settings" check off "Require an access code" and input whatever you want your code to be. The code can contain letters, numbers, and symbols. Also check off "Require scrolling to end of AUP" to be sure your users read the whole thing.

> ▼ **Acceptable Use Policy (AUP) Page Settings**
>
> ☑ Include an AUP page
>   ☑ Require an access code: [example1234]
>   ☑ Require scrolling to end of AUP

6. For "Authentication Success Settings" you have a couple of options; the ideal one is shown. Sending the user to their originating URL keeps the process the guest is going through nice and clean but it requires a supported device running Cisco IOS 15.2(2) E. Googling for "Web Authentication Redirection to Original URL" should get you the supported device list. If you can't support this, then the other two options are used equally, sending the guest to a generic success page or sending them to a designated URL like the company webpage. For most places we would recommend going the "Authentication Success Page" route for simplicity.

> ▼ **Authentication Success Settings**
>
> Once authenticated, take guest to:
>   ◉ Originating URL ⓘ
>   ○ Authentication Success page
>   ○ URL: [ ]

7. We'll enable the Support Information Page to assist guests in gathering information that can assist the Helpdesk in getting them online. Hiding the empty fields also keeps the page clean and simple, no need to complicate information here.

▼ Support Information Page Settings

☑ Include a Support Information page

Fields to include:

    ☑ MAC address

    ☑ IP address

    ☑ Browser user agent

    ☑ Policy server

    ☑ Failure code

Empty Fields

    ◉ Hide field

    ○ Display label with no value

    ○ Display label with default value:

8. We've finished the portal settings but we still need to customize some of the other aspects of the portal to meet our needs. Head over to the "Portal Page Customization" section and replace the default AUP in the "AUP Text" area with one provided by your company or write something generic to go in its place.

9. Finally, save the portal configuration and then click the "Portal Test URL" link at the top of the page to see the final outcome. You should be greeted by something similar to what is shown here.

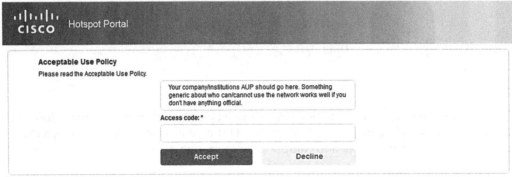

We now have a working Hotspot guest portal in nine easy steps! If you close out of the portal page and back to the list of Guest portals, you will see our new portal but it will have "Authorization setup required" listed under it and a yellow triangle. ISE knows that there are now AuthZ rules that point guests at this Hotspot so it warns you that more setup steps are needed. Since it's the next step, let's do that right now.

Guest Portal AuthZ Rules

Other than assuming we already have a portal configured, the only other assumption for this example is that you have a basic authorization framework created which contains a redirect ACL on your WLC(s). Check Chapter 6 for a good example if you need one.

First, we're going to want to configure our AuthZ result that will tell ISE to direct users matching a condition we define to the Hotspot portal we configured.

Authorization Profile

* Name	GUEST_WIRELESS
Description	Sends guests to the hotspot portal
* Access Type	ACCESS_ACCEPT
Service Template	☐

▼ **Common Tasks**

☑ Web Redirection (CWA, MDM, NSP, CPP)

Hot Spot ▼	ACL	ACL-REDIRECT	Value	Guest Hotspot ▼

☐ Static IP/Host name

This result is very simple; the only thing to note is that the web redirection type has a special "Hot Spot" value which is different than the normal "Centralized Web Auth" we would use for Self-Register or Sponsored portals. No other value is required in the result.

Next we'll configure the AuthZ rules themselves that will support guests getting redirected to the Hotspot and then after agreeing being granted normal guest access. This will happen with two rules like those seen here.

Status	Rule Name		Conditions (identity groups and other conditions)		Permissions
☑	GUEST_WIFI	if	**GuestEndpoints** AND Airespace:Airespace-Wlan-Id EQUALS 7	then	PermitAccess
☑	GUEST_WIFI_SIGNIN	if	Airespace:Airespace-Wlan-Id EQUALS 7	then	GUEST_WIRELESS

Since rules are processed in a top-down manner we have to build the rules in a way that can look a little bit backwards but makes sense once we step through. Both rules make use of the Airspace-Wlan-Id attribute, which in this case is 7 and maps to a dedicated guest SSID we've created. Since that SSID will only ever be used for guest access it's ok that we're using it like this. The other attribute checked is the Endpoint Identity Group which we set in the Hotspot guest portal configuration. Our traffic flow is going to look something like the following:

1. User connects to "guest" SSID whose Wlan-Id is 7.[7]
2. User matches the second rule by default and ISE sends the GUEST_WIRELESS results to the WLC.
3. Guest is shown the Hotspot portal, enters the access code, accepts the AUP, and is granted access. Authenticating device's MAC is also added to the GuestEndpoint group.
4. ISE sends a CoA to the WLC and the client starts the authorization process again.
5. This time because the guest has successfully gone through the Hotspot their devices' MAC is in the GuestEndpoint identity group and matches the first rule.
6. ISE sends the "PermitAccess" results to the WLC and the client is granted network access.

The rules defined in the previous image would also work for other types of guest portals; you would only need to adjust the AuthZ results so that it was correct and the same process continues to work.

Configuring Sponsors

Since sponsors, if you are using them, will be critical to guest access we'll want to ensure that the correct people have access and that it's easy for them to get access. Our assumptions here are that you are using AD for authentication, have AD groups already configured for your users and that they have already been brought into ISE via the External Identity Source area so they can be used. Our example will be similar to some of the examples used previously in this chapter so we'll be setting up access for three groups of people: Helpdesk personnel, Secretaries, and general employees.

We'll start with assigning our AD groups to sponsor groups; we'll utilize two of default groups that ISE has OOTB but we're going to create one more for the Secretaries because they are a unique case. Start in Guest Access → Configure → Sponsor Groups, create a new group, and assign the relevant AD group as a member.

Sponsor group name:* Secretary_Accounts

Description: Special permissions for company secretaries

Members...

Sponsor Group Members

Search

Name

LAB-AD:lab.local/LAB/Employee/Groups/Secretaries

[7]Another reasonable option for matching SSID is selecting the called station ID if the SSID is included by the WLC.

Our use case for this group is that they will be responsible for guests or groups that are coming to visit the organization. Schedules could rotate during the day so we want anyone who is in the front area/other location to be able to assist guests. Large groups may come in as well and so we want to be able to generate a batch of accounts with a unique prefix so we can identify the group as well as get them access quickly without having to create numerous individual accounts. In order to accomplish this the new group is going to be given the following permissions:

- Create "Daily" users
- Can select any supported location
- Sponsor can:
  - Create multiple guest accounts to be assigned to any guests (random)
  - Allow sponsor to specify a username prefix
  - Limit to batch of 30
- Sponsor can manage:
  - Account created by members of this sponsor group
- Sponsor can:
  - Do everything but use the guest REST API

Next we'll take our other two AD groups and assign them to the proper existing sponsor groups. Helpdesk will be placed into the ALL_ACCOUNTS group and general employees will be placed into the OWN_ACCOUNTS group. For the most part the default group's settings are fine but we'll want to adjust a couple of things to prevent possible abuse and make our guests a little bit happier:

- All groups:
  - Enable "Send SMS notifications with guest' credentials."
  - Enable "Require sponsor to provide a reason" under the "Suspend guests' account" option.
- OWN_ACCOUNTS:
  - Ensure only the "Daily" guest type is permitted for creation.
  - Disable "Multiple guest accounts assigned to specific guests."
  - Disable "Multiple guest accounts to be assigned to any guests."
  - Prevent accounts from being created with start dates more than 30 days in the future.

Now that our groups are created we'll configure the portal so that our sponsor can log in and create/manage guest accounts. Switch to the "Sponsor Portals" area and open the default portal. Enter the FQDN that sponsors will use to connect to the portal, something like "sponsor.example.com" and let your DNS administrator know that FQDN should be a CNAME to your PSN(s) A records.[8] You'll also want to ensure that the certificate you're using for portals has the portal FQDN as either the CN or SAN or use a wildcard certificate for your portals.

---

[8]When bookmarking the sponsor portal, make sure the bookmark is *just* the FQDN you pick. ISE handles the redirection to another port and appends some additional information. If you bookmark the specific link, you will probably get 404 errors down the road if things change.

The default ISS is fine but you may want to adjust it to fit your own needs; similarly you can leave the SSID section blank unless you want to create and add one. The only other change we'll make to the settings is to require scrolling to the end of the AUP, ensuring that our sponsors can't say they didn't "see" an important section of it.

Moving over to the Customization tab select "Acceptable Use Policy" under the "Portal Access" section and put in the AUP that is used by your company or edit the existing one so that it has your company name instead of "Cisco Systems." Under the "Create Accounts" section in "Guest Types" select the "Settings" tab above the preview window and check off "Hide guest type if only one is available to sponsor"; that keeps unneeded information off the page for our OWN_ACCOUNT sponsors. In the "Create Account for Known Guests" section go to the preview area settings and check off:

- Required fields:
  - First name
  - Last name
  - Email address
- Guests can choose from the following SMS providers[9]:
  - T-Mobile
  - ATT
  - Verizon
  - Sprint

We want to require those basic fields because everyone visiting should have them and the SMS providers selected are the major US ones and provide free SMS SMTP gateways for us to use. If you are somewhere else or are using another SMS Gateway service such as Click-a-Tell, then select that instead. Finally let's customize the Email and Print notifications to include the SMS provider in them. Right after the phone number line in each area insert the line "SMS Provider:$ui_sms_provider$".

```
Last Number $ui_last_name$
Phone Number:$ui_phone_number$
SMS Provider:$ui_sms_provider$
Valid From: $ui_start_date_time$
```

Add others as well if you like, using the variable button in the WYSIWIG editor. The SMS provider is a quick example of how we can add something and give our users a little bit more information about their account. It can also be helpful if you are doing SMS notifications and someone doesn't get one, quickly looking at an email or printed guest info will tell you if maybe the wrong provider was selected.

That should be all you need to get started. From here your sponsors given access via your AD groups will be able to log in to this portal and create guest accounts for people who need them.

[9]Using SMS for password notification is great but if you're unsure of cellular coverage in your physical location or the local provider isn't in your ISE list, it may be smart to disable SMS notification.

10

Deployment Strategies

It would be nice if we could assume that every network we work on every day is net new and doesn't otherwise have anyone currently connected on it. In that case, we wouldn't have to deal with any whiney end users until we're done configuring the network for their use. Unfortunately this is not our reality and almost all the time we have to implement a technology it's into an existing environment that has operational users that we need to be sensitive to. ISE is no different than any other technology in this regard. If you're evaluating or seeking to deploy ISE in your environment, you're going to have to do it in a manner that does not disrupt your current users' work flow, or at least minimally disrupts your users while you implement the desired network access restrictions. There are definitely techniques that can be employed to make this process smooth. We'll break these down between implementing wired networks and implementing wireless networks separately because from a technical perspective they tend to function distinctly but the process from a logical standpoint can happen at the same time. We'll start with wired networks.

Wired ISE deployment broadly breaks down into several phases:

1. Planning/design
2. Pilot
3. Implement monitor mode
4. Implement enforcement mode
5. Network operation/enhancement

ISE deployments around existing wired networks can become challenging because it may be presumed that a great number of devices currently connected to your wired infrastructure do not have an 802.1x supplicant and we may not have a complete inventory of the types of devices deployed. This is why we deploy monitor mode first. Let's define monitoring and enforcement for clarity:

- Monitor mode: A configuration where ISE will allow any device connecting to the network unrestricted access
- Enforcement mode: A configuration where ISE will enforce network policy on unknown or unwanted devices restricting them from accessing sensitive or internal corporate resources

Understanding the definitions of each of these is important and there are a couple of points you should be aware of. First, just because something is in monitor mode does not mean that

ISE does not control the function of the port. In the monitor mode deployment as we're going to detail below, ISE will control interfaces where authentication is configured, but ISE will allow any MAC address onto the network without restriction.[1]

Enforcement means that unknown devices[2] which connect to the network are restricted from network access. That restriction can take many forms including dACL restrictions or some kind of web authentication. Some of the following is purposefully vague because the enforcement mode is a relatively small part of the effort you will put in.

Getting the network into monitor mode is possibly the most challenging part of a wired ISE implementation. There are a few ways of doing this but we'll detail the method that we've found to be most effective.

Let's first go through the behavior of devices on modern networks with ISE authentication. Devices will be either authenticated with 802.1x or utilizing MAB functions. We may typically assume that devices that are corporate domain member PCs are going to be doing 802.1x. In the long term, devices that are doing 802.1x authentication are easy to manage because we don't necessarily need additional information about them (outside of their authentication behaviors) to properly apply network policy. Devices using MAB are the ones that do not have supplicant configurations for 802.1x for any number of reasons. Reasons may include:

- They are embedded devices that don't support 802.1x, for example, older printers, scanners, and non-Cisco APs.
- They are corporate domain member PCs that are not configured properly.
- They are PCs owned by contractors that perform required duties on site but the devices are not corporate assets.
- The device is rogue and should not be attached to the corporate network.

Without an absolute inventory of the first three sets of those devices (obviously you won't have an inventory of rogue devices), it may be very challenging to write ISE policy where when you deploy it you can go straight to enforcement mode without accidentally restricting access to users who may need access to resources that were not in production to your knowledge.

From an operational perspective, because none of those devices will typically have an 802.1x supplicant enabled by default, they connect to a switchport, and if it's enabled for ISE control, the authentication process that ISE will attempt to utilize is MAB. This is where the exact behavior of ISE is useful to understand. We're going to take a step back and do a little review of some key concepts that are required for monitor mode:

- In the ISE configuration provided in Chapter 7, each edge switchport will allow both dot1x and MAB. If dot1x is not utilized by the endpoint, the switchport will attempt to authenticate the endpoint in ISE with MAB.
- When profiling is enabled with the "RADIUS" probe on an ISE policy node, every MAC address that is sent to ISE is added to the Endpoint Identity store inside ISE.

---

[1]Because ISE is controlling network access even in monitor mode, it's important to understand that should ISE fail (or the switch lose network connectivity to ISE) that critical authorization be enabled to prevent connecting users from completely losing access to network resources.

[2]Devices that otherwise don't have an explicit authorization policy to permit access.

With that in mind, when you go through the AAA process of an endpoint that is presented to ISE with "RADIUS" profiling enabled, every AuthC operation will succeed in a typical ISE authentication policy.

That doesn't necessarily mean that every endpoint will be permitted network access; it just means that the AAA process will then move on to the AuthZ ruleset to determine if the endpoint is permitted, denied, and if any additional attributes are sent to a switch in the event of a successful authorization. This is where we can manipulate network permissions to achieve a successful monitor mode.

In the authorization ruleset, if we create a rule that matches just "Wired_MAB," we will match any possible MAC address that is learned by the ISE profiler.

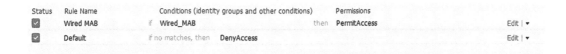

In the case above, we would achieve monitor mode for all wired connections; we also wouldn't have the capability of restricting what would or would not be in monitor mode. Obviously this will not scale because you would have no ability to bring segments of your network piece by piece from monitor mode to some type of enforcement. The easiest way to manipulate what is and is not in monitor mode is by creating a group of switches that are in monitor mode and a group of switches that are in enforcement mode. This way you need to only manipulate which group a switch is a member of to change its enforcement (monitor mode) behavior.

Groups of switches (or any network device) are created by browsing: Administration → Network Resources → Network Device Groups.

Most typically you will want to create a couple of different groups of device types. In this case we've created the following:

- Enforced-Switch: A group for switches that should perform some kind of network access enforcement
- Monitor-Switch: A group of switches that should be in monitor mode
- Wireless: A group for WLCs (not relevant for this section but since you are here why not create it)

You can then set the switch's group membership under the Network Device configuration.

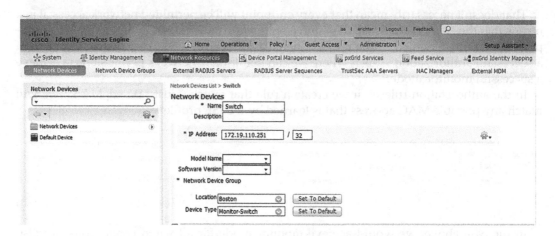

In this case our switch is set to be a member of the "Monitor-Switch" group. Now we can create an authorization policy that takes advantage of the network device groups we created.

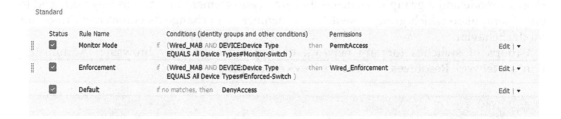

With that policy we can change how that switch authorizes devices centrally in ISE without any change in the actual end switch configuration. In this case all that is required for authentication to have the enforcement action is to change the switch configuration inside ISE.

The advantage of this type of configuration in monitor mode is that the level of effort to bring devices between monitor mode and enforcement is really easy. You also can perform reporting very easily based on network device group or authorization profile.

The behavior of this is also pretty low impact, so low impact that typically when we work with customers to bring them from monitor mode to enforcement, it can be done during business hours. Once we've run reports on a particular switch and found that there are no longer devices that require monitor mode for authorization, we can change the switch's membership to enforcement mode. When you change the switch's membership, it does not change the authorization of any existing switch authentication session to active. It simply changes the behavior for any further authorizations that are initiated by the switch.

Earlier in this chapter we said that getting into monitor mode was more challenging than enforcement. This is simply because the initial configuration of ISE control of edge switchports is typically service impacting to clients, at least briefly. Going from monitoring to enforcement mode, because it will not impact sessions that are established with ISE, is not itself service impacting. Let's talk about why this happens and what to expect on common devices.

When you're deploying ISE in monitor mode on a switch, here are the typical steps to follow. First, configure the switch (in ISE) as a network device in the monitor mode group. Then configure all the global parameters on the edge switch, RADIUS servers, AAA, device sensor, etc. Lastly, on the edge switchports that should be controlled with ISE, apply the authentication parameters required for the edge. That last step is where clients can experience a brief network outage. This outage is caused when the switch is suddenly asked to authenticate the edge client when it did not require authentication before. For a regular PC, when this happens, you might see a couple of pings lost if doing a continuous ping, but it's not an extended outage.

If your network has IP phones deployed on it, it's important to remember that a simple "monitor mode" rule result like the previous example is not going to allow a phone to connect on the voice VLAN. For it to get assigned to the voice VLAN it will need to be profiled such that we can provide the phone the authorization result containing the voice domain permission. This means, functionally, the phones will not, and cannot, be using the monitor mode rule; they'll have to be profiled. This may sound scary, but if you've tested profiling policies in advance, the risk that this does happen is pretty low. In any case, you should expect to see phones reregistering to the Cisco Unified Communications Manager (CUCM) or rebooting when you apply the authentication configuration to edge switchports.

If you are deploying ISE on switchports that have wireless APs on them, there are a few things to keep in mind. First, if you're using FlexConnect APs that have local switching configured at the AP, you should not deploying ISE on the edge switchport that connects to the AP. FlexConnect APs are best deployed with switchport that are set as trunks, and the authentication commands require that the switchport is in access mode. If you're deploying APs in standard local mode where all WLANs are fully tunneled back to the WLC, there is not an issue with authenticating the edge port that connects APs. During the initial configuration of authentication on the switchport, like a regular PC, a small amount of traffic loss should be expected while the MAC address of the AP is authenticated and authorized against ISE. Typically this packet loss is enough to cause the AP to deregister from the WLC. During this time the AP is unavailable to service wireless clients.[3] In the case of APs, because they don't require access to the voice VLAN, the monitor mode rule will function for them if profiling fails initially.

---

[3]This should probably go without saying, but if you're going to configure ISE on a switch, be sure you're not connecting to the switch wirelessly from an AP that will be on an ISE-authorized switchport. You'll lose connectivity to the switch when the AP crashes as it loses connectivity to the WLC. If this happens to you, you'll have no one but yourself to blame.

The last common device to deal with in deploying monitor mode is printers. These are typically the problem children of ISE monitor mode. Printers typically have a very lazy OS that runs them, lazy in that they normally don't send data to the network gratuitously; rather they sit there idle and wait for a job to be sent their way from either an edge client or a print server. As mentioned in Chapter 3 for MAB to function an edge device has to send the NAD a packet so that the switch can learn the port's MAC address and then that MAC can be sent to ISE for authorization. Well, in the case of a printer, if it does not ever send any information gratuitously and simply waits for something to connect to it, the ISE cannot authorize that port. Once the printer is made to send something (anything really) to the network, either it will profile properly or it can use the monitor mode rule. Because of this behavior, it's pretty common to have to reboot some number of printers in an office. When a printer is rebooted, the printer will have to do some of the following: require an IP via DHCP, or connect to an NTP server, or ARP for its own default gateway. Once it's done any of these, ISE will learn its MAC address and the port may become authorized. As part of any ISE monitor mode deployment it's important to run around and briefly test all the printers and be prepared to reboot them should they not immediately function.

Given all the potential things that can lose connectivity with the network while going into monitor mode, it should be pretty clear that in nearly every case it's important to do the monitor mode implementation during a maintenance window. You'll want someone onsite who has familiarity with how to make sure edge devices are generally functioning after you deploy monitor mode. This is not meant to scare anyone here because once you've pinged all your printers when you configure your switch for monitor mode, you're generally done. Devices that have any feature that does a keep alive will come back only pretty quickly.

Once you're into monitor mode, the day after your implementation you're going to want to spend some quality time reviewing your authorization logs and run report to see what is actually hitting your monitor mode authorization profile. These devices will have full network access on the data domain VLAN but if your goal is to get into a deployment with some level of enforcement you'll want to find out what kinds of devices are utilizing the monitor mode AuthZ profile. Reasons they may be using the monitor mode authorization profile may include:

- They are corporate assets that should be using 802.1x but for whatever reasons their supplicants are not configured as such. These would typically need to be repaired by support staff.
- They are devices that are not matching a profile configured. This may be because of the following reasons:
  - The profiler probes are not functioning properly. This would mean you would troubleshoot device sensor, IP helpers, or SNMP integration between ISE and the NAD.
  - Devices are not providing information that you were anticipating having. This may include DHCP information where in reality the devices are statically addressed.
  - The endpoint profile was not actually configured for use in the authorization ruleset.
- The device is an authorized noncorporate asset that would function in an enforcement scenario. This may be an onsite contractor who would not require access to internal corporate resources. These can typically be ignored.
- The device is malicious or rogue or otherwise not authorized to be connected to the network. In the case of these devices you would typically want to revoke their access if you're going to be in monitor mode for a while.

The next obvious thing you're going to ask yourself is "how long should I be in monitor mode?" In all honesty every deployment is different and there are lots of factors that can go into how long you stay in monitor mode. They can include:

- The level of effort involved in remediating devices that are hitting the monitor mode authorization profile but should not. This could be because there is a significate technical challenge that needs to be surmounted around implementing 802.1x supplicants, or just the sheer number of devices that need to be evaluated.
- The volume of staff resources dedicated to remediating devices. If it's no one's job to evaluate what is utilizing monitor mode, it'll be impossible to move to enforcement.
- The level of urgency around moving to enforcement. If there is no regulatory requirement around moving to enforcement mode, then taking one's time may be entirely acceptable.

When I look back on my ISE deployments, I have customers who experience monitor mode broadly differently in the amount of time they were in monitor mode. My maniac coauthor, Jeremy, completely skipped monitor mode and went directly to enforcement because he has an incredible handle on what devices were on his network—and has absolutely no regard for human life (Andy's right, it was pretty crazy—J.W.). Most people are in monitor mode between a week and a month. Some users may decide that they don't actually need to advance to enforcement because in monitor mode endpoint profiling and auditing provides them sufficient network visibility to meet their requirements.

The actual act of moving to enforcement mode involves just going into the network device inside ISE and changing its device-type group membership. When you do this, any new device connecting to the network will be subject to enforcement action if they don't match one of the other authorization policies above. That being said, if there are any active sessions on the switch when you change the device group membership, the active sessions will not be impacted, even if they're currently using the "monitor mode" authorization result. Any new sessions that are initiated from the NAD in question will then be subject to enforcement if the authorization doesn't otherwise match one of the authorization conditions above.

Now that we've talked about the mechanics of what monitor mode is actually, we actually need to think about what we can do for an enforcement mechanism. There are a few really good options for enforcement that ISE provides for us that we're going to talk about. It's possible that your environment may use more than one of these depending on your requirement and as you think about how you want your environment to behave do keep an open mind because when you really analyze, the functionality provided by any of them may change your mind from your initial instinct. Although there are possibly more, the following are the three most common enforcement types:

1. You can provide a dACL that restricts access to internal resources but provides the customer unfettered internet access. This would involve creating a dACL that restricts access to RFC1918 network and any network that your company happens to own and then permits connectivity to anything else. This is transparent to users as the ACL is applied and internet access is granted while quietly restricting access to internal devices.
2. Configure a CWA page that requires the user to log in to gain access to network resources. This lets you provide differentiated access between user types (guest vs. AD) and lets you apply different network restrictions based on who the user is. You may also

gain additional profiling information from this CWA based on the browser user agent and web kit from the web authentication.

3. You could provide a dACL that allows the endpoint to obtain an IP address but nothing else. This type of authorization allows the device to obtain no network access other than DHCP. Allowing the client to obtain an IP address lets us gain profiling information about the client without allowing them to gain access to any significant network resources.

There are a few other enforcement mechanisms that are optional, more of a second tier. They're valid design options but typically are problematic at scale, don't provide flexibility, or may not provide a great end user experience:

1. If you have a dedicated "guest"-type VLAN configured in your closets, you can do a VLAN override for unknown devices to that VLAN.[4] This can help you provide path separation for wired guest-type users where you feel that VLAN segmentation is more appropriate. The issue for this is that it may be more difficult to provide ISE with DHCP profiling information if device sensor is not available. Also, if a device is first connected to the network and does not initially have a profile determined in ISE, in this case it will be assigned to the guest VLAN. If the device is then properly profiled once it's connected to the network for some time, ISE will have to CoA the session and change the device's VLAN. This VLAN change means the client will have to change subnets. This CoA can be service impacting in a couple of ways. If it's done with a port bounce, the switch interface will be "shut/no shut" by ISE which will allow the client to obtain a new address. But this could obviously take some time and will be intrusive to whatever the endpoint is. If there are multiple devices connected to that port (like a phone), the other devices will lose connectivity to and could potentially reboot (in the case of the phone). If a "reauth"-type CoA is done, the whole port is left up but there will be no way for the client to know that its VLAN was just changed and without manual intervention the client will not be functional in the network until it obtains a valid address for its VLAN.[5]

2. If you're inclined to entirely deny network access to endpoints, you can create an authorization policy that has an "access-reject" result. This will provide the endpoint no network access. We typically don't use this because it's preferable to at least allow the endpoint to obtain an IP address so we can gain some additional profiling information.

We'd like to point out that as you go through and design your ISE policy, all of the options listed above are not mutually exclusive. Depending on how you deploy your NAD groups you could have a variety of styles of enforcement across your organization to suit different security needs and corporate cultures of each subgroup in your company. That being said, start with one and add additional ones if you find that the need suits you.

---

[4]The term "guest VLAN" in cases like this might not be 100% correct; in reality the VLAN would be used for any devices that otherwise failed authentication. Think of the VLAN more like an "unauthenticated" VLAN because occasionally you may have a misconfigured printer end up here.

[5]Beyond the fact that we generally think that VLAN override should be using sparingly, we also want to note that doing a VLAN override, in itself, does not necessarily restrict network access to devices that are being moved from one VLAN to another. You need to be prepared to have a scalable solution for actually securing the devices from one another if you're going to rely on VLAN override.

WIRELESS

Transitioning an enterprise wireless network from a pretty wide open design to a more enforced configuration is a much different animal from a wired environment. This is because we start out doing wired networks presuming that most devices in a corporate LAN do not do 802.1x by default or have not been required to yet. There is also often no logical differentiation in network access on edge networks beyond VLANs that often do not have ACLs associated with their switched virtual interfaces (SVIs). Wireless networks, by a few aspects of their nature, are a completely different animal:

1. Wireless networks use SSIDs to different use cases. These use cases are the same ones we've been discussing (guest, secure access, mobile device data offload, etc.).
2. Wireless devices' use of 802.1x is far more common in organizations than it is on wired network access. This is for a pretty simple reason; it's easier to install 802.1x on an SSID than a switch with a bunch of printers.
3. There is an expectation of network segmentation that typically does not exist on wired networks. This is, in my opinion, because wireless networks do not have really specifically physical limitations (you can get to them in the parking lot depending on your build's specific configuration); people expect to have their access tailored or restricted. If you plug into a corporate network from your office, people often expect to have really broad unrestricted access.

If you're looking to deploy ISE into an existing wireless network, it's often because you're looking to implement increased controls on the devices and who connects to your network. As such, you need to understand what use cases you're working with and what level of differentiation you're looking to do. Here are a couple of very common examples:

1. A corporate 802.1x wireless network has been using PEAP/MS-CHAPv2 authentication with a Microsoft Network Policy Server (NPS) for the past several years. The corporation now wants to provide differentiated access based on what type of device is connecting (corporate owned vs. BYOD).
2. A company's guest network uses a static username and password that has been widely distributed. This makes the username/password hard to control and you cannot be sure that the guest network is not exclusively used for guests.

Both of these use cases can be addressed by ISE but they have a common thread. In many wireless network implementations, without having done some amount of due care, the network administrator may open the network up for use cases that were not originally intended. Let's break down the issues above a couple of ways.

The first problem, a network where unrestricted user PEAP/MS-CHAPv2 is used, is a really tough one we've found. We can walk into an organization and when we ask how many mobile devices are connecting to a WLAN, the network administrator may look at me sheepishly and have no idea how many or what types of devices are connecting to the secure corporate SSID. We also find no shame in this. For many years simple PEAP-based authentication designs were popular because they were straightforward to implement and almost all the devices that were connecting to the Wi-Fi network were corporate-owned Windows XP systems. When we started deploying networks like these, there was no such thing as iOS or Android and OSX was not popular at all in the enterprise outside of marketing departments (and even then it wasn't ubiquitous). Typically these networks are deployed with RADIUS servers that don't support profiling. We most commonly see these being Cisco ACS or Microsoft NSP.

So where to start? Well, there a couple of recommended steps you should take. First, configure your wireless controller(s) to use ISE for its RADIUS server and configure your RADIUS AuthC and AuthZ policy to use PEAP for authentication just like it's configured on the legacy RADIUS server implementation. The reason this is the first step is because often times you may not have any idea exactly how many non-Windows mobile devices are associating with your wireless network. When you integrate ISE into the SSID, you will be able to enable device profiling and report on how many devices are joining the network that are not Microsoft Windows. Call the following: "Finding out how large your BYOD problem is." This doesn't mean you really know how many noncorporate devices are joining your network, because it won't account for things such as corporate/authorized OSX or mobile devices. Administrations normally will have a good idea of how many of those are to be expected. In a small/medium-sized network, if you are expecting 500 Windows PCs and a handful of OSX PCs but you end up seeing 400 iPhones being profiled, you'll understand the scale of the "BYOD problem" your organization has. What you do about this entirely depends on your security requirements in your organization, and the scale of the issue you discover but there are a few possible stances that organizations normally take.

It's entirely plausible that you find that there are actually very few mobile devices that are determined to be unauthorized on the WLAN. While your organization may choose to deal with these at a future date, if there is not a large problem, it may be possible to deal with this with "policy." Policy in quotes means that users are reminded that putting nonauthorized devices on the corporate network is a violation of corporate policy. In that case they may voluntarily disconnect their iPhones from the Wi-Fi and that could be the end of it.

If there are a decent number[6] of devices out there, and your organization requires segmentation of mobile devices, it's entirely possible and reasonable that steps from an ISE network access policy be taken to gather more information as to what devices are authorized versus the number that are actually unauthorized in a manner that provides greater fidelity than simple device profiling. Typically this would entail implementing a higher-fidelity authentication methodology on corporate-controlled devices, like the ones discussed in Chapters 12 and 13. You can implement EAP-Chaining or EAP-TLS or machine-only PEAP on corporate-authorized devices for wireless network access while leaving traditional PEAP enabled. This could include deploying AnyConnect via System Center Configuration Manager (SCCM), or changing the supplicant configuration of domain member systems with GPO.

This way, once you have your strong authentication method of choice deployed for authorized systems, when you run a report on what is connecting and authorizing with your legacy PEAP AuthZ rule, you'll know that because they used PEAP they were mobile devices.

This is, in our opinion, the best part of the implementation—when we've used network policy to match different sets of devices. You have a few choices here at this point. Typically

---

[6]A decent number being entirely subjective of the network/security administrator.

if you want to maintain Wi-Fi access for employee BYOD mobile devices, you can do that a few different ways:

- Create an AuthZ result that gives them an ACL that restricts them from accessing internal resources that mobile devices should not require access to.
- Create an AuthZ result that does a VLAN override on their airspace interface to put them on a guest-type VLAN where they have restricted access to internal resources.
- Create a NSP BYOD configuration with single SSID deployment for them and force them onboard. Then grant them a level of access like the above two examples.

If you configure the network restrictions in such a way that maintains access to resources that users reasonably expect and may be reasonably granted (active sync and internet), they likely won't even notice that they've had their access curtailed.

If you determine that you don't want any nonauthorized device to have any access to corporate Wi-Fi, then it's entirely reasonable to deny them access entirely to any resources including active sync and the internet. Once you have your corporate-authorized devices using a strong authentication methodology, you can simply disable or remove the legacy PEAP authorization rules you had configured. Once this is done, presumably any mobile device connecting with a user credential using PEAP/MS-CHAPv2 would simply hit the default authorization rule.[7]

The second problem described above is far simpler to deal with in general. Let's break down the problem and understand its ramifications first. In organizations who have guest networks with static credentials it's extremely common for virtually all of the employees to have put the credentials to memory when they want to put their personal device, or their kid's device, or any miscellaneous device around on that guest network. The issue with this is that, typically, the guest wireless network is explicitly slated for the guest users and employees are not guests.

We often hear from IT managers that they don't care at all if employees use the guest network; their concern is that guests don't get access to the corporate network. While preventing guests from accessing the corporate network is obviously important there is a serious case to be made around preventing employees from using the guest network.

First, guest network connections often do not have as robust web filtering implemented as a corporate network connection will. Categories of websites like social media are often liberally allowed on guest networks in many organizations while they are greatly restricted on the corporate LAN. Also, web security devices may be well suited to log what user is accessing what website on a corporate LAN; such devices typically don't exist on a guest network. As such, your users are easily going to be circumventing your corporate web policy by simply changing to the guest SSID and using it to access the internet.

A similar issue with employees using a guest network frequently with corporate PCs is that, if your guest network isn't implemented with web security filtering (Intrusion Prevention System (IPS), Advanced Malware Protection (AMP), etc.), if they use a corporate PC to check a website that is otherwise disallowed on the corporate network, they may inadvertently become infected with a virus or malware. Once they're done checking ESPN, they'll change back to the corporate LAN to continue doing their work. Once they bring the virus back to

---

[7]This is denying access by default.

your corporate LAN, the virus could easily spread inside your network since the virus has just bypassed all your strong perimeter defenses.

So how do you deal with this? We recommend simply implementing a captive portal on a guest network and requiring a sponsored login. To help restrict how the credentials are used we recommend implementing guest users via sponsorship with a couple of broad parameters:

1. Enforce guest user and endpoint lifetimes to something sensible for how long a guest may be around your organization. If guests are typically around only for 2–4 days, then don't allow a guest user or endpoint to be created for more than a week. If a guest happens to be around for more than a week, it's entirely reasonable to ask them to obtain a new account.
2. Restrict who the sponsor users are who have authorization to create users. Look toward users who can conveniently and centrally manage guest users. These types of people include front desk staff, office managers, IT helpdesk, or administrative assistants. If you provide these users the ability to create and manage guest accounts, the likelihood you'll have broad use of single credentials by all your employees becomes much lower.

The implementation of this design typically doesn't require much more than simply announcing that this will become the company policy/process at date X and then simply implementing CWA web authentication on your guest SSID on that date and removing the legacy username/password.

11

ISE Policy Design Practices

A decade ago, employees of companies would rarely personally own the mobile email device that provided access to corporate resources. In these days Blackberry by RIM was the ruler of the enterprise mobile email landscape with incredibly little competition. Companies loved Blackberry because it provided centralized management, provisioning, and security. They weren't particularly expensive and the workforce productivity enhancements were incredible. For market reasons, entirely out of the scope of this book, the Blackberry has been increasingly out of favor of users because other more user-friendly devices became available and popular. Specifically the proliferation of Apple iPhones and of Google Android devices is what virtually every enterprise's user base now prefers. How they voiced this preference when they started ditching their corporate-provided Blackberries and brought into work their own personal phones with the expectation that they'd get company email on it.

As such, BYOD, or Bring Your Own Device, is a huge buzz acronym in the industry today and it is having a big impact on how enterprises provide access to services to users. It means different things to different people and corporations. Most typically, BYOD literally means employees bringing in their own devices and wishing to get access to corporate resources and offload internet data from their cellular connection to Wi-Fi. Corporate resources in this case may include email, internal websites, file shares, and other internal apps. Occasionally BYOD policy may get mixed into company-owned, but nondomain devices such as OSX or company-owned mobile devices. That exact definition is entirely dependent on how your company defines access rules for different classes of devices. For our examples, we'll stick with what is most common in the field, employees trying to connect their personally owned device to corporate Wi-Fi.

The corporate policy around what network access will be provided to employee-used, but non-company-owned assets from which some level of business may be performed is a huge question. Companies break down generally into the following categories with regard to BYOD policy:

- BYOD devices are not allowed on corporate wired or Wi-Fi or VPN networks ever.

  - In the first case, only corporate-owned devices will ever be permitted access. I would call this device trust, with no trust put on the actual end user of the device.

- BYOD devices are unrestricted on corporate wired or Wi-Fi or VPN connections.

  - No differentiation is put on the physical device the user is connecting with. The user may connect to corporate resources with their personally owned phone, with the same network access level as their company-owned laptop.

- BYOD devices are allowed some level of access differentiated from what a corporate-owned device may have.

  - This is where things get interesting. We want the same user to have differentiated network access controls based on what device they connect from. This is where ISE provides us some really useful tools.

For our design discussion, we're going to make a couple of assumptions. While every company is different, we generally find the following to be true and reliable:

1. BYOD devices will not be members of the corporate Active Directory or other directory service.
2. Corporate-owned devices most often are members of Active Directory or other directory service.
3. Corporate-owned mobile devices are most often managed by a corporate MDM system.

The thing about BYOD design is that the most important part of BYOD design in my opinion is counterintuitively how you identify corporate devices with an authentication that provide a high fidelity identifying that the device is a corporate asset. What is a high-fidelity authentication? Great question. A high-fidelity authentication for corporate access has the following characteristics:

- Is strong cryptographically
- Has authentication that uses cryptography to secure client credentials
- Provides ability to authenticate that the device is corporate issued

If you rely on PEAP/MS-CHAPv2 domain user-type authentication for corporate-owned devices, you're never going to efficiently distinguish between domain member and non-domain member devices.

Looking at how a PEAP/MS-CHAPv2 authentication occurs is important:

- EAP session starts.
- RADIUS server (ISE) provides its certificate to the client for authentication.
- TLS tunnel is created.
- Client provides its MS-CHAPv2 credential (username/password).
- Access-accept or access-reject message is sent depending on AuthZ or AuthC.

There is nothing in the credential exchange to establish what is exactly the client device is. Any type of device out there can be set to provide your wireless (or wired) network a username/password. While you can do profiling to determine what the device is, there are two issues with that. First, if you're presuming that all your internal devices are Windows devices and you want to preclude non-Windows devices from connections, you still can't differentiate between a corporate Windows PC and a noncorporate Windows PC. Second, a determined attacker would have to do very little to bypass your AuthZ policy if user credentials are otherwise allowed to authenticate while obfuscating their actual device's OS. Basic ISE MS Windows profile policy at the time of this writing simply uses DHCP attributes that may be easily manipulated and this won't tell you if the device is actually corporate owned.

Because of this, PEAP/MS-CHAPv2 user authentication generally is insufficient to allow for a robust BYOD network access policy. The next two chapters will discuss a couple of aspects of deploying ISE to achieve robust access policy.

Chapter 12 is devoted to configuring strong network access policy with ISE and other components to strongly authenticate corporate devices. This, in my experience performing ISE implementations, is often the more challenging part.

Chapter 13 is devoted to discussing methods of authenticating BYOD-type devices to allow for effective differentiation.

12

Corporate Authentication Designs

So, the first step in BYOD design is to decide how to authenticate a corporate device and determine that this is a corporate device that deserves liberal or unrestricted network access. We have a few favorite designs to accomplish this that we'd like to go over:

- PEAP machine-only authentication
- X509 authentication
- EAP-Chaining
- MDM authorization

Each of these has advantages and disadvantages, and may be supported or unsupported on various operating systems. We'd take them step by step in discussing them. We would like to note that these may be mixed and matched depending on deployment requirements. It's entirely not uncommon to mix TLS, PEAP, and MDM through the same deployment should security and platform requirements dictate.

PEAP MACHINE-ONLY AUTHENTICATION

The advantages of this methodology are that it is easily configured from both a supplicant and an ISE policy perspective. PEAP machine-only authentication works by configuring the Windows supplicant to only ever provide its computer credential. A feature of Windows that not every administrator is aware of is that each AD member PC maintains an account in the AD, the username is the hostname, and a password associated with this account. This password for the machine account is even rotated occasionally depending on AD policy in the background. You can configure the native supplicant of a Microsoft Windows PC to always use this account for its authentication credential, never using a user credential. If you are to do this to every PC with wireless enabled on it in your company with GPO, you're going to give ISE a way to determine that each of these PCs is in fact a member of AD because it will present its AD credential. Any device authenticating with a user-type credential would then by definition not be a domain PC because each domain device would have already been configured via GPO to always only present a computer credential.

The disadvantages to this are that this can be an inflexible deployment option. First, it is generally available only to Windows PCs that are AD domain members.

Because each Windows PC is going only to dot1x authenticate with its computer credential always, it is impossible to apply network policy based on the user who is logged into the PC. ISE never actually learns who is logged into the system. If corporate policy requires that different network access policy be applied based on user security group membership, computer-only authentication is generally not an option.

Configuring a supplicant for this is actually really straightforward. Simply go into Advanced settings for the supplicant and set the suppliant for computer authentication.

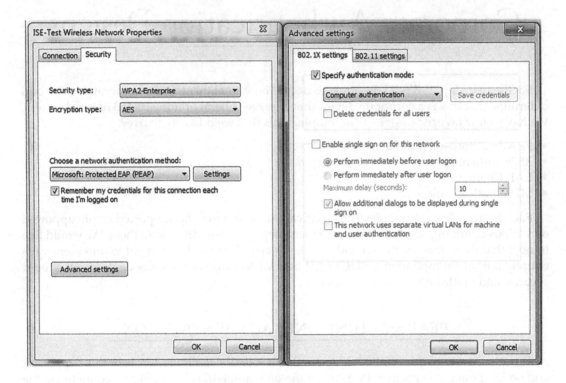

To allow the same thing in ISE authorization policy is really quite straightforward.

In this case we are going to validate the aspects of the authentication we expect to occur: wireless dot1x, PEAP, and Domain Computer membership. All other methodologies are going to be denied (until we allow a BYOD policy at least).

X509 Authentication

With EAP-TLS authentication while ensuring corporate authentication you're able to ensure the user authentication from a corporate device; policy may be applied based on user directory security group membership. This user directory group membership is otherwise not possible through PEAP computer-only authentication. Why user resource differentiation you ask? Some examples of policy to be applied may look like as follows:

- IT users may be assigned to a VLAN that allows access to network devices via virtual teletype (VTY) ACL.
- Finance users may be assigned a general VLAN without restriction to network resources servicing their needs.
- General users are assigned to a general VLAN but are provisioned an ACL that restricts access to services only R&D users may need.
- Computer-only authentication allows for access only to WSUS, AV servers, and domain controller services.

The disadvantages of this methodology are simply that the organization choosing to deploy this must maintain an internal PKI that allows for certificate distribution to client machines for authentication. If a PKI doesn't exist, one must be designed, and deployed prior to this architecture being selected.

EAP-TLS authentication in and of itself will absolutely not determine that a device is a corporate asset. On the contrary, there are places that we expect to use EAP-TLS to authenticate a BYOD, distinctly noncorporate asset. To accomplish EAP-TLS authentication while simultaneously providing sufficient differentiation between corporate and BYOD we need to accomplish two basic tasks:

1. Ensure that certificates issued to corporate devices have their private keys sufficiently secured to preclude users from applying a corporate certificate to a different device.
2. Issue certificate attributes that make it identifiable as a certificate issued to a corporate device.

It is critical that administrators of PCs in an enterprise environment take steps to secure the certificate store to preclude users from easily removing certificates and their corresponding private keys from devices. Should both the private key and the public certificate be removed, the pair may be installed a third-party device and joined to your network and ISE would not be able to differentiate between the malicious device and the corporate device it was removed from. Thus, security of the cryptographic material is truly critical. While key security is not exactly in the scope of this book, here are some tips that we give to customers typically when they look to ensure that private keys aren't compromised off corporate devices:

- Seems obvious, but mark the private keys as "no export" when creating the certificate templates in your AD.
- Remove the end user from the local administrator group so they are unable to access the local key store.
- Implement full disk encryption where possible to mitigate attacks at the local disk.
- Disable removable media access to make removal of key information directly from a system more difficult.

As to the second point above, making the certificates used for corporate authentication different from ISE-issued certificates, the most common way to differentiate certificates is at the time of their deployment through templates. There are three ways to issue certificates that are pretty common in ISE deployments:

- AD certificate enrollment with GPO
- ISE-issued certificate (SCEP or Internal CA)
- MDM-issued certificate

The ability to distinguish between AD GPO-issued certificates and MDM- or ISE-issued certificates is in the attributes the certificates have. Here are some common ones we may look for:

- AD-issued certificates typically have the username/hostname of the certificate in the SAN (subject alternative) field as the UPN or DNS name of the PC.
- MDM- or ISE-issued certificates typically have the username simply as the common name of the certificate.
- The attribute of the certificate may be set with a specific watermark to identify how or where it was issued from.
- The SAN of an ISE-issued certificate have the MAC address of the device the certificate was issued to.

Advantages in deployment of this methodology are numerous. X509-type authentication is considered the gold standard for network authentication. Properly implemented it provides strong authentication cryptographically and is efficient for the RADIUS server to process as it doesn't necessarily require queries to the external identity store for authentication, making it very efficient.

Because certificates may be issued to both the user and the machine (stored in different locations in the registry), both computer and user authentication may be performed. These specific authentications happen independently and, where possible, we recommend you perform both.

Let's take a second to talk about why doing machine authentication along with user authentication is important for a good user experience (and not only user). The reason for this is that if a user attempts to log in to a machine that has user-only authentication enabled on it, there are a variety of restrictions placed on it simply by the behavior of user-only authentication.

When a computer boots up, before anyone logs into it, when machine authentication is enabled, a machine is able to obtain an IP address, check in with any services that are available on the LAN that provide it security updates (WSUS and/or AV server), and connect to domain controllers. With connectivity to the domain controllers a few functions will be available that would otherwise be unavailable should the PC be disconnected from the network:

- If the user had not ever logged into the PC, they would not be able to log in without connectivity to the domain controller.
- If the user had previously logged into the PC but they were required to update their password per domain policy, they would not have the domain policy applied to them and they would not be prompted for password update.
- If the user had previously logged into that PC, but had changed their password in the interim since that PC had been connected to the corporate network, they would have

to log in with their old password since the PC in question would have no record of the updated password.
- Typically login scripts run when machine authentication is enabled, whereas when user-only authentication is enabled, this is less flexible.

The configuration of the supplicant is fairly straightforward where certificate authentication is set, and presuming both user and computer certificates are issued, user or computer authentication is configured. Typically using GPO to configure the SSID is easiest. Here are the screenshots of my recommended GPO settings. First create a Vista or later wireless policy.[1]

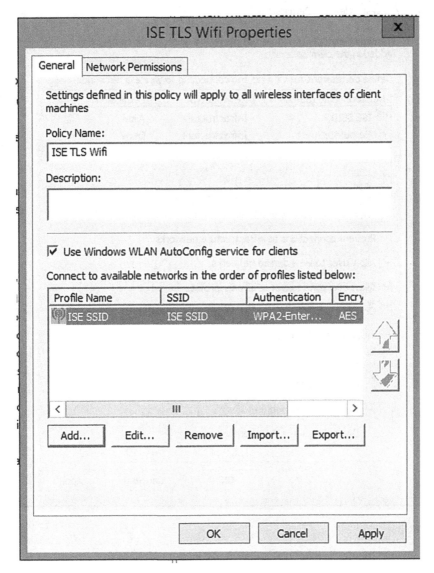

[1]No one should be using Windows XP at this point.

Under Network Permissions there are a few settings you should configure. First, deny access to the corporate guest network to corporate PCs. There is typically no reason a company-owned domain member PC should be connecting to the guest network. Next, prevent connections to *ad hoc* wireless networks. There is generally no reason for corporate PCs to connect to an *ad hoc* Wi-Fi network. Lastly, enable the "Block Period" and set it to 1 min.

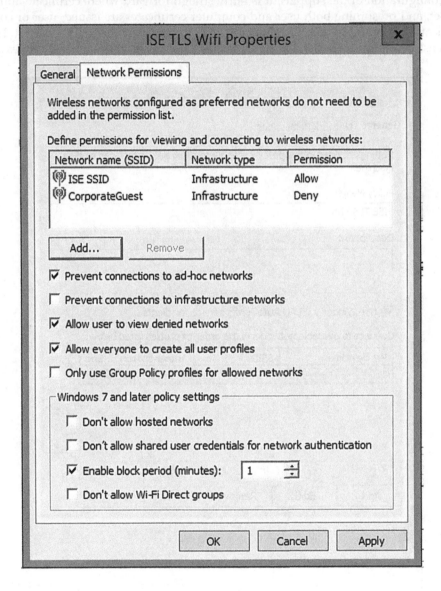

Add the SSID of the WLAN you're looking to use.

Set it for "Microsoft: Smart Card or other certificate" authentication which will set it for EAP-TLS and increase the maximum authentication failures to above 3. A good number to set this too is 5. It goes without saying that if you're using anything other than Wi-Fi Protected Access (WPA) 2/Advanced Encryption Standard (AES), you're nuts.

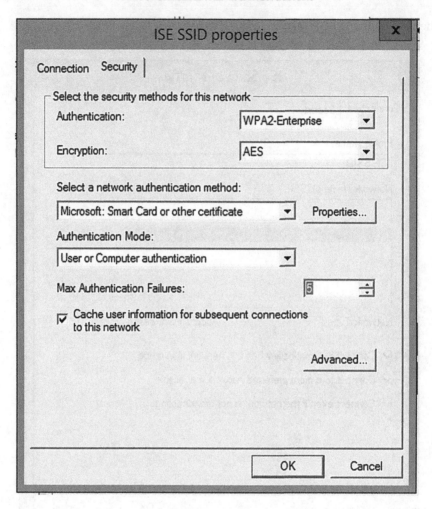

Under Properties next to the authentication method you should specify the CA that issued the certificates to your ISE servers. This helps prevent malicious actors from impersonating your enterprise wireless network.

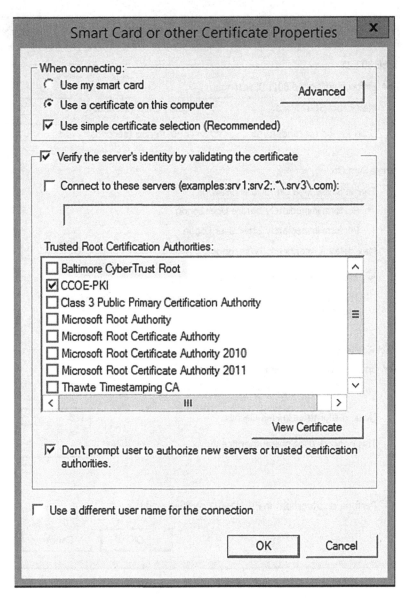

Under the Advanced settings field both enforce advanced 802.1x settings (to ensure consistent EAP timers across clients) and enable Single Sign On.[2]

---

[2]Enabling Single Sign On changes the behavior of the Windows login process and we've found the feature helpful. If you're unsure here, please check Microsoft TechNet for detailed information about its behavior.

Advanced security settings   **X**

┌─ IEEE 802.1X ──┐

☑ Enforce advanced 802.1X settings

Max Eapol-Start Msgs: `3`   Held Period (seconds): `1`

Start Period (seconds): `5`   Auth Period (seconds): `18`

┌─ Single Sign On ───┐

☑ Enable Single Sign On for this network

◉ Perform immediately before User Logon

○ Perform immediately after User Logon

Max delay for connectivity(seconds):   `10`

☑ Allow additional dialogs to be displayed during Single Sign On

☐ This network uses different VLAN for authentication with machine and user credentials

┌─ Fast Roaming ───┐

☑ Enable Pairwise Master Key (PMK) Caching

PMK Time to Live (minutes):   `720`

Number of Entries in PMK Cache: `128`

☐ This network uses pre-authentication

Maximum Pre-authentication attempts: `3`

☐ Perform cryptography in FIPS 140-2 certified mode

[OK]   [Cancel]

As for ISE policy, the authentication policy must take into account certificate authentication selecting the correct principal X509 username. In our case, being that the certificate is deployed via AD GPO, the SAN would hold the UPN of the user/machine.[3]

[3]This point is pretty critical. When deploying certificates via certificate templates in AD, you should be absolutely sure that the UPN is available in the SAN field of the certificate; otherwise our policies below will likely fail.

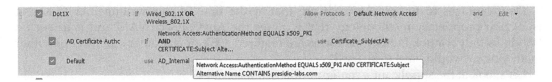

Looking at our authorization rules, they are more complicated than the AuthZ policy we configured for machine-only PEAP.

	Status	Rule Name	Conditions (identity groups and other conditions)		Permissions	
	☑	Wireless User - Corp Device	(Wireless_802.1X AND AD:ExternalGroups EQUALS presidio-labs.com/Users/Domain Users AND Network Access:AuthenticationMethod EQUALS x509_PKI AND CERTIFICATE:Subject Alternative Name CONTAINS presidio-labs.com)	then	PermitAccess	Edit | ▾
	☑	Wireless Corp Device	(Wireless_802.1X AND AD:ExternalGroups EQUALS presidio-labs.com/Users/Domain Computers AND Network Access:AuthenticationMethod EQUALS x509_PKI AND CERTIFICATE:Subject Alternative Name CONTAINS presidio-labs.com)	then	PermitAccess	Edit | ▾
	☑	Default	if no matches, then	DenyAccess		Edit | ▾

Standard (above table)

First off, there are two rules: one rule for machine authentication and one for user authentication:

- Machine authentication occurs when no user is logged into the PC.
- User authentication occurs when a user has logged in during the Netlogon process of Windows.

There are also more conditions in these rules than previously. Let's break them down one at a time:

- Wireless_802.1x: Specifying the media used and the authentication methodology, specifically excluding MAB methods.
- External Group membership: Validating that while we have authenticated the certificate as being valid, it is associated with a valid domain object in either Domain Users or Domain Computers security groups (per rule).
- Authentication Method: PKI authentication to be sure that we're identifying the specific method used in case password authentication is used elsewhere in our policy.
- Certificate Subject Name Contains: In our case, the domain we're using is presidio-labs.com. Because the UPN is used in the subject alternative, domain object will have presidio-labs in their UPN. This is the watermark I've chosen to use to validate this certificate was issued via GPO.

EAP-Chaining is a really effective feature when it comes to determining corporate access. It is effective in this case specifically because of our ability to simultaneously authenticate a device's membership to the directory, and the user logged into the PC simultaneously (or chained in the same authentication).

Advantages of this design methodology are basically twofold. First, implementation of PKI is not required for client authentication. This means that the server infrastructure required is simpler than it is for EAP-TLS. Second, because we have the user information as part of the authentication, we can apply network access policy based on the user's security group information along with the computer's own security group membership.

Disadvantages to this deployment are that at the time of this writing EAP-Chaining is a Cisco proprietary methodology that requires the AnyConnect NAM and is as such a Windows-only feature. If other platforms are required, OSX or any other mobile OS, another methodology would have to be used.

Let's look at the supplicant's configuration.

You have limited control over NAM from the UI exposed after it is installed so the first thing you are going to want to do is get ahold of the AnyConnect Profile Editor installer which will give you the tools you need to create the profiles you will be using. The NAM Profile Editor will give you a GUI front end to what will eventually be an XML file containing all settings needed by AnyConnect (AC) for your network configuration. After we create the file you will have a number of deployment options but we'll mainly concentrate on having ISE do that part.

Launching the Profile Editor will show you a GUI that looks similar to this.

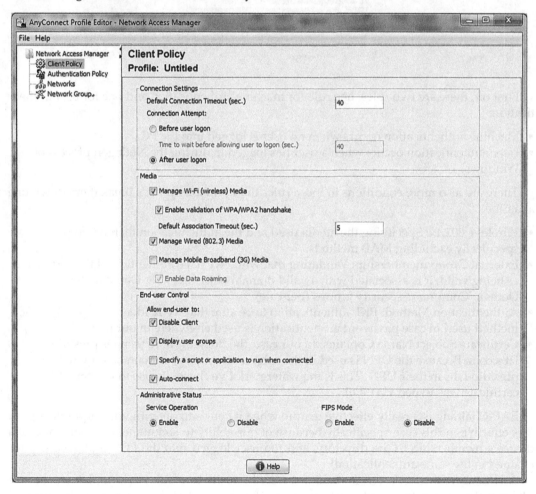

The initial Client Policy page is fairly straightforward and provides good defaults for most environments. If you need to manage mobile data connections or configure Start Before

Logon, this is where you can do that. Authentication Policy lets you define what methods you want the NAM module to use when authenticating to networks. Now this is important because unless you want to restrict your users from using some network types or you don't permit them to connect to unknown networks, these will impact the user connecting from home, hotel, airport, etc., which could result in some not-so-happy calls. If you are ready to deal with complaints and/or want only to ensure they are connecting only to absolutely secure network, then you can uncheck legacy options here. However, even though it should be fairly obvious that there are far better options to go with than Wired Equivalent Privacy (WEP), Temporal Key Integrity Protocol (TKIP), LEAP, etc., those should be retired if still in use; chances are that you will want to leave these settings alone.

Let's jump to Network Groups quickly since misunderstanding what it is will probably result in end user confusion and/or you having to redo your profiles. There is a single group listed by default and for the majority of deployments you don't want to change this. You will also probably want to keep all the networks you create in the global network list instead of adding them to the default network group. The global networks are always available no matter the network group that is selected.

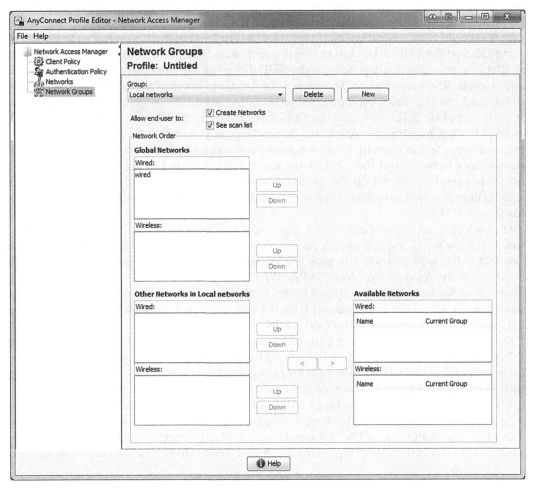

The one possible use case for separate network groups would be location-specific networks you want to define for your users that might not be available at every site. Then you can create a group called "Site A," add site A's networks to it, and have it there for your users. The gotcha is that users need to actively switch between network groups that aren't global. That is why creating something like "Widget Group Networks" and placing your networks inside that group and having another group called "Personal Networks" for users custom ones might seem like a good idea but is going to cause a lot of pain on the user end as they have to switch between groups. Moral of the story: Use network groups only when you know your use case needs them and your users can handle it. Besides ISE handling your networks you should be able to reduce the number of SSIDs you need to configure anyway!

The big section here is obviously the Networks one; it's here you will be creating the different definitions of the networks your users will be connecting to. The Profile Editor does a decent job of walking you through the steps needed to configure a profile and only presents the tabs to you that you need based on what options you have selected. You will start off selecting a wired or wireless connection type; note that if you select wired, it will show up for *all* wired connections; so whatever you name the connection will show up even when connected to a non-dot1x network. It's mainly an aesthetics issue but something that could confuse end users. If you select a wireless network, you have the option of telling ISE that the SSID is hidden or if it is a corporate SSID. The hidden SSID option tells ISE that it needs to actively probe for the SSID since the network isn't going to be broadcasting itself. The corporate SSID option tells AnyConnect that the SSID has the highest priority and should *always* be connected to if it's in range. This is generally a good option for your corporate SSID obviously and since we're running ISE you really need only one anyway! It's not required however and depending on your use case might not be appropriate—always test in your own environment. You can also tell AC to run a script when it connects to a network but the catch is the script isn't included in the profile and instead you are required to place it on the machine with some other method. If you package the AC installers together into your own setup package, you can include it there or even deploy it with GPOs.

After selecting the type of connection, you are going to be prompted to select the security level. Since we're talking ISE here, you are always going to pick Authenticating Network since that is the type that lets you pick 802.1x parameters. For a wireless network you will have to pick the Association Mode (WPA, WPA2, etc.). Wired profiles will require you to define a Port Authentication Exception Policy so that AC knows how to handle traffic when there authentication/key management fails. It's safe to leave these options alone unless you really need to tweak how the supplicant works.

Your next task will be selecting either Machine/User/Machine or User as an option for the type of connection the profile will be used for. This is mentioned earlier but it's important to reiterate it again: If you are authenticating machines joined to a domain, you should implement machine authentication or machine and user authentication; if you do only user authentication, your domain machines will have issues since they won't be able to connect to the domain controllers while booting. Issues from this won't show up right away (cached GPOs) but new GPOs or GPOs that can be applied only during startup will eventually cause you to start troubleshooting weird machine issues—do yourself a favor and address this issue now. Since we're talking about EAP-Chaining we'll want to select Machine and User Connection.

Next we'll configure our machine authentication; our EAP Method will be EAP-FAST and we'll want to leave all the defaults that show up after that. Make a note of the option to use unauthenticated PAC provisioning; make sure this is off unless there is a really good reason you need it. The names are a little misleading, but unauthenticated provisioning just creates a TLS tunnel between the machine and the ISE allowing potential bad actors to man-in-the-middle attack the exchange without any knowledge of the client/ISE. Instead, authenticated PAC provisioning will verify the certificate provided by ISE before the exchange, ensuring that the client trusted the endpoint. Within the certificates area you can configure trust rules that can further verify certificates being used by ISE to ensure they have the correct CN/SAN before sending credentials across. Security wise this is a good thing to do; rogue RADIUS servers configured on a cloned SSID that your clients use can be used to steal credentials and we don't want that. The issue can be that the rules you create can cause issues with certificate flexibility down the road, if you move to a new domain name or change the names of the ISE PSNs. Using the rules is recommended but just keep those issues in mind while creating them. If you plan on using a wildcard certificate and follow best practice of segmenting your domain, then you can safely add that same segment as a rule (something like ".ise.company.tld") and be covered for the most part. For CA trust you probably want to trust the OS's certificate store so you don't have to manage another certificate store. For credentials we'll want to use the machine credentials, but the usage of the "host/anonymous" unprotected identity is up to you. It is best practice to leave that there because it provides some additional security for your clients and under normal circumstances you would rarely see that information within ISE. However, there are times when having a real user/machine name in the unprotected identity can be useful for troubleshooting clients that are having problems and it can also cut down on some confusion for other people who might not understand the inner/outer identity concept.

The user section of the configuration will be almost exactly the same as the machine section; there are only a couple of small changes to make and the first is "Extend user connection beyond logoff." Enabling this setting results in users appearing to be logged in even after they have logged off in Windows. Now you could make use of this to permit access to machines for maintenance purposes or something else that might be environment dependent but we recommend disabling the option and relying on proper machine authentication/authorization instead. This option has the potential to throw off your accounting information so if you are heavily investing in accounting, then definitely turn it off. The second option is the user credentials that are used; you probably want this to be "Use Single Sign-On Credentials" so that the domain credentials of the user will be passed to ISE and they don't have to type anything in. This setting will also fall back to prompt the user for a username/password.

Once you've created your networks, save the entire configuration as an XML file and simply copy it to: "C:\ProgramData\Cisco\Cisco AnyConnect Secure Mobility Client\Network Access Manager\newConfigFiles\configuration.xml." Restart the service and the configuration will be applied. The name is important and must be "configuration.xml" or else AnyConnect will ignore it.

There are two steps in configuring the ISE policy for EAP-Chaining. First, you need to enable EAP-Chaining in the authentication result. This would be under the allowed protocols in Authentication results.

▼ ☑ Allow EAP-FAST

    EAP-FAST Inner Methods
    ☑ Allow EAP-MS-CHAPv2
        ☑ Allow Password Change Retries [3] (Valid Range 0 to 3)
    ☑ Allow EAP-GTC
        ☑ Allow Password Change Retries [3] (Valid Range 0 to 3)
    ☑ Allow EAP-TLS
        ☐ Allow Authentication of expired certificates to allow certificate renewal in Authorization Policy
        ⓘ
    ◉ Use PACs   ○ Don't Use PACs
        Tunnel PAC Time To Live   [90] [Days ▼]
        Proactive PAC update will occur after [90] % of PAC Time To Live has expired
        ☑ Allow Anonymous In-Band PAC Provisioning
        ☑ Allow Authenticated In-Band PAC Provisioning
            ☐ Server Returns Access Accept After Authenticated Provisioning
            ☐ Accept Client Certificate For Provisioning
        ☑ Allow Machine Authentication
            Machine PAC Time To Live   [1] [Weeks ▼]
        ☑ Enable Stateless Session Resume
            Authorization PAC Time To Live   [1] [Hours ▼] ⓘ
☑ Enable EAP Chaining
☐ Preferred EAP Protocol [LEAP ▼]

[Save] [Reset]

Then you need to configure an AuthZ policy to utilize EAP-Chaining. ISE authorization policy would typically look like as follows in most normal EAP-Chaining situations. Notice that you can use the Network Access:EapChainingResult AuthZ condition here.

We are validating independently when a user is authenticated to a domain PC, and also when a domain PC is authenticating without a user authenticated (user will fail in this case).

Lastly in our examples, using the external MDM feature of ISE to validate corporate device is a pretty powerful method to authorize devices that are not Windows. Previously we've given you some pretty powerful examples that require the corporate devices are running Microsoft Windows, but we all know that companies issue devices that are not necessarily running Windows. ISE utilizes REST API that may be used by a wide variety of MDM vendors. If an enterprise uses an MDM, chances are that MDM is in the ISE compatibility matrix for integration and if your corporate devices are managed by that MDM, ISE can query the MDM for useful information such as registration or policy compliance. If the enterprise registers their corporate devices to the MDM, regardless of platform, ISE can validate that these devices are corporate assets.

The advantage of this method is twofold. First, the client platform doesn't matter to ISE. If your MDM vendor of choice supports an OS, ISE won't necessarily care what that is. My examples will include using the Meraki Systems Manager Enterprise which supports Windows, OSX, IOS, and Android. Second, the policy configuration of this is extremely simple from an ISE perspective. Simply integrate ISE into the MDM and MDM conditions appear in the AuthZ ruleset.

Disadvantages are limited to the fact that this does require ISE APEX licenses which is the highest cost plus the cost of the MDM. From a licensing perspective this may be the highest software cost.[4] If you don't have an MDM and you're not sure what direction you may want to go in, it doesn't hurt to check out the Meraki Systems Manager MDM. It has a good feature set for many customers and you can onboard up to 100 devices without incurring a license charge.[5]

To register a device to the MDM if you're using the Meraki Systems Manager, the process is pretty straightforward. Under the Client List menu click "Add devices".

Under the Add devices menu, each supported platform has a different onboarding methodology. Select the platform of the device you'd like to onboard and follow the process.

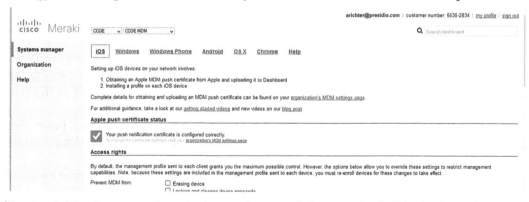

[4]Keep in mind that the cost overall may be cheaper when you calculate operational efficiencies that can be gained from an MDM.

[5]At the time of this writing.

If you're using another MDM solution, obviously, this will be very different.

From an ISE policy perspective here is what is required. First, integrate the MDM to ISE. To perform this task in ISE, browse through the UI Administration → Network Devices → External MDM. Then provide ISE the IP/hostname and API credentials to the MDM (from an ISE perspective, the process is exactly the same no matter what MDM you are using).[6]

External RADIUS Servers   RADIUS Server Sequences   Trusted AAA Servers

External MDM Server List > **Meraki**

MDM Server details

* Name	Meraki
* Hostname or IP Address	n131.meraki.com
* Port	443
Instance Name	
* User Name	ecdab5fe407839157065ca3b6c5
* Password	••••••••••••••••••••••••••••
Description	
* Polling Interval	240 (minutes) ⓘ

☑ Enable

Test Connection

Save   Reset

Finding those settings in Meraki you need to browse: Organization → Configure → MDM → ISE Settings. The ISE Settings menu is located at the bottom of the page.

Once the MDM is integrated to ISE, the MDM may be referenced in the AuthZ policy. For this to work smoothly you need two rules. You can use one rule to check for MDM registration

[6]You will need to be sure that ISE will trust the certificate for the API here. To do this you need to import the certificate chain used to secure MDM. In the case of Meraki it's a GoDaddy certificate chain that needs to be imported. When you import the chain, be sure to import each certificate in the chain individually and be sure to enable "Trust for authentication within ISE" in trusted certificates.

and later in the AuthZ policy you'll need to create a web authentication rule that references an MDM portal. Let's start by looking at an AuthZ policy.

| | | Corp MDM | if | (Wireless_802.1X AND presidio-demo:ExternalGroups EQUALS presidio-demo.com/Users/Domain Users AND MDM:MDMServerName EQUALS Meraki AND MDM:DeviceRegisterStatus EQUALS Registered) | then | PermitAccess | Edit \| ▼ |
| | | MDM Onboard | if | (Wireless_802.1X AND presidio-demo:ExternalGroups EQUALS presidio-demo.com/Users/Domain Users) | then | Wireless MDM Onboard | Edit \| ▼ |

If a device is known by ISE to be registered to an MDM on the MDM server named Meraki, it's given a "PermitAccess" result on whatever VLAN the WLC is configured for. For ISE to know to check the MDM for its registration status ISE needs to perform a web authentication to an MDM portal.[7] Here is the result that I'm using in this example.

Authorization Profiles > **Wireless MDM Onboard**
Authorization Profile

* Name	Wireless MDM Onboard
Description	
* Access Type	ACCESS_ACCEPT ▼
Service Template	☐

▼ **Common Tasks**

☑ Web Redirection (CWA, MDM, NSP, CPP)

| MDM Redirect ▼ | ACL | NSP-REDIRECT | Value: MDM Portal (default) ▼ | MDM Server: Meraki ▼ |

☐ Static IP/Host name/FQDN

☐ Auto Smart Port

The result is a web authentication that uses an MDM redirect action, has an ACL[8] (airspace), and points to a portal and MDM server.

The user experience of this is, if a device previously registered, the MDM portal page will display a "Success" page after ISE does a REST lookup to the MDM, a CoA is issued, and the result is matched where MDM registration is selected. If the device is not registered, it will be prompted to onboard to the MDM. In the case of a Meraki MDM the CWA portal will request a Meraki network ID. If the end user does not know this (typically this would be kept by IT), they would be unable to gain network access beyond the MDM portal.

---

[7]This behavior described here is for ISE 1.4 which supports multiple MDMs. ISE 1.2 and 1.3, which support only integration to a single MDM, do not require a webauth redirect to determine MDM registration.
[8]We generally use the same ACL that we use for Native Supplicant Provisioning (discussed in Chapter 13) but add DNS exception for the MDM. Skip ahead to the next chapter if you need the ACL details.

Back to the AuthZ policy; notice that there is an AuthZ rule that allows you to check for MDM compliance. This MDM compliance would be where you can create policy that the endpoint devices conform to requirements for network access. This may include preventing devices from connecting that do not have PIN lock configured, or preventing devices that are jailbroken. In Meraki to configure compliance policy those rulers are set in: Systems Manager → Configure → Policies.

Security policies

Back to list >

Security policy name	Passcode-Lock-Required
Desktop	☐ Screen lock after 15 ⇕ minutes or less.
	☐ Login required
	☐ Firewall enabled
	☐ Running apps blacklist ⓘ
	☐ Mandatory running apps ⓘ
OS X	☐ Disk encryption
Windows	☐ Antivirus running
	☐ Antispyware installed
Mobile devices	☑ Passcode lock
	☑ Device is not compromised ⓘ
All devices	☐ Application blacklist ⌄ ⓘ
	☐ Mandatory applications ⓘ
	☐ Device must check in every 30 minutes ⌄

Then you can apply this policy to all or some of the devices in your MDM by going through: Systems Manager → Configure → General and scrolling down to ISE Settings.

ISE settings

Security policy mappings	Systems Manager security policy	Tag scope	Tags	Actions
	Passcode-Lock-Required	With ANY of	Corp ✕	✕
	Add a new security policy scope			

This way, any devices associated with a tag may be determined to be compliant or non-complaint depending on which security policy you then associate with the tag.

CHAPTER

13

BYOD Designs

Now that we've beaten to death how to implement authentication and authorization for corporate devices, let's look into some options for our design in configuring authentication/ authorization for BYOD devices.

Looking at configuring high-fidelity authentication for BYOD is definitely an important goal, but typically the fidelity becomes slightly less critical for some organizations depending on the level of access and the sensitivity of connectivity in the case of BYOD.

Here are some common suggested configuration designs (obviously your design may differ, but these are common ones I've seen in the field):

- PEAP user authentication
- EAP-TLS user authentication (ISE-issued certificate)
- Web authentication

Each of these designs have their own advantages and disadvantages to weigh in your configuration. We'll be weighing them each, one at a time.

USER PEAP

For PEAP user authentication, this is exactly what we said you should not use in your design for corporate device access. If we ensured that corporate devices do not use PEAP user authentication, any other device that authenticates with PEAP (which is the default EAP type for most mobile devices) will connect and match your BYOD policy.

The advantage of this design is twofold. First, it is a very simple authorization rule to configure. Second, it's also very easy to connect mobile devices with this method because PEAP with MS-CHAPv2 is the default connectivity methodology for both Apple iOS and Google Android devices.

The disadvantage to this configuration is that it does not provide for very secure authentications compared to other methodologies. The user behavior is that any certificate that ISE presents, users will click accept to allow their username/password credentials to be passed to the RADIUS server. Accepting the certificate of your corporate RADIUS server is not a big deal, but if a malicious RADIUS server of a malicious wireless network is presented, you can be sure that a bunch of your users are going to accept it. If user credentials are not that sensitive to your company, or you are not prepared to exercise any control over the devices joining the network, this is the method for you.

The authorization rule for this configuration looks something as given in the screen shot.

Standard

	Status	Rule Name	Conditions (identity groups and other conditions)		Permissions
	☑	Wireless User - BYOD	if (Wireless_802.1X AND AD:ExternalGroups EQUALS presidio-labs.com/Users/Domain Users AND Network Access:EapTunnel EQUALS PEAP)	then	PermitAccess
	☑	Default	if no matches, then	DenyAccess	

[Save] [Reset]

BYOD EAP-TLS

A more advanced implementation would be to utilize EAP-TLS to the mobile devices your users have and to require them to authenticate to your network via certificates rather than simple username/password authentication. This design provides for some advantages; first, EAP-TLS authentication provides for cryptographically more secure authentication from the client perspective because we can also have ISE install the authentication settings into the client along with the certificate; we can ensure that the root CA is deployed to the client so that the client will properly trust the ISE server. This provides for a more secure method of operation for your clients as well as also provides the convenience of not having password rotation interrupt wireless authentications.[1]

The disadvantage to this configuration is again twofold. It is much more complicated to deploy than the generic PEAP user authentication methodology. When we deploy certificates, there are many moving parts that we need to ensure work properly. Since we have ISE deploy certificates to mobile endpoints it's important to note that there is a compatibility matrix that must be taken into account for your design. ISE supports the vast majority of mobile device operating systems and platforms for certificate deployment but not all. The following is supported:

- Apple iOS
- Google Android
- Microsoft Windows
- Apple OSX

Without getting into specifics, there are version requirements that do change from time to time. While typically the latest releases are supported shortly after their release from the manufacturer, there are generally minimum required versions. Please consult that compatibility matrix to be sure that versions supported at the time of your deployment are acceptable to you.

[1]Many customers complain that when they use username/password authentication for mobile devices wirelessly, the devices will silently fail having forgotten to rotate the password on their phones. Certificates, by contrast, need only to be updated when the certificate expires.

There are a few mobile platforms that aren't supported with ISE certificate deployment at the time of this writing:

- Microsoft Windows Mobile and Surface (ARM)
- Nook
- Amazon Fire

If your implementation requires support for the above platforms, you probably need to look at another design.

In any case, let's get into the steps required to implement certificate provisioning through ISE. The first step is to configure your CA and for our example we're going to configure ISE to be a subordinate CA to an AD CA. To do this we need ISE to generate a Certificate Signing Request (CSR) for a subordinate certificate authority certificate: Administration → System → Certificates → Certificate Signing Requests.

You'll see there is a big button labeled "Generate Certificate Signing Request." Press it.

Inside the generate CSR page you'll see, again, that there are a few settings for Usage. In this case, because we want to make ISE a subordinate to the corporate root CA we'll select "ISE Intermediate CA" and click "Generate."[2]

The CSR will be generated and you'll be prompted if you'd like to export the certificate.

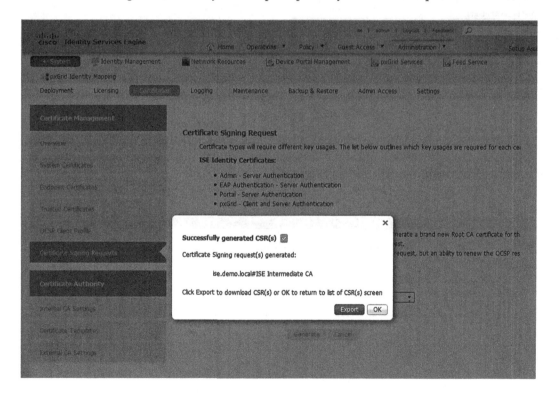

---

[2]Depending on your design it may be a good idea to keep your BYOD PKI distinct from your corporate PKI. If you're inclined to have ISE act a standalone root CA, you can skip this step and use the default ISE CA certificate.

Select Export.

Download that CSR you've created and then upload it in your CA for signature. If you have a Microsoft CA, like most of us, browse into the certificate UI and request a certificate.

Paste the contents of the CSR into the field.

Microsoft Active Directory Certificate Services -- CCOE-PKI   Home

Submit a Certificate Request or Renewal Request

To submit a saved request to the CA, paste a base-64-encoded CMC or PKCS #10 certificate request or PKCS #7 renewal request generated by an external source (such as a Web server) in the Saved Request box.

Saved Request:

Base-64-encoded
certificate request
(CMC or
PKCS #10 or
PKCS #7):

Certificate Template:

Subordinate Certification Authority ⌄

Additional Attributes:

Attributes:

Submit >

Select "Subordinate Certificate Authority" as the certificate template type. Click Submit.

You'll be prompted to download the certificate. Download it as a Base 64 encoded file. The file name of the certificate will be "certnew.cer".

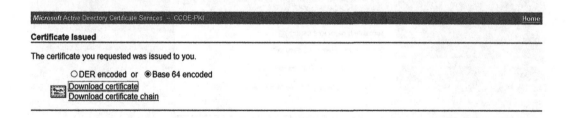

Microsoft Active Directory Certificate Services -- CCOE-PKI   Home

Certificate Issued

The certificate you requested was issued to you.

○ DER encoded or ⦿ Base 64 encoded
Download certificate
Download certificate chain

When you browse back to the CSR window in ISE, you'll see that there is a "Bind Certificate" button available. Select the CSR and click Bind Certificate.[3]

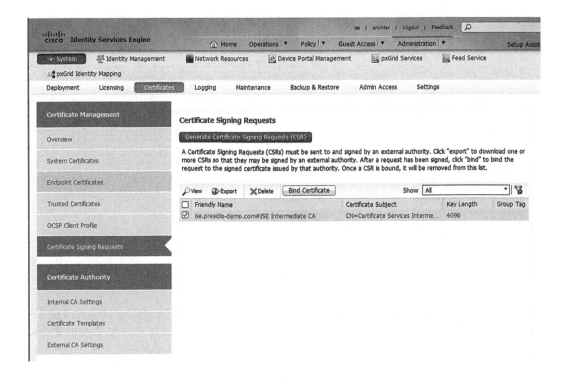

Browse to the certificate file and then click Submit.

The last thing you'll want to do to set up your ISE CA is to configure a certificate template. The certificate template will define all the subject fields in the certificates you're looking to deploy along with key size and validity period.

Subject fields are things like Common Name, Organization, City, State, and Country. You should fill these out and consider using one of the fields as a way to identify the certificate you're using as BYOD-type certificate. In our case we'll specify the OU of the certificate as BYOD and also show you how this can be used later. The common name is automatically filled with the username used in the authentication to get to the Native Supplicant Provisioning (NSP) portal (either EAP or CWA).

---

[3]This binds the issuing CA certificate to the primary admin node of the cluster. If you have redundant admin nodes, you will need to manually back up the public/private keys for the CA certificate and import them into your secondary admin node. There is capability in ISE to automatically sync the private key information of the CA. The commands to back up the key information are detailed in Chapter 17.

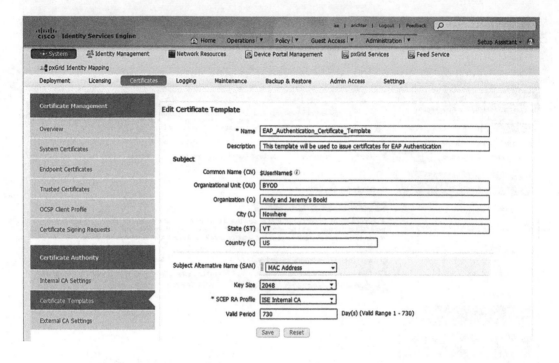

It's highly recommended you leave the defaults for key size and validity period. The key size default of 2048 is broadly compatible and considered sufficiently secure. If you reduce the key length, you may be susceptible to cryptographic attacks, and larger key lengths are not compatible with some supplicants (Apple iOS). In this case we've just edited the default template but feel free to create your own rather than edit the default.

At this point, when you issue certificates from your ISE CA, the certificates will be from your ISE subordinate CA. You're asking yourself, "How do I do that now?" Great question!

ISE can issue certificates through a process called "NSP." What NSP does is it allows ISE to push a supplicant configuration down to an end device. This supplicant configuration could technically be for wired or wireless connections but in reality, its is most commonly deployed for wireless connectivity.

If you had an external SCEP CA you were inclined to use rather than the ISE CA, this is where you would configure it.

Through NSP you can have the supplicant configured for a few different EAP methods including EAP-TLS, PEAP, or EAP-FAST but, for our purposes, the only one that will also have ISE issue a certificate is EAP-TLS.

NSP works by redirecting the clients to a web portal. The web portal can be deployed in two different ways:

- Single SSID method: This is where an SSID is configured for 802.1x. When a device connects to the SSID and authenticates with a username/password credential (most typically with PEAP), the device is set to redirect to the NSP portal for certificate/ supplicant provisioning. Once this is complete, ISE will send a CoA asking the client to reauthenticate. Because the supplicant was configured for EAP-TLS the client will then reconnect and authenticate with EAP-TLS. Presumably the AuthZ policy allows for full network access without the need for further provisioning (unless you're doing posture, which isn't all that common for BYOD).

- Dual SSID method: In this case you have two different SSIDs. One is unencrypted with MAC filtering and RADIUS NAC configured. The other one is 802.1x authenticated (presumably encrypted with WPA2/AES). The open SSID is configured with a CWA portal for authentication and after the user is web authenticated they're asked to perform the NSP operation. As part of that NSP the supplicant is configured to connect to the 802.1x-secured SSID with EAP-TLS.

There are advantages and disadvantages to each of these methods. The single SSID method is generally simpler and works well when you're using typical mobile devices such as iOS or Android devices (OSX also works fine). With this you're not relying on additional SSIDs that may be dedicated to provisioning and you're not asking the supplicant to have to make a service-impacting change as part of the onboarding task. The issue with the single SSID method is that Windows is often less cooperative when asking it to join the SSID when it's likely that the SSID will present a certificate as part of the PEAP authentication that isn't in the trusted store. If you use a certificate from a public CA, this can be easier on Windows devices. If you anticipate onboarding lots of Windows systems, single SSID method is probably not your preferred method. If you're going to be doing mainly iOS or Android devices, single SSID is definitely the preferred method.

When using the dual SSID method, you don't have to worry about the EAP certificate in use because you can use a publically trusted certificate tagged for your CWA portal. This means that the onboarding method can be more secure if you're worried about certificate trust issues. This makes the Windows process a little easier. The challenge is that you're going to rely on the supplicant to change SSIDs once NSP is complete. This has two caveats to remember. First, on your WLC you need to have "fast SSID change" enabled; otherwise the WLC will not allow your client to gracefully change from one SSID immediately to another.[4] The next issue is that iOS will not automatically change SSIDs and requires manual intervention by the end user (they're going to have to manually change their own SSID). If you're going to be onboarding a lot of iOS devices, it's not recommended to use the dual SSID method.[5]

One other aspect of this design that is not always brought up is that the single and dual SSID methods are not necessarily mutually exclusive. You could configure them both and recommend the users onboard whichever way they are more comfortable or whatever works better for their platform. The issue with this is that it could be more confusing for your users and you may be able to provide them better support by using only one of them and giving them clear guidance. If you're unsure which one will work better for you, then you should definitely test both out.

[4]This is in the General Controller configuration tab. It's pretty safe to enable.
[5]If you have a bunch of iOS and Windows devices to onboard, there isn't a technical reason why you couldn't enable both the single and dual SSID designs at the same time. You just have to make sure your users could be adequately trained so they can onboard their devices without a lot of Helpdesk intervention.

First, we'll go through the configuration of the single SSID method and then add on the dual SSID method afterwards. We'll assume that you have an 802.1x SSID setup similar to the example provided in the NAD example.

First, we're going to authorize a person who's authenticating via 802.1x with PEAP and a username/password and is a member of domain users.

| | ☑ | BYOD Onboard | if | (Wireless_802.1X AND Network Access:EapTunnel EQUALS PEAP AND presidio-demo:ExternalGroups EQUALS presidio-demo.com/Users /Domain Users AND Network Access:EapAuthentication EQUALS EAP-MSCHAPv2) | then | Wireless BYOD Onboard |

The users will be provided an authorization result that sends them to a NSP web redirection.

Authorization Profiles > Wireless BYOD Onboard
Authorization Profile

* Name   Wireless BYOD Onboard

Description

* Access Type   ACCESS_ACCEPT

Service Template ☐

▼ **Common Tasks**

☐ VLAN

☐ Voice Domain Permission

☑ Web Redirection (CWA, MDM, NSP, CPP)

Native Supplicant Provisioning ▾ ACL NSP-REDIRECT   Value BYOD Portal (default) ▾

That NSP web redirection requires two attributes:

• An airspace ACL that will govern the web redirection
• A specific BYOD portal to be used (I've used the default, but feel free to customize)[6]

The ACL here is a little different from a regular guest ACL because NSP uses an additional protocol as part of the device onboarding. NSP uses TCP 8443 as the web port for the operation but it also uses TCP 8905 for the actual onboarding traffic.

[6]You can customize the portal look and feel in the BYOD portal under: Administration → Device Portal Management → BYOD. Portal customization is covered in some detail in Chapter 9.

Access Control Lists > Edit   < Back   Add New Rule

General

Access List Name	NSP-REDIRECT

Deny Counters	0

Seq	Action	Source IP/Mask	Destination IP/Mask	Protocol	Source Port	Dest Port	DSCP	Direction	Number of Hits	
1	Permit	0.0.0.0 / 0.0.0.0	0.0.0.0 / 0.0.0.0	UDP	Any	DNS	Any	Inbound	0	▾
2	Permit	0.0.0.0 / 0.0.0.0	0.0.0.0 / 0.0.0.0	UDP	DNS	Any	Any	Outbound	0	▾
3	Permit	0.0.0.0 / 0.0.0.0	172.19.110.164 / 255.255.255.255	TCP	Any	8443	Any	Inbound	0	▾
4	Permit	172.19.110.164 / 255.255.255.255	0.0.0.0 / 0.0.0.0	TCP	8443	Any	Any	Outbound	0	▾
5	Permit	0.0.0.0 / 0.0.0.0	172.19.110.164 / 255.255.255.255	TCP	Any	8905	Any	Inbound	0	▾
6	Permit	172.19.110.164 / 255.255.255.255	0.0.0.0 / 0.0.0.0	TCP	8905	Any	Any	Outbound	0	▾

There are a few pieces of configuration that are available in the portal's configuration:

- You can have the device added to an endpoint identity group (MAC address group). This can then be referenced in the authorization policy.
- By default devices are added to the "RegisteredDevices" group and are purged every 30 days.[7]
- You may require acceptance of an AUP.
- You can potentially configure what page the client is redirected to on successful provisioning.[8]
- You may enable a device support page. This page is useful when you're troubleshooting client onboarding issues because it can provide information to the administrator about the client NSP session including browser agent, IP, MAC, policy node, and failure reason.

Once you've done that, we need to configure the NSP operation itself. First, we need to go into the Client Provisioning results in client provisioning: Policy → Policy Elements → Results → Client Provisioning → Resources.

We need to do two things here. First, we need to configure a supplicant provisioning profile. This profile is the SSID settings we want to push down. Click Add and give the profile the configuration you're inclined to have.

---

[7]You may want to adjust the purge policy or add the devices to a different endpoint identity group. We're not thrilled with the default behavior here and don't really love relying on identity groups.
[8]Not all NADs support this.

Native Supplicant Profile > CCOE

Native Supplicant Profile

* Name	CCOE
Description	
* Operating System	Apple iOS All
* Connection Type	☐ Wired
	☑ Wireless
*SSID	CCOE
Security	WPA2 Enterprise ▼
* Allowed Protocol	TLS ▼
* Certificate Template	EAP_Authentication_Certificate_ ▼

▼ **Optional Settings**

▶ Windows Settings

▶ iOS Settings

[Save] [Reset]

Once you've added the supplicant configuration profile, you'll need to download any required wizards for either Windows or OSX. These NSP wizards are required for those operating systems to perform the NSP actions. To enable them go back to "Resources" and select Add "Agent resources from Cisco.com"; this will let you download the wizards straight from the Cloud. Download the appropriate wizards for Windows or OSX for your version of ISE.

Now that you have the required Client Provisioning results we can go in and actually configure your client provisioning policy.

That web portal will detect their OS through profiling of the device browser and initiate the NSP operation differently depending on what kind of OS is requesting the supplicant configuration:

• Apple OSX uses an application provisioned by the ISE node.[9]
• Apple iOS uses the native XML configuration profile functionality.

[9]ISE used to use a Java-based wizard in versions 1.2 and earlier. If you're still using the Java-based version, we highly recommend you upgrade as the new application is much easier.

- Windows uses a Java-based wizard.[10]
- Android requires the download of an application to perform the configuration.

You need to create a provisioning policy per operating system that specifies both the NSP profile with your SSID settings and also a wizard where relevant. You can also configure other conditions; typically I include AD group membership where possible but it's not required.

Client Provisioning Policy

Define the Client Provisioning Policy to determine what users will receive upon login and user session initiation:
For Agent Configuration: version of agent, agent profile, agent compliance module, and/or agent customization package.
For Native Supplicant Configuration: wizard profile and/or wizard. Drag and drop rules to change the order.

	Rule Name	Identity Groups	Operating Systems	Other Conditions	Results
☑	iOS NSP	If Any and	Apple iOS All and	presidio-demo:ExternalGroups EQUALS presidio-demo.com/Users/Domain Users	then BYOD SSID Config Edit | ▾
☑	Android NSP	If Any and	Android and	presidio-demo:ExternalGroups EQUALS presidio-demo.com/Users/Domain Users	then BYOD SSID Config Edit | ▾
☑	Windows NSP	If Any and	Windows All and	presidio-demo:ExternalGroups EQUALS presidio-demo.com/Users/Domain Users	then WinSPWizard 1.0.0.43 Edit | ▾ And BYOD SSID Config
☑	OSX NSP	If Any and	Mac OSX and	presidio-demo:ExternalGroups EQUALS presidio-demo.com/Users/Domain Users	then MacOsXSPWizard Edit | ▾ 1.0.0.30 And BYOD SSID Config
☑	AV posture	If Any and	Windows All and	Condition(s)	then NACAgent 4.9.5.4 And Edit | ▾ NAC-Profile And ComplianceModule 3.6.9938.2

For Windows, iOS, or OSX the configuration for provisioning of supplicants is done at this point.

If you're using Android, there is an additional step you'll need to take to make this work. You noticed that we said that Android requires an application to perform the configuration, and that application isn't listed as a wizard in our client provisioning policy. That's because the application is actually provisioned from the Google Play store, the store native to Android where you get your apps. To enable this, we'll need to adjust our ACL to allow access to the Google Play store.

The easiest way to do this is to go back into our WLC and add a DNS-based rule to our NSP-REDIRECT ACL.[11] Hover over the blue drop down next to your ACL and select "Add-Remove URL".

Access Control Lists

Enable Counters ☐

Name	Type	
ACL-REDIRECT	IPv4	▾
MDM-Redirect	IPv4	▾
Student	IPv4	▾
NSP-REDIRECT	IPv4	▾

[10]It's assumed that the Windows BYOD device already has a version of Java installed on it.
[11]This is not supported before version 7.6 or some older access points. If you are looking to do this and you're on earlier code, we highly recommend you upgrade. When in doubt here, please consult the configuration guide around the feature restrictions.

Once in the URL List, add the URL for Google Play store which is "play.google.com" at the time of this writing.

ACL > NSP-REDIRECT > URL List		< Back
URL String Name [ ]	Add	
URL Name		
play.google.com		☑

The way this works is that the WLC will snoop DNS requests looking for requests going to play.google.com and whitelist up to 20 IP addresses for those transactions dynamically. This is generally sufficient for the client to download the application from Google Play.[12]

At this point you're ready to actually onboard a device but not so fast. You still need AuthC and AuthZ rules that you will use after you're done onboarding to gain network access. Those rules should have a couple of important attributes:

- The AuthC rule should be sure to identify the common name as the user identity.
- The AuthZ rule should identify with a high fidelity that these devices are who they say they are when we provide them network access.

The easiest way to create the AuthC rule that gives you the behavior you're looking for here is to utilize the fields that we created in the certificate template earlier on. For example, the issuers of the certificates we create are all going to have the Common Name ISE in them, so we can identify the certificates that are issued to BYOD devices by ISE by just checking for that field.

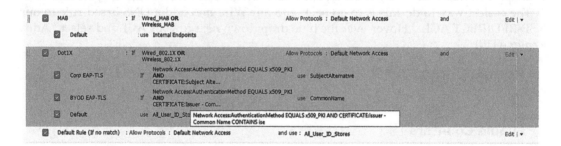

The exact conditions are as follows:

- Authentication Method = x509
- Issuer Common Name Contains ise

---

[12]Just note that when you look at configuring DNS-based ACLs, they only work right now in support of web authentication redirection with RADIUS NAC. If this ACL is also used for MDM, then add meraki.com (or your MDM) to this for web authentication to an MDM portal.

If both of those conditions are met, then ISE will use the common name in the certificate for the identity field so we can then use the username in AuthZ to validate that the AD user is still authorized.

The specifics of the authorization rule that you would typically use are a little more complicated because we do want to ensure that the authorization result being provided is correct for these users and devices.

| | ☑ | Wireless BYOD User | if | (Wireless_802.1X AND presidio-demo:ExternalGroups EQUALS presidio-demo.com/Users/Domain Users AND presidio-demo:IdentityAccessRestricted EQUALS False AND Network Access:AuthenticationMethod EQUALS x509_PKI AND CERTIFICATE:Issuer - Common Name CONTAINS ise) | then | Wireless BYOD | | Edit \| ▼ |

The conditions have the following attributes:

- Wireless dot1x
- External Group membership = Domain users
- IdentityAccessRestricted = False
- AuthenticationMethod = PKI
- Certificate Subject Issuer Contains ise

This provides us pretty specific functionality here:

- First, we're making sure we have the correct medium and access methodology with wireless dot1x.
- Next we're going to make sure that the object we're checking is a user in a proper group.
- By checking "IdentityAccessRestricted = False" we're making sure that the user is not otherwise disabled in AD.
- Then we're going to be sure that we're authenticating with a certificate.
- Lastly we're making sure that the certificate template we're using is from the ISE CA because no other sensible certificate that we can validate ourselves we'd see in the wild may have their issuer set as "ISE."

With those rules configured, now we're ready to actually start onboarding devices onto your LAN.

The dual SSID design for NSP onboarding provides similar functionality but instead of relying on a single dot1x SSID, we have a separate open unencrypted SSID that we will use for onboarding and configure the end client to join the dot1x-encrypted SSID with EAP-TLS once we have gone through the NSP process. There are some basic pieces of configuration both on the WLC and in ISE we need to do to make this work.

On the WLC we need to have enabled "Fast SSID change" under Controller → General. This is important because when we have the client switch from the unencrypted SSID to the encrypted SSID, we need the controller to allow this change with minimal disruption. Otherwise the settings for the WLC and WLAN are the same as a typical guest SSID with ISE.

Inside ISE you need to configure a CWA guest page for sponsored guest login (or self-service if you are inclined). There are a couple of pieces of configuration to adjust to make this a NSP page also.

First, be sure that the ISS of the guest portal page is configured to allow authentication from the external identity source that your corporate users use. If this is AD, this will work by default since the Guest_Portal_Sequence includes all AD join points. If you are using LDAP, you'll need to be sure you add that manually.

Once you've validated your ISS, you need to check a single box. Scroll down to "BYOD Settings".

▼ BYOD Settings

☑ Allow employees to use personal devices on the network

Endpoint identity group: | RegisteredDevices ⌄ |

Configure endpoint identity groups at
Administration > Identity Management > Groups > Endpoint
Identity Groups

Purge endpoints in this identity group: | 30 | days
Configure endpoint purge at
Administration > Identity Management > Settings > Endpoint
purge

☐ Allow employees to choose to guest access only

☐ Display Device ID field during registration

Configure employee registered devices at
Administration > Device Portal Management > Settings > Employee
Registered Devices

After successful device configuration take employee to:

○ Originating URL ⓘ

◉ Success page

○ URL: [   ]

And check "Allow employees to use personal devices on the network." Once you check this, you'll see that a BYOD flow is enabled in this portal. When a person logs in with an employee credential, they will automatically be delivered to the NSP BYOD flow.

At this point you need to be sure you've configured the Client Provisioning rules and results just the same way you'd configure them for single SSID NSP design and the client will have a certificate provisioned to the end device and the supplicant configured for EAP-TLS.

WEB AUTHENTICATION FOR BYOD ACCESS

Lastly, if you are providing BYOD access to employee devices and you're disinclined to provide them access with encryption on a WLAN, it's possible to have them use the guest SSID with their employee credential and not require BYOD. ISE provides ways for this to happen relatively gracefully, more gracefully than a guest SSID controlled with Prime or Wireless Control System (WCS) created guest users.

Typically when we go into an organization where the employees are using the guest SSID, the guest credentials are static, haven't been changed in years, and are known by everyone. In this situation if an employee is fired, or an employee was violating the web terms of service, it can be difficult to identify the end user of the device.

The configuration for this is also very simple. There are two steps. First, make sure the authentication in the guest portal allows for authentication to the identity store that is used by employees. Like I mentioned before, the default "Guest_Portal_Sequence" allows for AD authentication.

Second, you need an AuthZ rule that allows for employees to successfully be allowed on the LAN. This is what a typical AuthZ policy looks like when I'm deploying it.

⠿	☑	Wireless Employee Guest SSID	if	(Wireless_MAB AND presidio-demo:ExternalGroups EQUALS presidio-demo.com/Users/Domain Users)	then	Wireless_Guest	Edit | ▾
⠿	☑	Wireless Guest User	if	GuestEndpoints AND Wireless_MAB	then	Wireless_Guest	Edit | ▾
⠿	☑	Wireless Splash Page	if	Wireless_MAB	then	Wireless_Splash_Page	Edit | ▾

The bottom rule is the rule that allows devices to use the web splash page. Then either users who have successfully authenticated as guests (and are using their registered endpoint identity group) or those who can be identified by an AD group membership are allowed to connect to the guest LAN.

Obviously in this case the employees may be provided a different AuthZ result, providing them access to potentially some internal resources (active sync maybe) while providing true guests nothing. That's entirely up to you and your specific deployment but this design will allow both guests and employees to directly log in to the guest splash page and gain access.

14

ISE Posture Assessment

INTRODUCTION

The role of posture checking within ISE is to check one or more attributes on an endpoint and use those checks to determine if a client is "fit" to access the network. These attributes can include:

- Antivirus/spyware installation/definition verification
- Windows updates
- If a service/application is running
- Files existing/dates checked
- Registry keys existing/containing specified values

These posture rules/conditions are extremely flexible and with a little ingenuity you can check almost anything about a computer and use the outcomes to make policy decisions.

POSTURE BASICS

The first thing to know about posture is that the outcome for each client is Boolean; either you pass or you don't. You can't make policy (AuthZ) decisions based on the condition of rules being checked so keep that in mind while trying to determine if/where/how this will be used in your environment. Posture policy rules also operate differently than other sections of ISE. Where AuthC/AuthZ rules process in a top-down, first-match order, all posture rules that have their conditions match a user will be run for that user. The list of available attributes that you have to craft is also reduced so you might need to rethink how you handle multiple groups of people so that each group runs only the rules that they should.

You should also take into account that running posture will probably require you to deploy another piece of software to machines running it. Depending on the route you take this may not be the case but let's look at our options first:

- AnyConnect ISE posture module (Windows and OSX): This is the preferred way to do posture; it supports all features, remediation actions, and conditions as long as they are relevant to the underlying OS (you can't check for registry entries on an OSX machine, e.g.).
- NAC Agent (Windows and OSX): The legacy posture method. This agent is supported but End of Life (EOL) at this point; only legacy NAC deployments should consider using it at all. Even then this should be phased out and moved to AC as soon as possible.

- Temporal web agent (Windows): This lets you perform most posture checks without the need to install software onto the machine. The downside is that no remediation actions are available so the user has to manually fix the issues themselves.

There is a clear winner here that covers most use cases and that is AnyConnect. If you are deploying it as your chosen supplicant (say for EAP-Chaining), then you have a single software stack that's responsible for network access and only single new icon users see in their taskbar. Now there are cases where maybe you don't want to (or you can't) install software on machines and in those cases you are going to want to utilize the Web Agent but there is a catch here and it's something anyone coming from NAC will miss; users don't have an option on which agent to use. If you have a group of users, like vendors, where sometimes the full AC module is appropriate but sometimes the Web Agent would work better, you will need to pick the one that will work the best for *all* the users in that group unless you want to create some more Client Provisioning Portal (CPP) rules that target your users more.

You will want to turn on updates for posture rules/definitions so that ISE will always have the latest information to check your clients against. These updates pull down updated Cisco rules (file/registry-based patch checks, OS version checks, etc.), new supported AV/AS platforms, and information about the latest definitions for AV/AS products. After all, you don't want to set up all the rules to check for definitions and then have ISE not know what they are. You can get to the update area by going to Administration → System → Settings → Posture → Updates.

Posture Updates

⦿ Web   ◯ Offline

* Update Feed URL `https://www.cisco.com/web/secure/pmbu/posture-update.xml` [Set to Default]

Proxy Address

Proxy Port   HH   MM   SS

☑ Automatically check for updates starting from initial delay [01 ▼][00 ▼][00 ▼] every [24] hours ⓘ

[Save]   [Update Now]   [Reset]

▼ Update Information

Last successful update on	**2015/06/18 00:27:23** ⓘ
Last update status since ISE was started	**Last update attempt at 2015/06/18 00:27:23 was successful** ⓘ
Cisco conditions version	**200011.0.0.0**
Cisco AV/AS support chart version for windows	**135.0.0.0**
Cisco AV/AS support chart version for Mac OSX	**57.0.0.0**
Cisco supported OS version	**13.0.0.0**

Scheduled updates are not enabled by default so make sure that you run this at least once before starting to create your own posture conditions/requirements. You really don't need to schedule to run more than once every 24 h in most cases since almost every AV vendor only releases definitions daily. Here we've chosen a time of 1 a.m. so that when our users start the next day, any checks are operating off the latest info. We're also pulling directly from Cisco's update feed but for any air-gapped/high-security networks you have the option of going through a proxy server or downloading an offline update file from Cisco's site and then uploading it yourself. If you are in the latter situation, it might be easier to use conditions within ISE that don't rely on the posture updates (definition checking based on dates and no versions, non-registry-based Windows Update checks) so that you don't have to upload the files as often.

Up until recent versions of ISE there was something that anyone coming from NAC would have missed—a "persistent" posture state/session. NAC would keep a list of MAC addresses that had successfully logged on and ran posture so when they were seen again they just got the access they needed without going through the whole process again. This was good because it meant that users had a faster login because their device had already been deemed to be compliant. Normally with ISE your posture state follows your authentication session; so if you disconnected/rebooted/tripped over a cable when you reconnected, that would look like a new session and you would need to run all the posture checks again. Depending on the type/number of rules this might not be a big deal but it still introduces some lag time that doesn't need to be there. With ISE 1.3 and later the concept of "posture leasing" was introduced and it permitted a client's posture state to be remembered even if they disconnected. Once enabled, any of the previous scenarios that would have caused the posture module to run again now allow the client to get online right away. The lease also moves between media types, meaning if a client runs posture from a wired port in the morning and then they get up in the afternoon to go to a meeting, they don't need to posture on the wireless connection since ISE already knows that the machine checks out.

Posture General Settings (i)

Remediation Timer	4	Minutes (i)
Network Transition Delay	3	Seconds (i)
Default Posture Status	Compliant ▼ (i)	
☐ Automatically Close Login Success Screen After	0	Seconds (i)

Posture Lease

○ Perform posture assessment every time a user connects to the network

◉ Perform posture assessment every [1] Days (i)

[Save]   [Reset]

A lease time is global for all clients and is configured under "Administration → System → Settings → Posture → General Settings"; the value can be between 1 and 365 days; setting this to 7 days is a good starting point. Only AnyConnect clients can make use of this feature so keep that in mind if you are moving from versions older than 1.3.

Also you can see there are some general timers/options that are set that impact all clients running posture in your deployment if you don't have a more specific setting inside the Client Provisioning area. The first one is important and one that you will probably want to change since it's the amount of time that a client has to complete the posture process before they are deemed noncompliant. Err on the higher side for this value since there isn't really any harm that can come from a long timer here; 60 min is a good place to start if you need a number. The network translation delay is the amount of time the posture process waits before kicking off a network "refresh" and getting its new AuthZ policies. The default should be fine unless you are switching client VLANs (which, while said in other sections, should be reiterated here too: please avoid this) and in that case you will want to tweak this for your own environment. The default posture status is used for client that can't run posture but AuthZ policies say that they should, like Linux machines. This setting determines how the devices are treated; a setting of Compliant will allow those machines access after they hit the Client Provisioning page while a setting of Non-Compliant forces all machines to run posture and those that can't won't be granted network access. The final setting, Automatically Close Login Success Screen After, is applicable only to the NAC Agent and cleans up the login process a bit. If you are migrating off NAC, this is probably a good thing to enable.

The last feature you will want to know about related to posture is something called passive reassessment (PrA), located under Administration → System → Settings → Posture → Reassessments. PrA allows you to run the same posture checks you run on clients when they access the network at defined intervals after clients are already online. This would let you, for example, to continue passively checking on machines that might go through the normal posture process only once a week because of posture leasing. Checks are executed transparently in the background so users don't see anything is happening unless the enforcement type is configured to do something. If you are running checks on AV install/definitions when clients access the network and had PrA enabled, then even if the client uninstalls AV mid-day they would be exposed only for a little while before the posture check would fail and action could be taken. When that happens, there are three options that can be taken on how to deal with that failure:

1. Continue: Silently log the fact the posture checks failed and permit the client to continue accessing the network normally.
2. Logoff: The client is removed from the network and has to start their authentication like it's a fresh network login. This means any failed posture rules caught by PrA would then be remediated through the normal remediation process.
3. Remediate: AnyConnect will pop up and allow the user to fix any failures just like during the initial authentication but they will retain their current network access during this time. If they don't fix the issues within the grace period, then the session is terminated and they start a fresh network login.

Reassessment Configurations List > **New Reassessment Configuration**

Reassessment Configuration

* Configuration Name	All-Users
Configuration Description	
Use Reassessment Enforcement ?	☑
Enforcement Type	remediate ▾
Interval	240 minutes. *i*
Grace Time	30 minutes. *i*

Group Selection Rules

1. Each configuration must have a unique group or a unique combination of groups.
2. No two configurations may have any group in common.
3. If a config already exists with a group of 'Any', then no other configs can be created unless -
    i. the existing config with a group of 'Any' is updated to reflect a group (or groups) other than 'Any', or
    ii. the existing config with a group of 'Any' is deleted
4. If a config with a group of 'Any' must be created, delete all other configs first.

* Select User Identity Groups   Any ⬦

Now, this seems like it would be a great feature with a lot of potential; however, in practice it's hindered by the inability to use anything other than ISE user identity groups for targeting of configurations. This means that unless you are a major corner case and for some reason creating local accounts in ISE for user network access, you have the ability to set only a single PrA configuration that will apply to every single user. If you have some groups that should be logged off right away and others that you are OK with, failing posture checks you have to accept that either everyone is going to fail or everyone is going to get kicked off. Now, if you have a very locked down homogeneous environment, then this feature might give you some extra piece of mind; otherwise it might be better to forgo this particular feature.[1]

REQUIRED AUTHZ COMPONENTS

Before we dive into configuring posture we'll need to configure some AuthZ components so that clients are correctly redirected to posture portals when needed and then granted network access when they pass posture. We'll make the assumption that you followed the NAD section and that you have the "POSTURE-REDIRECT" ACL deployed on your NADs already.

First, we will need to create a new AuthZ result that directs clients to the Client Provisioning Portal that we'll configure later. Head into Policy → Policy Elements → Results → Authorization → Authorization Profiles. Typically when naming these profiles it's good to call out they are used for posture so our new AuthZ profile will be called "Employee-PostureDiscovery." The difference between a normal production AuthZ result and this is that we'll be checking off the "Web Redirection" option.

---

[1]There is some potential here for a home-grown solution using PrA with an enforcement type of "continue" and the posture status report. The report could be scheduled to run hourly, exported to a remote repository, or parsed for identity/PrA information, and then an external script could make decisions (ignore the PrA result, log off the client via the API, etc.) based off of its own logic.

▼ **Common Tasks**

☑ DACL Name | PERMIT_ALL_TRAFFIC   ▼ |

☑ VLAN   Tag ID **1** | Edit Tag | ID/Name | 10 |

☐ Voice Domain Permission

☑ Web Redirection (CWA, MDM, NSP, CPP)

| Client Provisioning (Posture) ▼ | ACL | POSTURE-REDIRECT | Value | Client Provisioning Portal (def: ▼ |

☐ Static IP/Host name

You can see that we're still passing a dACL and VLAN back to the client but we're also forcing the client to get redirected to the default Client Provisioning Portal and telling the NAD to use the "POSTURE-REDIRECT" ACL to determine what is redirected to ISE and what isn't. The dACL chosen here is actually OK because the redirection ACL will push almost everything to ISE but if you wanted to be extra cautious you could duplicate the access granted/needed for your redirect ACL into a dACL and stop non-HTTP traffic from being redirected to ISE at all.

Once we have that created, we'll need to create the AuthZ rules to support posture and this typically involves two stages. The first one is duplicating the existing AuthZ rule for the group of people you want to posture and modifying the conditions to check for a posture state and then push them toward posture; the second part is modifying the original AuthZ rule to check for the successful posture status before granting access.

| ☑ | Employee-Compliant | if | (Wired_802.1X AND LAB-AD:ExternalGroups EQUALS lab.local/LAB /Employee/Groups/Employees) | then | **Employee-Compliant** |

This shows what our normal employee rule looks like before posture is implemented. We're just checking to see if the user is a member of the "Employees" group and based on that we grant them access with the "Employee-Compliant" result that puts them into VLAN 10 and applies a permit-all dACL. After we duplicate the rule and modify both our Employee AuthZ looks like this.

☑	Employee Compliant	if	(Wired_802.1X AND LAB-AD:ExternalGroups EQUALS lab.local/LAB /Employee/Groups/Employees AND Session:PostureStatus EQUALS Compliant)	then	Employee-Compliant
☑	Employee NonCompliant	if	(Wired_802.1X AND LAB-AD:ExternalGroups EQUALS lab.local/LAB /Employee/Groups/Employees AND Session:PostureStatus EQUALS NonCompliant)	then	Employee-NonCompliant
☑	Employee PostureDiscovery	if	(Wired_802.1X AND LAB-AD:ExternalGroups EQUALS lab.local/LAB /Employee/Groups/Employees AND Session:PostureStatus EQUALS Unknown)	then	Employee-PostureDiscovery

We've added an additional check on the "PostureStatus" session attribute to see if the user has run posture yet or not. The first rule now checks to make sure that the user's posture status is equal to compliant before it grants network access while the third rule checks for a PostureStatus of Unknown (meaning posture has never run) and when matched will use the AuthZ result we previously created to ensure the user is redirected to the CPP. The second rule checks to see if the PostureStatus is NonCompliant and thus the device failed posture for some reason and applies a special AuthZ result that cordons the device off, providing access only to resources needed to become compliant again. This is an optional rule but very helpful; other options for addressing the condition include letting the user hit a default "deny all" rule toward the bottom of the list or gain guest access if you have rules that permit that. Order wise you typically want to keep the noncompliant AuthZ rules under the compliant ones although only in complex rulesets will that become a true issue.

If you have only a single group or a single all-encompassing rule for your organization, then you are all set but if you have other groups that you would like to have posture apply to then you should make similar modifications to those AuthZ rules to support them.

CLIENT PROVISIONING

Before your clients can actually get to the posture stage they need to have AnyConnect installed on them. You can handle this a couple of different ways, a dedicated tool such as SCCM, AD, or through ISE itself. We'll concentrate on deployment through ISE since it can cover both installations and upgrades of existing installations but depending on the rights your users have on their machines you might need to explore one of the other options for installation.

Flow wise the Client Provisioning (CP) process has a couple of twists and turns in it but is fairly simple. We'll be assuming a Windows AnyConnect-only flow but it's similar for OSX:

1. Client hits an AuthZ rule that pushes them to a CP portal.
2. CP rules are run against the client, top-down, until a matching rule is found. That result is used to determine the data sent to the authenticating client.
3. If the user already has AnyConnect ISE posture installed, then the local AC client pulls down the configuration from ISE, applies any needed updates based on the included settings, and then proceeds to start the posture process.
4. If the user does not have anything installed, then they have to launch a browser and are presented with a 10-s countdown. The countdown is there to prevent AnyConnect from being mistaken for not running when it's just taking a bit longer than normal.
5. Once the countdown expires, the AnyConnect installation is launched, using ActiveX for IE and a Java applet for non-IE browsers. If both of those fail, there is the option to download a bootstrap executable that will start the process.
6. AnyConnect now downloads, installs, and is launched.
7. The process is now the same as step 3.

That process has multiple components in it that you will have to configure including the CP result and the AnyConnect profiles that are handed to the client. The first thing we'll want to do is get the AnyConnect packages that will be uploaded to ISE, which unfortunately right now requires you to login to CCO and download manually. Go to http://www.cisco.com/

go/anyconnect → "Download Software for this Product" → "AnyConnect Secure Mobility Client v4.x" and download the Windows and OSX "Head-end deployment (PKG)" files.

After you have those two files you will need to upload them to ISE; head into Policy → Policy Elements → Results → Client Provisioning and add "Agent Resources from local disk." Select "Cisco Provided Packages" and then browse to where you downloaded the PKG file(s) and submit. Repeat if you need to upload for another OS. The last software piece we need is the AnyConnect Compliance module that will be included when we build our configuration profile later on. The Compliance module is what handles checking all the AV/AC/patch Management products that ISE supports and since it's a separate component from the ISE posture module it can be upgraded independently and much more easily. Users see a quick message in AC but it's fairly transparent when it happens. Click "Add," and then "Agent Resources from Cisco site" and check off the AnyConnect Compliance modules for the OSs you will be supporting and then click "Save." ISE will download them and you should see them show up in the resource list in a few seconds.

Now that we have the AnyConnect package(s) uploaded we'll create the ISE Posture Profile that will be used by our clients, "Add" → "NAC Agent or AnyConnect Posture Profile" → "AnyConnect." The profile contains settings that can be changed/tweaked to fit your environment but there are really only a couple you need to touch:

- Remediation timer: The note is misleading because there is already a value filled for this and as it turns out the value can't actually be empty. Put in the amount of times you want clients to be able to remediate before they are automatically flagged as noncompliant.
- IP address change: This entire section can be ignored unless you are doing VLAN changes for your clients. Again, please try not to do that.
- Discovery host: This value is safe to leave blank; the posture module has its own discovery that is able to pick up on the HTTP redirect and trigger posture. There might be some corner cases where this is needed but those should be few and far between.
- Server name rules: This needs to be filled in and should probably be "*.your.tld" unless you have a good reason to just go with "*." If you have multiple domains, then you can do something like "ise.lab.local, *.my.tld, *.other.tld" to cover all of them.

Agent Behavior

Parameter	Value	
Enable debug log	No ▼	
Operate on non-802.1X wireless	No ▼	
Enable signature check	No ▼	
Log file size	5	MB
Remediation timer	60	mins

Posture Protocol

Parameter	Value
PRA retransmission time	120 secs
Discovery host	
* Server name rules	ise.lab.local

There is also a note that you should have separate Posture profiles for Windows and OSX. This is true for VLAN change use cases because the optimal settings for Windows and OSX are different; you can safely use the same profile for both otherwise. Submit your profile and then "Add" an "AnyConnect Configuration" profile. You will be asked the select an AnyConnect package that this is for and you should note that once you make that choice and then save this profile that value cannot be changed. You should incorporate the AC platform and version you selected into the name of the configuration so that it's clear when you use it in Client Provisioning rules.

AnyConnect Configuration > **New AnyConnect Configuration**

* Select AnyConnect Package: AnyConnectDesktopWindows 4.1.2011.0

* Configuration Name: Employee AC Win 4.1.2011.0

Description:

After selecting the version of AnyConnect you will need to choose, at a minimum, the Compliance module you previously downloaded as well as the ISE Posture profile you created. Should you want to also deploy VPN, AMP, Diagnostics and Reporting Tool (DART), etc., you can check off those options and select a profile for them, but those profiles need to be created externally and uploaded; ISE currently supports only creating/ editing the Posture profile with the WebUI. If you want an example with NAM, check out Chapter 12.

Once the profiles are chosen, you have two more sections to cover, Deferred Updates and Uninstalling the Cisco NAC Agent. The latter should be checked if you have any existing NAC Agents out there you want to get rid of and will ensure that it's removed while AnyConnect is pushed down. If you can't follow this route, then know that AC ISE Posture and the NAC Agent can coexist but there are some semicomplicated rules as to which one ends up running and performing posture plus you could lose some posture features if NAC ends up running.

You should keep the amount of time they coexist to a minimum if you need to go that path. As for the Deferred Update settings, here are some recommended settings that strike a good balance between usability for the client and ensuring proper updates are on the client.

Deferred Update

Allowed for AnyConnect Software	Yes ▼
Minimum Version Required for AnyConnect Software	4.1.0
Allowed for Compliance Module	No ▼
Minimum Version Required for Compliance Module	0.0.0.0
Prompt Auto Dismiss Timeout	60
Prompt Auto Dismiss Default Response	Update ▼

We're going to let our users defer updates for anything higher than version 4.1 of AnyConnect but not let them defer Compliance module updates. Since Compliance modules provide the core functionality we're looking for and they update quick/seamlessly it's a good route to take. AnyConnect itself though might require a few minutes to update and if that happens as our users are starting a meeting or something else there might be some frustration. We also are going to timeout the deferral after 60 s and automatically run the update if there is one. Since our reason for deferral is getting people online quickly, if that prompt times out, then we can probably safely assume we aren't keeping anyone from doing something if we then run the update. Once you are happy here, save this policy and we can then actually deploy it to clients.

Now we need to configure the Client Provisioning policy so that people we want to run posture will get the correct AnyConnect installation/settings sent to them. Go to Policy → Client Provisioning and you should see an area that either has existing CPP rules (so insert a new rule) or has a blank rule ready for you to fill in. Like everything we've done, name the rule something you will recognize and pick your OS, which will impact the results you can choose from later. Other Conditions is a good place to target users based on AD group or another attribute but we've got a limited set of attributes to work with so you won't have all the options available that you might in the AuthZ policy. Finally, pick the AnyConnect Configurations we just saved and then save the policy or add another OS rule if you need to.

Rule Name	Identity Groups	Operating Systems	Other Conditions	Results
☑ Employee AC Posture	If Any	and Windows All	and LAB-AD:ExternalGroups EQUALS lab.local/LAB/Employee/Groups /Employees	then AnyConnect 4.1.2011.0 Configuration

That's it! Users logging in and getting the proper AuthZ posture redirect will now have AnyConnect + ISE posture module installed on their machine if they need it and will be ready for the posture policy which we will build next.

POSTURE RULES

Each posture rule contains four key parts: Identity Group, Operating System(s), Other Conditions, and the Requirements to get run when the first three are matched. The Identity Group attribute is useful only if you are running posture for guest users or if you use locally created ISE accounts, so even though posture can be run against a computer (more on that later) you can't use endpoint groups in your rules. Operating Systems is self-explanatory; you will mostly use this to target specific checks (like Windows Update Remediation) so that they run only on the correct OS version. Other Conditions is typically where you will use things such as AD group, EAP-Chaining Result, or ISE Use Case to really get exact with your rules. Once all of those match, the Requirements are what is sent to the NAC Agent/AnyConnect posture module and run on the client in question. Requirements use checks like those in the beginning of this chapter and then contain the remediation rules that should be run if those checks fail. Let's take a closer look at the out-of-the-box requirements that ISE has.

Requirements

Name	Operating Systems	Conditions	Remediation Actions
Any_AV_Installation_Win	for Windows All	met if ANY_av_win_inst	else Message Text Only
Any_AV_Definition_Win	for Windows All	met if ANY_av_win_def	else AnyAVDefRemediationWin
Any_AS_Installation_Win	for Windows All	met if ANY_as_win_inst	else Message Text Only
Any_AS_Definition_Win	for Windows All	met if ANY_as_win_def	else AnyASDefRemediationWin
Any_AV_Installation_Mac	for Mac OSX	met if ANY_av_mac_inst	else Message Text Only
Any_AV_Definition_Mac	for Mac OSX	met if ANY_av_mac_def	else AnyAVDefRemediationMac
Any_AS_Installation_Mac	for Mac OSX	met if ANY_as_mac_inst	else Message Text Only
Any_AS_Definition_Mac	for Mac OSX	met if ANY_as_mac_def	else AnyASDefRemediationMac

We can see in here that by default ISE has rules for all supported versions of Windows and OSX that check to see if any ISE-supported AV/AS version is installed on the client as well as definition checks for those products. Should the installation rules fail, we can see that the remediation action is to display some message text to the user but if the definition version rules fail we run a different action but it isn't clear what. Since the rules are similar for both AV versus AS and Windows versus OSX, let's break down the Windows AV rules to see what they are made of.

CONDITIONS

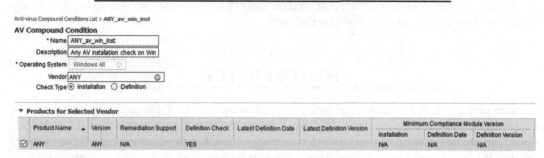

As the name of the condition above hints to, it is checking for any supported vendor's AV product installation on all Windows OSs. What's a "supported vendor/product"? The easiest way is to check http://cisco.com/go/ise in the "Software Downloads, Release and General Information" → "Release Notes" area and look for the supported products documentation. This list is updated frequently to include newly supported vendors and newer versions of existing products. You can also go into the posture conditions, create a new AV/AS rule, select an OS, and then look in the Vendor dropdown. The list is extensive and chances are if you have a product, it's supported in ISE.

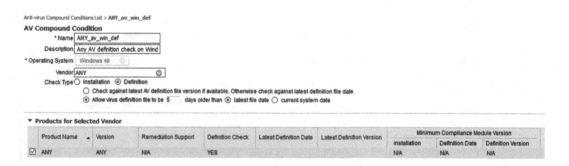

The condition used for a definition check looks pretty much the same but you can see some other options under Check Type. Here we are checking to see if the virus definition files installed on the machine are no more than 5 days older than the versions that ISE knows about. If you change these rules or create your own, it's generally recommended to allow definitions to be at least 1 or 2 days older on your machines unless your machines and AV solutions have timers that are finely tuned. If ISE gets a posture package update that includes, say, version 20 of AV definitions but your centrally managed AV system hasn't pulled that update yet and thus none of your machines have it, you could put yourself in a situation where your machines can't actually get online even if they are working perfectly. The only time you may want to forgo that recommendation is if you are in an outbreak scenario and you need to keep machines without the absolute latest definition filing off the network.

In general, conditions are used to define some sort of check you want to run on a machine. There are 10 different types of conditions that can be configured for posture; however, there is some overlap; let's dig into each one and see what it's made of:

- File condition: Checks all attributes (date, version, CRC32, existence) related to a single file. Can check both absolute and relative paths like a user's home directory or $SYSTEM32.
- Registry condition: A Windows-only condition, this checks registry keys/values based on existence or data within the value.
- Application condition: Checks to see if a specified application is running or not.
- Service condition: Checks to see if a specified service is running or not; OSX changes the value to loaded or unloaded for services.
- Compound condition: Will be discussed in more detail later on but simply put it allows you to take file/registry/application/service conditions and combine them into a single condition using Boolean operators.
- AV compound condition: Checks installations and definitions of supported antivirus software.
- AS compound condition: Checks installations and definitions of supported antispyware software.
- Dictionary simple condition: Checks a single AuthZ attribute from a limited list.
- Dictionary compound condition: Similar to the dictionary simple condition but allows you to combine multiple attribute checks into a single condition.
- Patch management condition: Checks OS vendor or third-party patch management platforms to verify that the software is installed and, if supported, whether the solution is enabled and all required patches are installed.

Compound conditions are an important part of ISE and if you have already been through Chapters 5 and 6 then you have seen some of how they work. The two dictionary conditions are exactly like AuthC/AuthZ conditions with the exception that not all of the attributes available in those rules are available to us in posture; however, you should be able to cover almost anything you need to unless you start getting really crazy. Posture compound conditions allow you to form rules like this.

Compound Conditions List > **pr_CSA_Agent_Version_5_0**

Compound Condition

        * Name   **pr_CSA_Agent_Version_5_0**

      Description **Cisco Predefined Rule: CSA 5.**

   * Operating System | Windows XP (All)   ⟡ |

| pc_CSA_Version_5_0_0_0_gt&pc_CSA_Version_6_0_0_0_lt |

This is a Cisco-provided rule that checks for version 5.x of the Cisco Security Agent; it does this by making use of two registry conditions, both of which have to result in a "true" verdict.

Registry Conditions List > **pc_CSA_Version_5_0_0_0_gt**

Registry Condition

* Name	**pc_CSA_Version_5_0_0_0_g**
Description	**Cisco Predefined Check: CSA l**
Registry Type	RegistryValue
Registry Root Key	HKLM
* Value Name	FullVersion
Value DataType	Version
Value Operator	later than
Value Data	**5.0.0.0**
* Operating System	Windows XP (All)

* Sub Key **\ SOFTWARE\Cisco\CSAgent**

Registry Conditions List > **pc_CSA_Version_6_0_0_0_lt**

Registry Condition

* Name	**pc_CSA_Version_6_0_0_0_lt**
Description	**Cisco Predefined Check: CSA ⟨**
Registry Type	RegistryValue
Registry Root Key	HKLM
* Value Name	FullVersion
Value DataType	Version
Value Operator	earlier than
Value Data	**6.0.0.0**
* Operating System	Windows XP (All)

* Sub Key **\ SOFTWARE\Cisco\CSAgent**

These images show the two rules that are used in the CSA compound condition and as you can see both are registry conditions that are checking a specific value for its version. The first one makes sure the version is later than "5.0.0.0" which means something like "5.0.0.1" or "5.3.8.1234" would correctly evaluate as true but so would "8.4.2.1" or "6.1.2.3." The second condition checks to make sure that same registry value is a version number less than "6.0.0.0" so that same version numbers of "5.0.0.1" or "5.3.8.1234" would correctly match but so would "0.0.0.0" or "4.3.8.1." Neither registry condition by itself is able to satisfy our needs of checking for just 5.x versions of CSA but a compound condition that combines both of them would be able to and that's exactly what happens in this case.

Compound conditions use Boolean logic which allows you to make use of AND (&), OR (|), and NOT (!) operators to control when the condition evaluates as true. The option to utilize parenthesis in order to group conditions together is also available and very useful for writing more complex conditions like this.

Compound Conditions List > **Example-Condition**

Compound Condition

* Name	Example-Condition
Description	
* Operating System	Windows All

Select a condition to insert below   ⊘   ( )   !   & |

!pc_IE11_0 | ((pc_IE6_0 & pc_RDPC_LATER_6) | (pc_IE7_0 & pc_RDPC_LATER_7))

Validate Expression

Our example condition, which should be stressed is just an example and while a valid expression would never evaluate correctly nor be useful on a client system, uses a combination of registry and file conditions to verify Remote Desktop Protocol (RDP) and IE versions on a client system. This condition uses multiple sets of parenthesis to group checks together which lets us form a condition that can account for multiple possible machine conditions all in a single rule. Now it's important to note that you shouldn't try and cram all of your checks into a single compound condition and call it a day; it would become increasingly difficult to handle the logic inside the rule and you wouldn't be able to later assign meaningful remediation rules that can provide your users with information about fixing the issues they might be having. A great example of how Cisco uses compound conditions is in the "pr_<OS>_Hotfix" conditions that are shipped in the posture data feed. These conditions use multiple file/registry checks to verify that critical OS patches are installed and since each compound condition is designed for a single OS it makes sense to group them together like this. It also means as consumers of those conditions we could use them in any posture policies we design and don't have to worry about updating anything when Cisco pushes updated versions; other methods of doing multiple checks like within the definition of the posture requirement don't offer that flexibility.

REMEDIATION

Once we've done the checking, we probably don't want to just leave the end user either guessing what's wrong or on their own to fix the issues. Using "remediation actions" you can however try to automatically repair and/or provide the user with information on how to fix the issue before they can continue. For example, if you are checking for

AV definitions and they are out of date, AnyConnect agent can automatically kick off the AV program's update process, wait until the update is complete, and then rerun the check to see if the machine now meets the set criteria. You can also use the application check to see if a machine has any P2P applications installed and present the user a warning page and link to the company policy forbidding these applications. Remediation actions come in eight flavors:

- AS Remediation: Used to define how to update the clients' antispyware program if they fail a posture check.
- AV Remediation: Same as AS remediation but used for antivirus programs.
- File Remediation: Used to provide the client with a single file.
- Launch Program Remediation: Does exactly what the name specifies, launches one or more programs.
- Link Remediation: Directs the client to a specific URL.
- Patch Management Remediation: Allows ISE to check/utilize third-party patch management software to ensure machines are compliant.
- WSUS Remediation: This rule is a little misleading; you can use it to query your own WSUS server and install updates from it but you can also contact Microsoft servers with this.
- Windows Update Remediation: This can be used to set/override settings for installation and checking of updates by the local Windows Update Agent.

Now, a couple of notes on these since some of them are not as straightforward as they might sound. Unless you have a very good reason, you shouldn't use the File Remediation method. It requires that TCP/443 is open to the ISE nodes for the client to download the file (which means the port used to administer ISE is now open to these possibly nontrusted clients) and the file can only be 50 MB in size. If you are going to be using posture, it would be much more beneficial to have a dedicated web server setup that can house these files as well as other helpful documentation that clients might need in order to get onto the network. The WSUS Remediation rule provides you with very good control over your endpoints in terms of making sure they have the exact/latest updates applied but it comes with a significant price and that is the time required to run this check. The client must contact the local or remote WSUS service and compare information it receives to what is stored in the local updates store. Not only is there latency with the checking (even if the WSUS server is local), but also any sort of corruption on the client can lead to timeouts and angry users waiting for the process to complete. Unless you have a good reason to use this check you are probably better off with the Windows Update check which is extremely fast because it's just checking local registry keys.

Back to our example rule now, we have covered the conditions used in the requirement; let's look at the remediation actions that get used. Since the action for the AV installation check is just to display a message, and you will notice in the list of remediation actions above there isn't a "Display message" action; you can simple set the message in the posture rule remediation section.

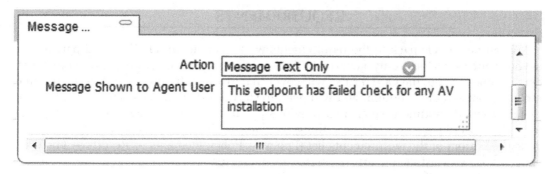

Simple and straightforward. The AV definition rule is similarly straightforward in what it does.

AV Remediations List > **AnyAVDefRemediationWin**

AV Remediation

* Name	AnyAVDefRemediationWin *(i)*
Description	Remediation for any AV
Remediation Type	Automatic ▼
* Interval	20 (in secs) (Valid Range 0 to 9999)
* Retry Count	1 (Valid Range 0 to 99)
Operating System	● Windows ○ Mac
* AV Vendor Name	ANY ▼

Save   Reset

The Remediation Type can be either Automatic or Manual and determines how the agent will behave when the client machine's definitions are out of date. Automatic remediation causes the agent on the machine to, with a supported product, kick off the update process without any user interaction. Manual on the other hand requires the user to either click a button in the agent window or go into their AV product and update that way before continuing. The interval and retry values are available only when using the automatic method; they control how long between and how many times the agent should try to get new AV definitions on its own. The OS value should simply reflect the OS you are targeting with your action. The vendor name can safely be the value of "ANY" and you don't necessarily need to pick a specific vendor; however, if you know that your company will be running products only from Vendor X, then you can safely choose just that vendor.

REQUIREMENTS

We can now circle back to the requirements we looked at earlier. The good part is that if you want to perform only generic AV/AS checks on your machines, then your work here is done for you; the OOTB rules will cover that just fine. If you wanted to create some more customized ones though, you will need to start doing that. Let's say we want to use that compound condition we created previously and a simple message as a new requirement; how would we do that? First thing we want to do is create a new requirement so go to the bottom of the requirements list (Policy → Policy Elements → Results → Posture); click the downward-facing arrow on the bottom most requirement and select "Insert new Requirement." Give your new requirement a name; we'll use "Lab_Example_ Condtion_Win" and select "Windows All" for the OS. Now we'll need to add the condition we created, but when we do that you will notice there are options here on how to treat the conditions.

Since we have only a single condition here the box is grayed out, but "All selected conditions succeed" also permits two other conditions—"Any selected condition succeeds" and "No selected condition succeeds." By putting two or more conditions here we can take conditions designed to check for one thing and combine them to do something else and reduce your need to write more conditions and duplicate effort. Two good examples of using this are as follows:

- Handling P2P applications for different groups of users. You could have conditions that check for specific applications but then use them once in an "Any selected condition succeeds" requirement for a group you want to warn about P2P but still allow through and then use them again in a "No selected condition succeeds" requirement for a group where you don't want to permit them online if they have a P2P application.
- If departments for some reason use different AV products (some use Symantec, some McAfee, others NOD32, some mixed, etc.), you could create compound conditions that check for the installation + service running for each provider and then reuse them without having to create compound conditions for each department.

Again though we run into a situation of when is it the right time to use this and when would something else (compound condition) be more appropriate. The decision will ultimately be yours and how you feel it works best in your environment. The good thing about ISE is that all this flexibility means that if you discover a better way to handle this down, the road migrating to it is fairly easy so don't worry you will be stuck in a single path forever.

POSTURE POLICY

The final part to getting posture doing what you want is to take those requirements you created and pairing them up with any identity groups, OS definitions, and/or other conditions you may want to assist you in targeting specific requirements to specific groups—that process creates the posture rules that will form your overall policy. By default there is nothing defined here so you will need to do 100% of the setup; some things to consider when formulating your policy are as follows:

1. All posture rules are cumulative.
2. You can run posture on machines.
3. Your OS choice will affect the requirements you can choose from; if you know you have a requirement that isn't showing up, then check this.

Use #1 to your advantage; instead of looking at the posture policy as "group" based and having multiple rules checking the same thing for multiple groups, look at it more from a global perspective (assuming that works for your organization). A simple example would be the AV requirement for employees; since this is the same for everyone just create one instance of it and make that rule apply to all your employees via an AD group. Assuming we then have two subgroups we want to customize (maybe patch checking for HR, HIPS product install check for Finance) we can target just those specific rules to users in those AD groups. When the posture rules are evaluated for an HR user, ISE will send down both the patch checking requirement and the overall AV requirement for evaluation. We keep our policy simple, clean, and straightforward.

The second point presents us with some interesting options, for example, if you have workstations that are shared among a group of users, you may want to apply a set of posture requirements to that group of machines that is independent from the users logging into them. To accomplish this you need to do only computer authentication with those machines since if you were to do user authentication, it would take precedence because posture runs after the user logs into the machine. The section "Examples" goes into a sample scenario a bit more if you are considering using this.

EXAMPLES

Basic Company Posture

We've covered remediation actions, conditions, and the rules they go into; let's take and put them all together into a nice policy for the Widget Group. We are going to want to run posture for multiple groups of users (HR, Finance, and Contractors), excluding Windows IT folks because they are using EAP-Chaining, as well as some computers that will be used for time keeping. We'll assume that our users and computer are in separate AD groups.

The first thing we want to do is create the conditions we'll be using that aren't provided out of the box. For this example we're going to assume that the Widget Group is using McAfee™ as their antivirus provider and want to make sure that not only is the product up-to-date but also both the AV and management components are actively running. Cisco provides a rule to check for the AV service but we'll need to create our own for the management service. The service is named "McAfeeFramework" so we'll create a simple Service Condition check for it.

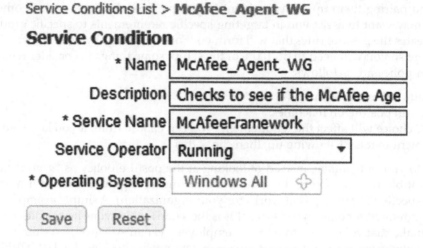

Next we're going to want to define AV install conditions for our Windows and OSX users. WG has decided that since they know all of their machines are (or should be) running version 8.8.x of McAfee Enterprise AV for Windows and version 2.1.x for OSX they are going to check for that exact version instead of using the Cisco-provided Any AV or event permitting any McAfee product. This is common when you are using a centrally managed AV product and is handy to catch machines that may have issues with their AV programs but are still getting definition updates.

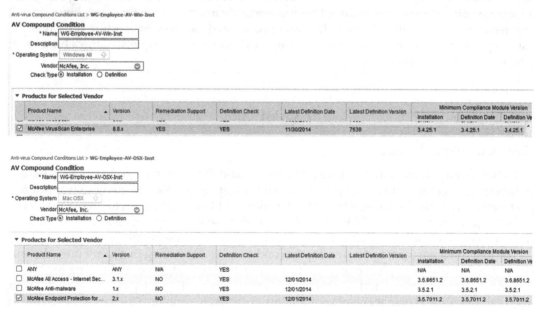

We've created two new AV compound condition rules, one for each OS. Notice that we have selected McAfee, Inc., as the vendor and that changed the listing shown at the bottom of the rule to show multiple versions of McAfee products that we could choose from. We've picked the versions that we know WG is running and nothing else. If we wanted to be more liberal with our policies, we could select the "ANY" option which would allow the posture check to succeed as long as any McAfee AV product was detected on the machine but that could be undesirable as a home user with the home version of McAfee AV could successfully pass that posture check. Now technically in this case they would fail the previously mentioned management service checks so it wouldn't matter here, but it's something you should consider in your own deployments.

Also take note of the additional information that ISE shows us for the AV products which includes support for remediation (supported on our Windows conditions, but not our OSX conditions), definition checking, latest definition date/version, and minimum Compliance module version needed to detect the product version. If we look at the Windows condition, we can see that ISE is able to detect both the date and the version number of the definitions that we are using but the OSX rules are able to detect based on only definition date. Depending on your AV/AS products, the options may be different as well so make note of them while building your conditions.

That covers the custom conditions; now we have to create the remediation actions that will be used when we build our posture requirements. Since we will be using the Cisco-provided AV definition remediation action we will need to create only two custom actions for our use case: one Link Remediation action and one Windows Update Remediation action.

Link Remediations List > WG_AV_Install_Link

Link Remediation

* Name	WG_AV_Install_Link
Description	
Remediation Type	Automatic
Interval	0 (in secs) (Valid Range 0 to 9999)
Retry Count	0 (Valid Range 0 to 99)
* URL	http://www.widgetgroup.local/it/av.html (enter a valid url such as http://www.cisco.com)

Save   Reset

For this rule we are simply automatically (for full Windows agents) launching a browser to the page http://www.widgetgroup.local/it/av.html with the assumption that the site will contain more information for the users. This is a good task for the remediation web server we referenced before. We've set the interval and retry values to 0 so that we attempt to launch to the site only once as more times wouldn't be very relevant in this case.

For the final policy elements work, we can take our custom and Cisco-provided conditions/actions and create a list of requirements that will be used when we build the posture policy. This process is mostly matching up conditions and actions for each OS/type we want and then naming them so let's look at a completed example and then call out some of the important things.

Requirements

Name	Operating Systems	Conditions	Remediation Actions
WG_AV_Install_Win	for Windows All	met if WG-Employee-AV-Win-Inst	else WG_AV_Install_Link
WG_AV_Install_OSX	for Mac OSX	met if WG-Employee-AV-OSX-Inst	else WG_AV_Install_Link
Any_AV_Installation_Win	for Windows All	met if ANY_av_win_inst	else Message Text Only
Any_AV_Definition_Win	for Windows All	met if ANY_av_win_def	else AnyAVDefRemediationWin
Any_AV_Installation_Mac	for Mac OSX	met if ANY_av_mac_inst	else Message Text Only
Any_AV_Definition_Mac	for Mac OSX	met if ANY_av_mac_def	else AnyAVDefRemediationMac
WG_McAfee_Service_Check	for Windows All	met if pc_McAfee_Service & McAfee_Agent_WG	else Message Text Only

For ease of reading we've removed the antispyware requirements from this list but other than that it should be similar to what you might see if you followed along with this process. We've taken the AV install conditions we created for both OSs and matched them up with the Link Remediation action that directs users to a specific URL for more information. Lastly, our McAfee service check uses the prebuilt condition and custom condition we made to ensure services are running but uses only the Message Text remediation action telling them "Your machine does not have the proper McAfee services running on it. Please reboot to see if this error goes away, if not please contact the Helpdesk at x1234." We decided that telling the user to reboot should be clear enough and that if something was still wrong after that they should call the Helpdesk anyway to get it resolved as there isn't much they could do on their own to fix it.

That completes our work creating conditions/requirements/actions in the policy elements area and now we get to tie those requirements to specific users in the posture policy section. Some of the settings seen here will make you go "Wait, didn't I just set these?" and you are partially right; you did but settings for conditions and OS are used differently in the posture policy. In the conditions they are used to determine validity; in the policy they are used to actually determine what requirements to apply to the device in question. It's like driving to a gas station with your vehicle; the conditions are all the different grades/types of fuel and the policy is the type of fuel your vehicle can actually accept.

Status	Rule Name	Identity Groups	Operating Systems	Other Conditions	Requirements
☑	WG-Employee-OSX-AV	If Any	and Mac OSX	WG-AD-Employees	then WG_AV_Install_OSX & Any_AV_Definition_Mac
☑	WG-Employee-Win-AV	If Any	and Windows All	WG-IT-Without-Successful-EAP-Chain AND (WG-AD-Employees)	then WG_AV_Install_Win & WG_McAfee_Service_Check & Any_AV_Definition_Win
☑	WG-TimeKeeping-Machines	If Any	and Windows 7 (All)	WG-AD-TimeKeepingMachines	then WG_AV_Install_Win & Any_AV_Definition_Win & WG_McAfee_Service_Check

This is our completed posture policy! Look at how we can have multiple require-ments per rule which helps cut down on the number of rules we need to cover all sce-narios. Best practice here is to group together common requirements (like our AV install/ definitions) into a single rule for (almost) all Employees since we want all of them to run it. It's almost all Employees because our Windows rules contain an additional condition called "WG-IT-Without-Successful-EAP-Chain"; this is a compound condition, which we learned about in the Policy Elements section. With that condition we will run the rule for all employ-ees but IT users that have successfully had their user and computer authentication together. We want that additional EAP-Chaining check as opposed to just checking the group to make sure we don't open a hole for IT users to possibly bring in their own devices, assuming we don't want that of course.

The last rule in our set is important to look at. We know our time keeping machines are all Windows 7 so we need to target only one OS (which also makes checking hotfixes easy) and we've added our AV install/definition/service checks to there as well. You might ask yourself why we did this and that's because it's the computer object we will be running posture against and not the user which prevents the previously defined employee rules from matching. Which really brings us to an important ISE concept; an object authenticating, be it computer or user, is basically the same from an ISE perspective. Almost any AuthZ, posture, SGT, etc., that you can apply to a user can also be applied to a computer and can open up a lot of possibilities when you are determining access on your network.

Patch Checking

While AV/AS-based checks might be one of the first things you start checking with pos-ture, patch checking will probably be the second thing you start doing. In general, the best way to handle this is to utilize the Cisco-provided compound rules that check for critical security patches with registry/file conditions. The only two reasons you might not want to go this route would be:

1. You have a dedicated patch management platform that is supported by ISE and so you can leverage the patch management conditions.
2. You are doing some highly customized patch staging where not all users' machines could have the latest patches and this is acceptable.

The first case is actually ideal; you can let the system(s) designed to do patch management do what they were designed to do and ISE just has to check the result. It also means you are verifying posture based on your own patching policy/practice and not one dictated by some-one else. In the second case you won't be able to use the Cisco-provided rules because they will conflict with your patching process.

Patching scenarios are quite straightforward and most of the time we need to build only the remediation action because the compound conditions for actually checking for the patch-es are already provided. If either of the two exceptions at the beginning applies to you, then you will need to perform an additional step here to create the condition that will check your machines. In this case we'll assume it is WSUS but the same methods could be used for any other product.

Patch-Management Conditions List > **Windows_Agent_PatchCheck**

Patch Management Condition

* Name	Windows_Agent_PatchCheck
Description	
* Operating System	Windows All ⟡
* Vendor Name	Microsoft Corp. ▾
Check Type	○ Installation ○ Enabled ⦿ Up to Date

▼ **Products for Selected Vendor**

	Product Name ▲	Version	Enabled Checked Support	Update Checked Support
☐	Microsoft SMS 2003 Advanced Client	7.x	YES	NO
☐	Microsoft Windows AutomaticUpdate	7.x	YES	YES
☑	Microsoft Windows Update Agent	7.x	YES	YES
☐	System Center Configuration Manager	4.x	YES	YES
☐	System Center Configuration Manager	5.x	YES	YES

This shows the options needed to make the Windows Update Agent check work how we want it, which is to ensure that all patches approved for the machine are installed and thus the machine is "Up to Date." Make sure you change that Check Type; the default of "Installation" will always succeed and won't check for patches. From here on out when we use the Cisco-provided compound conditions in the example just replace those with the condition you just created.

Head into Policy → Policy Elements → Results → Posture → Remediation Actions → Patch Management Remediation and "Add" a new action.

Patch Management Remediations List > **PMR-WUA-Install-Missing**

Patch Management Remediation

* Name	PMR-WUA-Install-Missing ⓘ
Description	
Remediation Type	Automatic ▾
* Interval	240 (Valid Range 0 to 9999)
* Retry Count	3 (Valid Range 0 to 99)
Operating System	Windows
* Patch Management Vendor Name	Microsoft Corp. ▾
Remediation Option	○ Enable ⦿ Install missing patches ○ Activate patch management software GUI

▼ **Products for Selected Vendor**

	Product Name ▲	Version	Enabled Remediation Support	Update Remediation Support
○	Microsoft Windows AutomaticUp...	7.x	YES	NO
⦿	Microsoft Windows Update Agent	7.x	NO	YES
○	System Center Configuration M...	4.x	YES	YES
○	System Center Configuration M...	5.x	YES	YES

This shows a remediation action that will automatically tell the Windows Update Agent to start installing any patches it needs as well as includes some retries to make sure that unless things go really wrong the patches should get installed.

We can now build our requirement, go down into the Posture Requirements area, and insert a new requirement. For our example the requirement will be checking Windows 7 patches.

| Win7 Hotfix Check | for Windows 7 (All) | met if pr_Win7_32_Hotfixes & pr_Win7_64_Hotfixes | else PMR-WUA-Install-Missing |

For hotfix checks like this it's important to select the specific OS you are checking since the compound conditions are valid only for a specific OS; if you select "Windows (All)," none of these checks will show up so double check that. Second, we add both the 32-bit and 64-bit conditions into the rule and ensure that "All selected conditions succeed" is selected. This might seem strange because 32-bit patch checks would fail on 64-bit Windows and vice versa but at the beginning of each of those compound conditions is a check to see if the machine the rules are being run on is of the opposite architecture (so if the rules are for 32-bit Windows, the conditions checks first for 64-bit Windows) and to return a success message. Basically what really happens here is that assuming the OS is correctly patched, each machine has a "success" verdict returned for both hotfix checks. If a machine is missing patches for its architecture, it will still fail those checks but pass the opposite architecture checks and overall, because both checks must pass, correctly result in a failed check and lead to the remediation action being run. Even if you are running only one architecture, you should really include both just in case; if you include only the checks for the 64-bit machine and that check is run on a 32-bit machine, the requirement will always succeed and that machine will never get its patches checked. Better to spend the 2 extra seconds and build the requirement for both architectures. The remediation action in this case is the patch management action we built previously that will trigger the Windows Update Agent to begin installing any missing patches.

Finally we'll go into our posture policy and create a new rule for the requirement we just created.

Posture Policy

Define the Posture Policy by configuring rules based on operating system and/or other conditions.

Status	Rule Name	Identity Groups	Operating Systems	Other Conditions		Requirements
☑	Windows 7 Hotfix Check	If Any	and Windows 7 (All)		then	Win7 Hotfix Check

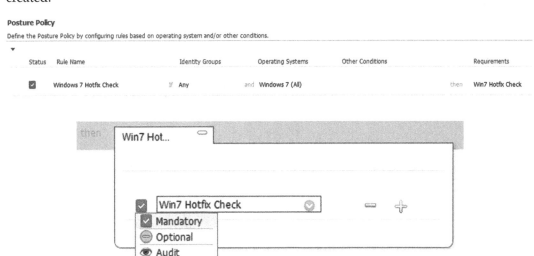

Again, like the requirement, it's important here to select the OS that we're targeting here or the Hotfix requirement won't be available to select. In the second to last image we aren't using any other conditions (like AD group) to determine who the rule should be run against but you will probably want to do that in your deployment. You could also make the requirement optional to start off with while you are testing things out or make it an audit only (users won't see anything about the rule) and you can run reports from ISE later to determine what your posture looks like. Other than those two things, once you save this posture policy your machines will begin checking and remediating their missing Windows updates.

That's it; you have covered posture within ISE! Now when you apply this to your own network, it will take some time to determine what you want to check but starting small can really simplify one of the more complex areas of ISE.

VPN Integrations

Configuring ISE for use with VPN use takes up only a relatively small section of this book not because it's not effective, but because it's really easy to deploy. We're going to talk about a couple of our favorite VPN designs and deployment examples of configuring a Cisco ASA with AnyConnect SSL VPN while using ISE as the backend RADIUS authentication store.

There are a couple of things to keep in mind while configuring ISE and AnyConnect VPN integration:

- ISE profiling in the traditional sense doesn't work. The endpoint identity for VPN users is the remote public IP address making resolution of the endpoint MAC address for profiling impossible.
- While you're used to having lots of flexibility doing EAP methodologies with 802.1x, that functionality isn't nearly as mature with VPN connectivity such that PAP is generally the standard RADIUS authentication methodology.
- There is a *lot* of functionality to take advantage of in AnyConnect that augments features/functionary in the ISE/ASA integration.

Let's start by looking at a basic configuration for VPN portal on ASA controlled by ISE:

```
aaa-server ISE protocol radius
 authorize-only
 interim-accounting-update periodic 1
 dynamic-authorization
aaa-server ISE (inside) host 10.128.2.3
 key RADIUS-KEY
 authentication-port 1812
 accounting-port 1813
tunnel-group ISE type remote-access
tunnel-group ISE general-attributes
 address-pool VPN_POOL
 authentication-server-group ISE
 accounting-server-group ISE
 default-group-policy GP_INTERNAL
tunnel-group ISE webvpn-attributes
 authentication aaa
 group-url  https://vpn.example.com/ise enable
```

There a few parts of this configuration to point out. First, we're configuring a RADIUS AAA server group using interim update, dynamic authorization (CoA), and standards complaint UDP ports (by default ASA will use the Cisco propriety legacy ports).[1] We'll also configure the RADIUS preshared key (PSK) we'll be using between ISE and the ASA.

Beyond that, you'll want to configure the other typical things you'd need to configure on a tunnel group:

- Specify address pool.
- Specify ISE as the RADIUS authentication server group.
- Specify ISE as the RADIUS accounting group.
- Specify default group policy you'd like to use.

You'll notice that I've enabled a specific group-url in this tunnel group. If there are going to be multiple use cases deployed on VPN (internal users and contractors), then multiple URLs is a good way to differentiate between them.

Once you add the configuration on the ASA, you'll want to configure the ISE side of the house.

First, add the network device to ISE. All you need is the RADIUS shared secret and IP address. Nothing else is explicitly required.

Network Devices List > **ASA**
Network Devices

* Name: ASA
Description:

* IP Address: 10.128.11.254 / 32

Model Name:
Software Version:
* Network Device Group

Location: All Locations — Set To Default
Device Type: ASA — Set To Default

▾ Authentication Settings

Enable Authentication Settings
Protocol **RADIUS**
* Shared Secret: •••••••• [Show]
Enable KeyWrap ☐ ⓘ
* Key Encryption Key [Show]
* Message Authenticator Code Key [Show]
Key Input Format ◉ ASCII ◯ HEXADECIMAL

[1]The configuration example here uses syntax available in ASA 9.2 and later. If you wish to use ASA 9.1, ISE will absolutely work for your configuration with the exception of posture assessment since CoA isn't available before ASA version 9.2.

Next you'll want to configure the authentication policy. The authentication default authentication conditions will specify wired or wireless authentications for MAB or 802.1x. VPN authentication won't match either of those since the compound conditions governing those conditions don't include the "Virtual" RADIUS NAS-Port-Type. As such you'll need to create a separate authentication policy rule.

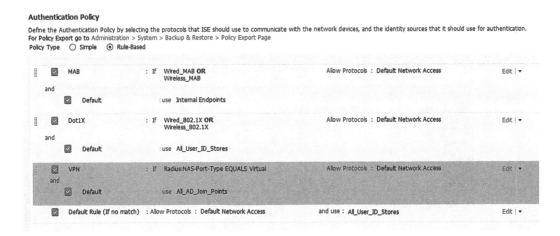

In this case we'll be matching the NAS-Port-Type of Virtual and using AD as our identity store.

You'll notice that we'll also be using the "Default Network Access" result in the rule. By default PAP is enabled in this result but if you've disabled PAP as an allowed RADIUS authentication protocol, you'll need to create a separate authentication result that allows PAP for VPN.

Authorization rules look remarkably similar to the conditions you'd specify for a wired or wireless 802.1x deployment.

In the conditions of the picture rule, we've specified both the media that the user is connecting with (virtual) and the external identify store group that the person is a member of. Easy right?

Now that we have some understanding of the AuthC and AuthZ conditions we need, there are a few options we have available for authorization results to actually give us a great deal of flexibility in our deployments. The two most popular ones are as follows:

- dACL
- Group policy override

We're pretty familiar with how dACL overrides work from wired network integration with ISE. You have the functionality for dACL on VPN with ASA but the actual behavior is a little different when applied to a VPN session. First of all, ASA VPN doesn't use wildcard mask ACL syntax by default.[2] Let's create a simple dACL to start out where we deny some destinations and then permit all access.

Downloadable ACL List > **VPN-dACL**
Downloadable ACL

* Name	VPN-dACL
Description	

* DACL Content

```
1 deny ip any host 10.128.2.12
2 deny ip any 192.168.0.0 255.255.0.0
3 permit ip any any
4
5
6
7
8
9
10
```

▶ Check DACL Syntax   ⓘ

Save   Reset

Then simply reference this in an authorization result.

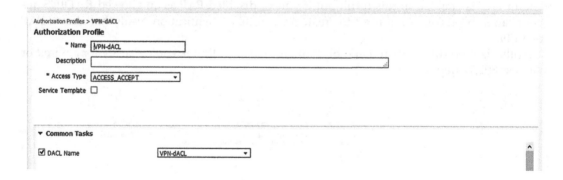

Authorization Profiles > **VPN-dACL**
Authorization Profile

* Name	VPN-dACL
Description	
* Access Type	ACCESS_ACCEPT ▾
Service Template	☐

▼ **Common Tasks**

☑ DACL Name   VPN-dACL ▾

And lastly in an authorization rule.

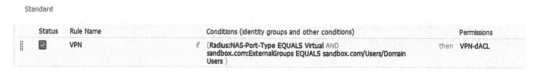

Standard

	Status	Rule Name	Conditions (identity groups and other conditions)	Permissions
⠿	☑	VPN	if (Radius:NAS-Port-Type EQUALS Virtual AND sandbox.com:ExternalGroups EQUALS sandbox.com/Users/Domain Users)	then VPN-dACL

[2]It's possible to configure the ASA to use wildcard syntax, but unless you really need to, we recommend you to not bother.

The next time someone authenticates to the VPN they'll have that ACL set on their VPN session. You can verify that through the following commands to see what the name of the ACL that was actually applied was (it is hashed when it's applied on a NAD). Below output has some information removed to save space:

```
ASA# show vpn-sessiondb detail anyconnect filter name arichter
Session Type: AnyConnect Detailed
Username     : arichter          Index       : 118
Assigned IP  : 10.128.14.21      Public IP   : 1.2.3.4
Protocol     : AnyConnect-Parent SSL-Tunnel DTLS-Tunnel
License      : AnyConnect Essentials
Encryption   : AnyConnect-Parent: (1)none  SSL-Tunnel: (1)AES256  DTLS-Tunnel: (1)AES256
Hashing      : AnyConnect-Parent: (1)none  SSL-Tunnel: (1)SHA1  DTLS-Tunnel: (1)SHA1
Bytes Tx     : 30731             Bytes Rx    : 19441
Pkts Tx      : 225               Pkts Rx     : 188
Pkts Tx Drop : 0                 Pkts Rx Drop : 0
Group Policy : GP_INTERNAL       Tunnel Group : ISE
DTLS-Tunnel:
Tunnel ID    : 118.3
Assigned IP  : 10.128.14.21      Public IP   : 1.2.3.4
Encryption   : AES256            Hashing     : SHA1
Encapsulation: DTLSv1.0          UDP Src Port : 61441
UDP Dst Port : 443               Auth Mode   : Certificate and userPassword
Idle Time Out: 30 Minutes        Idle TO Left : 30 Minutes
Client OS    : Windows
Client Type  : DTLS VPN Client
Client Ver   : Cisco AnyConnect VPN Agent for Windows 3.1.04063
Bytes Tx     : 27793             Bytes Rx    : 19596
Pkts Tx      : 281               Pkts Rx     : 200
Pkts Tx Drop : 0                 Pkts Rx Drop : 0
Filter Name  : #ACSACL#-IP-VPN-dACL-5580e7e2
```

Then you can see the actual syntax of the ACL with the following command:

```
ASA# show access-list #ACSACL#-IP-VPN-dACL-5580e7e2
access-list #ACSACL#-IP-VPN-dACL-5580e7e2; 3 elements; name hash: 0xe9385428 (dynamic)
access-list #ACSACL#-IP-VPN-dACL-5580e7e2 line 1 extended deny ip any4 host
10.128.2.12 (hitcnt=0) 0x991dd990
access-list #ACSACL#-IP-VPN-dACL-5580e7e2 line 2 extended deny ip any4 192.168.0.0
255.255.0.0 (hitcnt=0) 0x8757b095
access-list #ACSACL#-IP-VPN-dACL-5580e7e2 line 3 extended permit ip any4 any4
(hitcnt=66) 0x817204de
```

While doing dACLs with VPN clients is super easy it doesn't always give you the flexibility you need to provide granular access for different users groups. If you need to regulate more than just access control, you need to override the group policy assigned to the user.

When we say that you may want more flexibility, group policy override gives you the maximum amount of flexibility you'd get in terms of attributes you could apply to a particular user. Here are some of our favorites (in no particular order):

- Max simultaneous logins
- DNS configuration

- Tunnel protocol (full client VPN vs. clientless or both could be allowed)
- Idle timeout
- Address pool
- VLAN
- Access list

The purpose of this chapter is not to explain all the ins and outs of ASA configuration but you get the picture that you can configure a great deal by setting the client's group policy once it's logged in.

So let's go back into our same configuration and create a group policy and let ISE apply it. Here is an example group policy:

```
group-policy GP_ISE internal
group-policy GP_ISE attributes
 dns-server value 10.11.1.80 10.128.2.2
 vpn-simultaneous-logins 5
 vpn-tunnel-protocol ikev1 ssl-client
 split-tunnel-policy tunnelspecifi ed
 split-tunnel-network-list value SPLIT
```

Create an authorization result that references that group policy with the common task "ASA VPN".[3]

Authorization Profiles > **VPN-GP**
Authorization Profile

* Name	VPN-GP
Description	
* Access Type	ACCESS_ACCEPT
Service Template	☐

▼ **Common Tasks**
☐ NEAT

☐ Web Authentication (Local Web Auth)

☐ Airespace ACL Name

☑ ASA VPN   GP_ISE

Then apply that to an authorization rule (in this case we'll use the same AuthZ rule as before).

---

[3]This actually just references a standard RADIUS class 25 attribute.

Standard

	Status	Rule Name		Conditions (identity groups and other conditions)		Permissions
⠿	☑	VPN	if	(Radius:NAS-Port-Type EQUALS Virtual AND sandbox.com:ExternalGroups EQUALS sandbox.com/Users/Domain Users)	then	VPN-GP

When I log back into VPN, I'm then assigned to that group policy and my session has inherited all its settings.

```
ASA# show vpn-sessiondb anyconnect
Session Type: AnyConnect
Username     : arichter            Index       : 126
Assigned IP  : 10.128.14.22   Public IP    : 8.8.8.8
Protocol     : AnyConnect-Parent SSL-Tunnel DTLS-Tunnel
License      : AnyConnect Essentials
Encryption   : AnyConnect-Parent: (1)none  SSL-Tunnel: (1)AES256  DTLS-Tunnel: (1)AES256
Hashing      : AnyConnect-Parent: (1)none  SSL-Tunnel: (1)SHA1  DTLS-Tunnel: (1)SHA1
Bytes Tx     : 245300              Bytes Rx     : 30127
Group Policy : GP_ISE              Tunnel Group : ISE
Login Time   : 02:42:32 UTC Thu Jun 18 2015
Duration     : 0h:00m:23s
Inactivity   : 0h:00m:00s
NAC Result   : Unknown
VLAN Mapping : N/A                 VLAN         : none
```

These authorization results work across ASA platforms that go back to current supported platforms so as long as you're on an ASA that has a supported OS, both of those results are supported. That can be refreshing if you're doing a complicated wired deployment where older platforms may have software-supported IOS but not have all relevant features that ISE may want for device sensor or Security Group Tag (SGT).

There is a design element that we haven't gone over that is on the top of mind for most customers that is pretty important. For VPN users, how would you differentiate between devices that are corporate-owned devices that are BYOD but have the AnyConnect VPN client installed on them? This functionality isn't always that easy to deploy. There are methodologies that include posture assessment[4] but they wouldn't pass a test of a "high-fidelity" authentication where we would say that circumventing the check wouldn't necessarily be cryptographically trivial.

In our opinion the best way of validating that a device is a corporate-owned device when connecting to an AnyConnect VPN portal is to require a certificate authentication as part of

[4]Posture assessment could occur via dynamic access policy (DAP) on the ASA or through ISE on ASA 9.2 or later. For this specific use case the functionality is the same from a security perspective. You can check domain membership through registry settings through both ASA hostscan functionality and ISE posture assessment.

its authentication. For better or worse, this isn't necessarily an ISE-specific feature. ISE has the capability to check a user certificate first[5] in an authentication sequence and then secondarily an AAA password. This is actually a pretty straightforward configuration. From an ASA perspective. The first thing you need to do to accomplish this is to configure your corporate PKI as a trustpoint in your ASA. This can be accomplished either through Adaptive Security Device Manager (ASDM) or on the ASA CLI.

Once that's established, you need to enable the tunnel group configuration to require certificate authentication along with AAA:

```
tunnel-group ISE type remote-access
tunnel-group ISE general-attributes
  address-pool VPN_POOL_INTERNAL
  authentication-server-group ISE
  accounting-server-group ISE
  default-group-policy GP_INTERNAL
  username-from-certificate UPN
tunnel-group ISE webvpn-attributes
  authentication aaa certificate
  pre-fill-username ssl-client
  group-url  https://vpn.example.com/ise enable
```

While the authentication methodology listed there is "AAA certificate" the functional process is to require a certificate first and then an AAA authentication. If the certificate can't be validated by a trustpoint on the ASA, the person is never asked for a username/password. You'll also notice that we included the "pre-fill-username" configuration in there as well as "username-from-certificate." This is a pretty useful feature where you can actually have the username populated from a certificate attribute. If the certificate you're using is the same type of certificate we discussed in Chapter 12, then we know the user principal name is in the SAN field of the certificate and that can be used as the username for an AD authentication)

---

[5]As with EAP-TLS 802.1x authentication, private key security is absolutely essential to make this methodology effective. Typically this would include preventing end users from being local admins on their PCs and the use of full disk encryption.

The user can see the username there, and then they're prompted for their password. This isn't exactly an ISE trick *per se*, because from an ISE perspective we're still only checking the password.

So far we've been using AD username/password authentication but for users of RSA SecurID integrating ISE into an RSA Authentication Manager (AM) is very straightforward. While you can integrate your ASA directly into the RSA AM, using ISE along with AM and ASA provides you some additional functionality and convenience:

- Including ISE with AM gives you a single pane of glass to view all your authentications including wired and wireless and VPN all from the same authentication window.
- RSA AM doesn't provide as robust a set of authorization conditions and results, in particular dACLs.

To integrate RSA AM into ISE, there are a couple of steps. First, log in to the Security Console as an administrator. Browse Access → Authentication Agents → Add New.

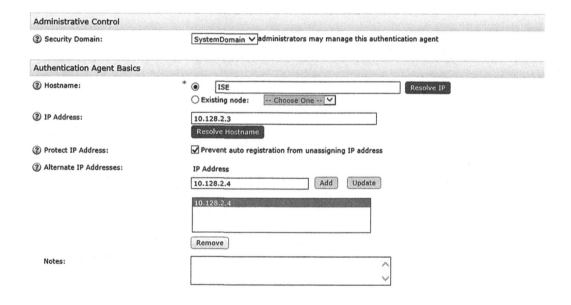

Add the hostname and then the IP address of your policy node. If you're inclined, you can add all your policy nodes as alternate IP addresses under the single authentication agent.

Once you've done this, you need to download the configuration file to upload to ISE. Browse Access → Authentication Agents → Generate Configuration File.

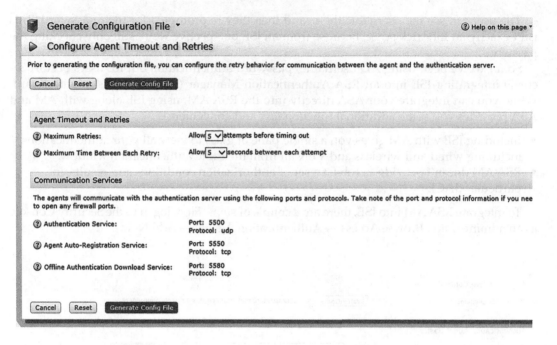

Click "Generate Config File" and you'll be prompted to download a ZIP file that contains the sdconf.rec file. This file contains the information ISE needs to locate the RSA AM servers and authenticate to them.

Inside ISE browse: Administration → Identity Management → External Identity Sources → RSA SecurID and select Add.

Select Browse and select your sdconf.rec file. Once you've done that, ISE should be able to authenticate to RSA AM.

Lastly, if you want to enable the AnyConnect client to display RSA SecurID-type message at login (prompting for passcode rather than password), you need to enable SDI messages in the tunnel group. That's also a single command:

```
tunnel-group ISE webvpn-attributes
 proxy-auth sdi
```

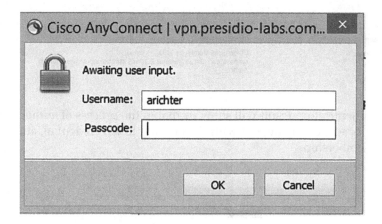

Once you enable that, you'll see that the login prompt requests passcode.

There are a couple of things about the RSA integration with ISE that you should keep in mind:

- The Identity Source will be called "RSA SecurID."
- ISE can integrate into only one AM cluster at a time so if you have more than one, you will likely have to configure it as a RADIUS proxy rather than native SDI.
- The RSA AM doesn't distinguish between a failed authentication and an unknown user. If you're going to add RSA AM to an ISS, then you should configure an "access reject" as a "user not found." That field is in the "Authentication Control" tab under the RSA SecurID External Identity Source.

Applying authentication policy based on AD user group policy once the person has authenticated with AD is also completely possible. Just like we were able to authenticate users with an X509 certificate in the EAP-TLS sections of this book and then authorize the end user with AD, we can do the exact same thing with SecurID and AD.

Let's look at the configuration.

The authentication rule will look exactly like you'd expect it to look.

We're using a condition to identity VPN authentications and then using the RSA SecurID External Identity Source.

The authorization rule looks very similar. It identifies the media type through a condition and then selects an AD user group that my user happens to be a member of (and provides an appropriate result, in this case a dACL).

Standard

	Status	Rule Name		Conditions (identity groups and other conditions)		Permissions
⠿	☑	AD Authorization	if	(Radius:NAS-Port-Type EQUALS Virtual AND sandbox.com:ExternalGroups EQUALS sandbox.com/Users/Domain Admins)	then	VPN-dACL

The actual authentication result will show us that in the process of authenticating and authorizing the VPN session, it checked with RSA for my token credential, and then looked to AD for group membership.

Lastly, if you want to combine both a certificate-based authentication and a RSA SecurID-type authentication on the ASA, that is also possible with a caveat. The methodology we used above when doing the AD password check to prepopulate the username field from the UPN isn't possible in the exact same way. The reason is that the RSA AM server will not by default use a fully qualified UPN as a user credential; it will want only the simple username. The work-around is to use the "strip-realm" feature of the tunnel group and remove the parts of the username after the @. The ASA configuration would look something like as follows:

```
tunnel-group ISE type remote-access
tunnel-group ISE general-attributes
 address-pool VPN_POOL_INTERNAL
 authentication-server-group ISE
 accounting-server-group ISE
 default-group-policy GP_INTERNAL
 strip-realm
 username-from-certificate UPN
tunnel-group ISE webvpn-attributes
 authentication aaa certificate
 proxy-auth sdi
 pre-fill-username ssl-client
 group-url https://vpn.example.com/ise enable
```

In this way, the ASA functionality is basically the same as before, but RSA SecurID authentication can be additionally utilized.

POSTURE

There are use cases where posture assessment is required on VPN sessions and in those cases, enabling posture assessment on your ASA VPN with Cisco ISE is pretty straight-forward. Posture assessment with your AnyConnect VPN does work a little different and has some slightly different caveats than you would typically see on a wired or wireless connection just because the media (VPN) does function a little different. From an ISE configuration perspective the policy is basically identical to a typical wired or wireless configuration.[6]

The ASA configuration is the same as above with one exception. You need to configure a redirect ACL in similar fashion to the ACLs created to support posture on a wired implementation where denied traffic isn't redirected and traffic permitted by the ACL is redirected per the policy:

```
access-list POSTURE-REDIRECT extended deny udp any any eq domain
access-list POSTURE-REDIRECT extended deny tcp any host 10.128.2.3 eq 8443
access-list POSTURE-REDIRECT extended deny tcp any host 10.128.2.3 range 8905 8909
access-list POSTURE-REDIRECT extended deny udp any host 10.128.2.3 range 8905 8909
access-list POSTURE-REDIRECT extended permit ip any any
```

With this, basic posture AuthZ policy can be created for your configuration.

Standard

	Status	Rule Name		Conditions (identity groups and other conditions)		Permissions
⠿	☑	VPN	if	(Radius:NAS-Port-Type EQUALS Virtual AND sandbox.com:ExternalGroups EQUALS sandbox.com/Users/Domain Users AND Session:PostureStatus EQUALS Compliant)	then	VPN-GP
⠿	☑	VPN Posture Discovery	if	(Radius:NAS-Port-Type EQUALS Virtual AND sandbox.com:ExternalGroups EQUALS sandbox.com/Users/Domain Users AND Session:PostureStatus NOT_EQUALS Compliant)	then	VPN-Posture-Discovery

As to the posture discovery AuthZ result, it looks very similar to the AuthZ result you'd use with wireless posture since a separate dACL isn't required.

[6]This design requires ASA 9.2 or later because that was when CoA support was added to ASA. For those of you who say you can do ISE posture assessment on VPN connections with an inline posture node, you're right but the inline posture node design is definitely inferior and should be avoided. If you must do posture on ASA versions 9.1 or earlier, we'd recommend looking at DAP rather than IPN.

Authorization Profiles > **VPN-Posture-Discovery**

Authorization Profile

* Name	VPN-Posture-Discovery
Description	
* Access Type	ACCESS_ACCEPT ▼
Service Template	☐

▼ **Common Tasks**

☑ Web Redirection (CWA, MDM, NSP, CPP)

Client Provisioning (Posture) ▼   ACL POSTURE-REDIRECT   Value Client Provisioning Portal (def: ▼

☐ Static IP/Host name

The main distinction between wired or wireless posture assessment and posture assessment on a VPN is that when implementing posture assessment on a VPN tunneling policy is important. Tunneling policy means that what networks are being tunneled over the VPN is very important during posture discovery. In almost all implementations we would recommend, as a best practice, that posture discovery occur over a VPN that has full tunneling (all traffic is tunneled) configured on it. That way when VPN connectivity happens, if the device ends up not being posture compliant, it isn't otherwise allowed to connect to other devices when remediation happens and it ensures consistent user experience during discovery or client provisioning. If split tunneling is configured and the client does not have the posture agent deployed, they may have access to internet resources but no internal resources until they attempt to connect to an internal website. Overall this can lead to a poor user experience.

All this talk about full tunneling may start to turn people who really prefer split tunneling as a much more efficient way of managing client traffic; you'd find that you have friends here. The way to implement this is pretty straightforward. Simply implement different group policies in different AuthZ rules for posture unknown versus posture compliant. That means that your posture unknown (discovery) rule should result in a group policy that requires full tunneling while the posture compliant rule should then have the split policy. In this way you can both accomplish effective full tunneling for posture checking and allow for split tunneling once a device is determined to be compliant.

16

ISE Reporting and Logging

INTRODUCTION

A lot of what we do within ISE covers things happening in real time; anything AAA related is occurring "right now"; profiling happens while a device is actively connected, data in the authentication view is all real time (or at least an active session) but what about when we want to go further back than 24 h? That's part of what reporting provides to you as well as being able to look at guest access, ISE deployment stats, and if you are wild enough TrustSec info.

REPORTING

Reporting is located under: Operations → Reports and the reports are broken down into five categories:

- Authentication Service status: This report focuses on machines/users and their AAA interactions with ISE.
- Deployment status: Information about your ISE deployment such as administrator logins, audit/change logs, and misconfigured supplicants/NADs.
- Endpoints and users: Profiling, posture, Adaptive Network Control (ANC) (formally Endpoint Protection Service [EPS]), MDM, and Supplicant Provisioning reports are here. This area does have some overlap with the first category but the authorization reports are more cumulative in nature.
- Guest access reports: Anything specifically guest related will be here such as sponsor logins and AUP acceptance.
- TrustSec: This area provides reporting for some specific features dealing with TrustSec but it's not widely deployed right now.

When you first start using reports, be ready to run a couple of different types to really figure out what you want to find. Like we mentioned above, there is some overlap in different categories that can cause some confusion right off but hopefully we can provide some common examples to smooth out the edges.

Globally there is one setting that can impact your ability to look at reporting data in ISE and that is the Data Purging setting. Administration → Maintenance → Data Purging should be configured to retain as much data as your institution feels necessary to get what it might need for historical reporting. When deciding what to set this value, too, there is a really quality chart that's available on the ISE Hardware Installation guide under VMWare (http://bit.ly/1LVSVdu).

This chart should hold true for most deployments. If you have a low number of authentications from your endpoints (they aren't moving around or you have long/no reauthentication timers), then you will probably see more days than listed here. Conversely, if you have a highly dynamic environment with people moving around, bringing on new devices, etc., you might see a smaller number of days than listed above. You of course can't have 50,000 endpoints with a 200-GB monitor node, set the data purge value to 365 days, and expect to keep those many days. Data will be purged as needed to reclaim space but keeping the value set to what you really need will keep your monitor nodes nice and snappy—and everyone likes that!

If you have a Security Information and Event Management (SIEM) that you use for security event monitoring and correlation, keeping logs on the ISE monitor nodes for a long period of time may not even be desirable. In that case, feel free to reduce the data purge timeout to what you feel would be useful for troubleshooting and then configure syslog export for your historical data needs.

Running reports in ISE is pretty easy; to get basic output for your selected report just click Run and you will see the relevant data for "today." You have other time range options as well but anything more than 30 days will inform you that the report can take a fair amount of time to run. You can either let it run normally (if you don't think the report will generate that much data) or tell ISE to let the report run in the background. The background option prompts you to select a repository where a CSV file of the results will be saved.[1]

After the time range selection, you will probably notice that there is a whole lot of data there that might not be relevant to you; this is where filters come in. Adding filters is as easy as clicking a button and then checking off what you want to filter by. You will probably use Identity (username) and Endpoint ID (MAC or IP address) the most but anything in the report can be used as a filter. When inputting your filters, ISE will help you out if it can; Identity/Endpoint ID fields will search through the information ISE has already to let you select something. If a field has only a few fixed values, then ISE will give you a dropdown that lets you select the possible options. Some reports have very few filter options, such as the AAA Diagnostics Report (which out of the box won't produce anything as it requires you to enable specific logging categories), so don't expect to always be able to filter by user/MAC/IP. Here is a quick example of how to get quality information from a report. One of our favorite reports is the posture details report. You may want to know all the times a user may be complaint with posture or uncompliant and on what identity (MAC) they're using over a specific time period. Here we selected time period, an identity (username), and the posture state we want to report on.

---

[1]We recommend having a TFTP server on your PC to have the CSV copy go to when generating a larger report.

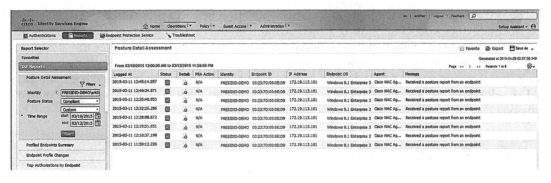

The final section of reporting is in the top right corner of the reports area. Here you will see options to favorite a report, export the report data, and save the report as a custom report or schedule it to run on its own. Favoriting a report adds it to the Favorites section on the left-hand side of the page and is handy if you are running a single report a fair amount. We recommend adding the RADIUS Authentications and the Current Active Sessions reports right off; you will more than likely use them a lot but add others as needed. Exporting a report lets you dump the contents to a configured repository as a CSV file to you can do more with it (creating graphs, advanced filtering, etc.). Saving custom reports lets you save the additional criteria you might define while trying to filter specific data, so if you find yourself always running the RADIUS Authentications report looking for failed attempts because a subject wasn't found in the identity store then you can save that information into its own report. When you get back into ISE to run the report later, it's only a single click instead of having to add the filters again. Similarly if you are exporting a reports data a lot, you can schedule that report to run once, daily, weekly, monthly, etc., and then export out to a repository of your choice as well as optionally sending you an email to let you know it was run/exported.

Scheduled reports open up a lot of possibilities for automating reporting; exporting to a system with some scripts/programs running to consume the data and reformat it can greatly improve your view of ISE when starting your day.

Let's look at some common scenarios and some reports that might help out with them.

Scenario: Management wants to see weekly views of a new ISE deployment.

Report: Authentication Summary with time range set to "Last 7 days." This report has some good information including a daily bar chart of passed/failed authentications, a table of the same information with some addition context, and failure reason/NAD/location summaries.

Scenario: Some users are reporting their mobile devices are no longer getting network access one morning and a profiler feed update was performed the previous night.

Report: Endpoint Profile Changes with the filter "Show only changes due to feed service" added and checked off. This report will let you know if any of your devices had their profiles changed because new/more exact profiles were synced to ISE. From here you could either roll back the change or (since you are following best practices and using logical profiles) add the new groups to your logical mobile device profile so your users can gain network access.

Scenario: You have deployed a wired deployment in monitor mode and you want to see how many clients are hitting your monitor mode rule before you change the deployment to enforcement.

Report: Radius Authentications in the Authentication Services report menu will help you determine which clients are hitting which authorization rules. In this case simply configure your filters to specify which authorization profile (result) you would like to see the utilization on. You'd need to be sure you had a specific authorization result if you care about a specific rule, but if you're looking to see what devices are using monitor mode, you'll see both their MAC addresses but also the switches they're utilizing and what switchports they're connecting on.

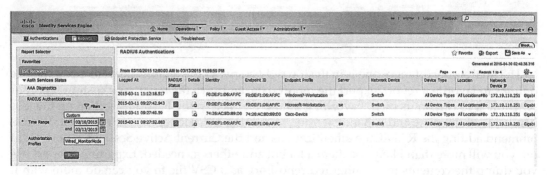

Scenario: Clients are failing posture rules after a deployment and you want to know which rules and what clients.

Report: Posture Detail Assessment with the Posture Status filter set to NonCompliant. You will be shown a list of failed posture reports from clients that includes their username, MAC, IP, OS, and the posture agent being used (NAC or AnyConnect). From here you can get detailed reports per client to see which rules are failing and why. If you need more information, you can run the Posture Troubleshooting tool under Operations → Troubleshooting.

LOGGING

When it comes to logging, ISE has a few options available to you depending on what you prefer to use or what you might already have deployed in your own environment. Logging categories list the types of messages that ISE can generate, their targets, the severity level, and whether they are being logged locally. Targets are remote machines that ISE will send events to so they can be stored there; we'll cover them more in a bit. The severity level is mainly cosmetic; if you don't think an event is important or you want to rate another more critical, then you can change the category. Local logging, out of the box, is enabled for all categories except passed authentications (those are passed to the monitor node(s) anyway) and can be useful for debugging issues that may come up during operation. The logs are purged from the local store after 30 days by default but that is generally a good enough value and should really only be changed if you have good reason. Like purging on the monitor nodes, space will be reclaimed as needed.

Remote targets are basically just syslog servers that ISE sends information to. ISE will define between two and three on its own; one of them will be used for RADIUS profiling information and one or two more will be defined for your monitor nodes. The ProfilerRadiusProbe target can't be deleted or edited in any meaningful way since doing so would break some functions of profiling; the LogCollector targets can be disabled if you want to turn off all logging but again this is not recommended. Normally the logging connection between the PAP/PSNs and the monitor nodes is UDP based since it provides low overhead. However, if you require it, you can enable the TCP logging target and replace the UDP target with that instead. TCP provides some benefits if your connection is prone to packets dropping/arriving out of order but it's slightly more resource intensive because packets need to be acknowledged by the receiving monitor node. If you have network conditions that cause you to evaluate TCP for the above reasons, it's highly suggested that you resolve the root issues if possible since those issues between nodes can be problematic for other things besides logging; see the deployment section for more information.

Now if we want to define our own log targets, then we have three options: UDP, TCP, and Secured. UDP is the most commonly seen syslog method since it is easy, stateless, and more widely supported by receiving systems. A downside though is that since UDP doesn't provide acknowledgment of packets ISE will never know that messages didn't reach your server. TCP on the other hand provides ISE with the ability to detect that a syslog server has gone down and actually buffer messages for a period of time. When the server comes back online, ISE will begin sending those messages, clearing the buffer by First-In, First-Out (which is also the method used to purge messages if the buffer becomes full). Secure syslog builds on TCP syslog and adds public-key encryption to the mix so that messages between ISE and your syslog servers can't be tampered with or seen by prying eyes. To set up a secure syslog target you need to select a CA certificate that ISE already trusts and is the CA that signed the certificate of the remote server. If you are using a self-signed certificate on your syslog server, then you must upload that certificate as a trusted certificate and trust it for client authentication and syslog. If you're using a signed certificate in your secure syslog environment, the CA chain of the certificate should be uploaded and also trusted for client authentication and syslog.

Usage

Trusted For: ⓘ

☑ Trust for authentication within ISE

  ☑ Trust for client authentication and Syslog

☐ Trust for authentication of Cisco Services

All remote targets you create have the option to also include alarms as well as the selected categories of messages but chances are you won't use this option. Sending alarms might be useful if you have a central platform that handles alerting and you want to only send alarm data to it instead of ISE doing its own alerts but if you are sending typical logging categories then you will see duplicate information by including alarms. The last thing to consider is your maximum message length which will determine how big the syslog message will be before ISE splits it into multiple individual messages. In a small or simple deployment your messages may always be less than 1024 bytes so you don't have to worry about fragmentation or split messages but in larger and more complex deployments with large AD infrastructures with lots of groups, EAP-Chaining, etc., you can quickly go over even larger packet sizes due to more complicated authentications. ISE does include unique ID per entire message (even if it's split across multiple packets) but the system you are sending that data to has to be smart enough to stitch them together if they are split up. Without stitching events together you will have partial events that don't contain relevant information and can cause complications if you are trying to correlate events.

Once you create your remote targets, you need to assign them to logging categories so ISE knows to send that information to your destination. If you are sending messages off for more historical archiving/report running, then you would probably want to duplicate what ISE itself sends to the monitor nodes, so going into each category that already has a "LogCollector" target and adding your remote target probably would fit well. If you want to send information off to another system to be there if you need to troubleshoot ISE system issues down the road, you might want to add your target to all the categories that have "WARN" level severities and contain diagnostic information. If you have SIEM and want to correlate/log user sessions, you would probably want to send Passed Authentications, Failed Attempts, and RADIUS Accounting.

Check with your SIM/SIEM vendor before configuring ISE to send data; you might be able to send more categories and glean more valuable information from what ISE has to offer. There is an ISE/SIEM compatibility matrix that may help you evaluate the correct version of SIEM you should run. ISE supports many popular SIEM platforms.

Logging categories also impact reports you run since the report data is pulled of the monitor nodes. If we go back to the AAA diagnostics report we looked at in the reports section and we run it, we'll see that, with a default configuration, we get no results. This is because the report looks at diagnostic categories (Authentication Flow, Identity Store, Policy and RADIUS Diagnostics) that aren't logged by default. In order to run this report you should add your LogCollector target(s) to each of those categories and then rerun the report.

Along with operational and diagnostic logging, ISE also allows you to centrally control the debug logs of your entire deployment right from your PAN. Going to Logging → Debug Log Configuration should show you the list of all your nodes and selecting one will show you a large list of logs that can be tweaked based on your needs. Until you are comfortable with ISE you should probably mess only with these when told to by TAC since making can potentially lead to reduced performance as applications have to log more data about what they are doing. However, if you know what component of ISE is having issues, this area is also a good way to gather information that can possibly lead you to your own answer or make finding Bug IDs on Cisco's site easier. After you have adjusted the logging level you can get to the logs two ways. The first way is going to Operations → Troubleshoot → Download Logs → ⟨node name⟩ → Debug Logs tab. You might have to do some checking to find the correct log file (try matching the description from the debug log configuration page with the log description) but you will be able to download individual files here. The second way is using the CLI from the node you have enabled debug logging on; running "show logging application" will list out the files you can select and then running "show logging application ⟨log file⟩" will paginate the output for you. From the CLI you also have the ability to pipe data through other programs (very similar to how you can in IOS) in order to find some specific data. For example, if we wanted to find any errors in ISE's main logging file, we could run "show logging application ise-psc.log | inc ERROR" from the CLI and we would see only log lines that have the word ERROR in them.

During upgrades all diagnostic/debug logging is disabled during upgrades or restored from backup operations. If you use this information for day-to-day operations,[2] you should make note to re-enable it.

MONITORING

Both reporting and logging are handy and important parts of ISE but once you have your deployment up and running there is a pretty good chance you are going to want to keep it that way. Since ISE is going to play a key role in giving your users access to the network (and in more advanced deployments, controlling access at all levels of the network including servers) you will want to know if something is or starts to go wrong. That's what we'll talk about in this section.

When you start off and log into ISE for the first time, what's the first thing you see?

Alarms

Name	Occurrences	Last Occurred
⚠ Supplicant stopped responding	15 times	4 hrs 29 mins ago
ⓘ No Configuration Backup Scheduled	53 times	11 hrs 46 mins ago
⊗ Insufficient Virtual Machine Resourc...	197 times	17 hrs 56 mins ago
⚠ License About to Expire	28 times	2 days ago
ⓘ Configuration Changed	151 times	4 days ago
⚠ RADIUS Request Dropped	4 times	9 days ago
⊗ High Load Average	11 times	14 days ago

ISE has a ton of alarms to let you know when something is going wrong, or even normal events that you should be away of such as configuration changes/missing configuration backups. Head to Administration → Settings → Alarm settings; ISE 1.3 has 73 alarms built in for you which is good because you can't create your own—not that there is much else you can cover that isn't already. From here you can also set up who should get emails when alarms are triggered and the sending email address. It's highly recommended that you configure these settings before going into production so you can detect if things start to go wrong.

Most of the events and their severities are pretty spot on but you will see in your deployments that some can be a little noisy while others you might way to pay some more attention to:

- Configuration Changed: This event is fairly important for auditing and especially if you have more than one administrator making changes. The downside is that some changes can be very noisy; adding a profiling rule to the "Workstations" profile, for example, can generate >100 emails as the profile is reordered and each step counts as a change.

[2]Which you shouldn't do.

- Slow Replication: There are three events here that are similar: info, warning, and error. Each one triggers at a certain threshold level when messages for a specific node had queued up beyond a safe level. You should really never see these events at all unless you have a node purposely offline or have WAN replication issues and nodes in other locations. If you see this event, even the info level, you need to look into it.
- Misconfigured Network Device/Supplicant Detected: These events are probably going to be noisy and unless you have complete control over all your supplicants the second one definitely will be. From a NAD perspective bugs in all supported WLC versions until 8.0 will cause this to always fire for WLCs. The recommended configuration for NADs in this book should give you the correct settings needed without having to worry about these alarms.
- CoA Failed/Supplicant Stopped Responding: Similar to the misconfigured supplicant, unless you have perfect control over your supplicants and endpoints these events are going to be very noisy. Neither event indicates anything is wrong and it's safe to turn them off.
- RADIUS Request Dropped: Another event that can be disabled although could have some valuable information/alert value. This event can fire if users enter the wrong password, supplicants send duplicate information, user wasn't found in your identity store(s), supplicant abandons its session, etc. Some events could indicate that something is wrong but other alarms should alert you and be much more exact/less noisy.

Now the above is just a guide since you will probably want to enable alarm notifications but also don't want to get flooded with emails. If you leave notifications turned off, then leaving all the categories turned on can give you a good idea of what you might be seeing and then disable those categories if needed. You also have the option of sending the alarms off to another system via syslog for more specific alerting, throttling, etc.

Besides the alarms ISE also gives you the ability to filter data all over the place within the GUI. Typically you will see blank boxes at the top of columns that let you input strings along with basic patterns to match, like in the authentications activity view. Patterns allow you to expand the traditional searches you could do in previous versions of ISE that only looked to see if what you typed in was contained anywhere in the target strings. You can still just type part of a username into the Identity field and have it match but you can also put "!jdoe" to match all identities that don't have "jdoe" in them. Along with that, the following patterns are available to you in ISE 1.3 and higher:

- {}: Empty values
- !{}: Not empty
- john*: Matches when the value starts with john
- *doe: Matches when the value ends with doe

If you need a quick reference, hover over the little "i" in each column name.

In other areas, like the endpoint/identity views, you have to click the filter button on the upper right of the window listing the results and that will let you put text filters (but not patterns) in to search. These areas will also let you create advanced filters that contain multiple conditions and then save them for later use if you want. Text filters are straightforward so let's look at the advanced ones and see what we can do with them. First, we'll want to actually get them on the screen, so go to the "Show" dropdown and select "Advanced Filter".

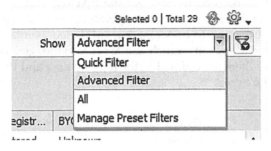

Once you do that, you should see the first line presented to you where you can select the property and what value you want to search for. Clicking the "+" next to that line will add another property that can be checked as well as give you the option of making the query match all values you input successfully before matching or if an entry can match only a single one. If we construct a simple advanced query, it might look something like this.

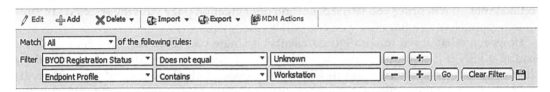

We're looking for any device that has a BYOD status that isn't unknown (so it's done something with the BYOD flow) and has a profile that has "Workstation" in its name. If this is a query we routinely want to run, maybe it's part of a checkup; we can click the Save icon, give the query a name like "BYOD Workstations," and then the query will be ready for us to use at any time in the future without having to recreate it.

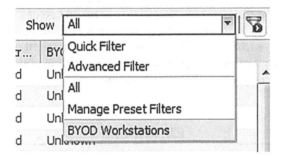

You can also select the "Manage Preset Filter" option to edit or delete any saved filters.

What if you are seeing information from clients that you don't want to? Collection filters let you do just that, using attributes such as username/MAC/NAD to filter passed/failed/all events for specific clients. Once created, the rules are sent to the policy nodes and impact the PSN's sending events to the syslog servers defined in your deployment (including the MnT nodes). You can create any number of rules here but for performance reasons it's recommended to keep the number under 20.

A common use for this would be to filter out the RADIUS test user that is used by your NADs to test the PSNs to make sure they are operating correctly (see Chapter 7 for more information). Since you are going to be seeing passed/failed events from this user roughly every 5 min per NAD and there isn't much use for it to be logged you can safely drop all events from it. Collection filters are defined in the logging area and this example would look something like that shown here.

	Status ▲	Attribute	Value	Filter Type	Time left (in minutes)
☐	☑ Enabled	User Name	radius-test	Filter All	Unlimited

You can also bypass any collection filters should you need to get additional events for troubleshooting some clients. Bypass can be configured from the same area we created the example filter, which would also let you define a duration up to 8 h to apply the bypass, or you can do it directly from the authentications live view. Right-clicking the MAC/username of an event will give you the option to bypass suppression for 1 h or if you select "Modify Collection Filter" it will bring you to the collection filter creation page with the selected attribute already populated in a filter that you can edit before saving.

However, what about misconfigured clients? A single bad client can introduce a sizable load to a PSN if it continually tries to authenticate incorrectly. In order to deal with these clients you can configure Anomalous Client Suppression to both detect and then optionally block attempts by these clients to authenticate until they are correctly configured. Anomalous Client Suppression is configured under Administration → System → Settings → Protocols → RADIUS (easy to find right ☺). By default this feature is enabled and its options are turned on which can sometimes make first-time deployment troubleshooting a challenge. If, in the initial stages of your ISE deployment, you would like more real-time information about authentications without suppression, this is safe to disable.[3] The default intervals don't require much tweaking to them out of the box; the only one you may want to change is the rejection interval based on the types of clients you are having issues with. If your anomalous clients are typically misconfigurations and you have lots of transient users, then it might benefit your users to move from 60 to 30 or 15 min. If you have tight control over your supplicants, then you might want to extend 60 to 120 or 240 min giving you time to find and address the endpoint before it can try and authenticate again.

EXAMPLES

How about some real-world examples of using logging functions to make use of the information ISE has to help us out?

---

[3]If you have a production ISE environment, take care before you disable this feature because it can severely reduce your cluster's scalability. If you have an ISE environment that is utilized in production and you need to disable this to troubleshoot, we recommend you do this in a maintenance windows if possible.

Send Events to Remote Servers

This is a pretty basic thing and we discussed it a little bit earlier in this chapter but since it is required for the following examples we'll make sure we cover it well so you have a good starting point.

First, head into Administration → System → Logging → Remote Logging Targets and click the "Add" button. We'll go through each of the three types so our bases are covered but make sure you are picking the target type that fits you best—secured syslog is pretty cool but unless you have regulatory requirements or traverse untrusted networks you are probably just setting yourself up for more complexity than is really needed.

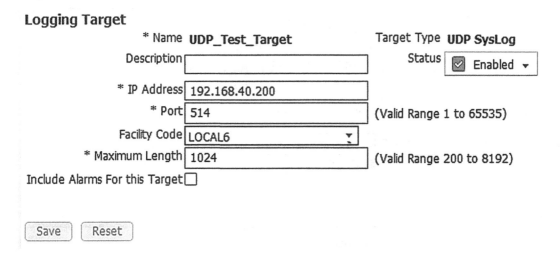

Kicking off with UDP, you can see here our setup is basically right out of the box and we have put in only the name of the target and the IP address that is hosting the syslog server.

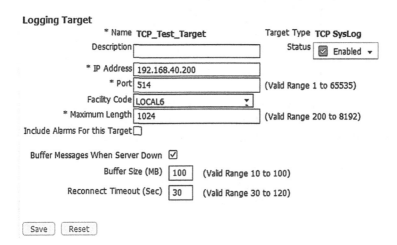

This shows that our setup for a TCP log target is similar. In this case our test server's port is still 514 so we've changed that and we've also enabled buffering of messages if the syslog server goes down. The amount of data the buffer can hold depends entirely on how active your ISE environment is but in most cases it should be plenty to support rebooting the syslog server for updates or something similar. For 90% of installations this is probably the type of log target you will want to use.

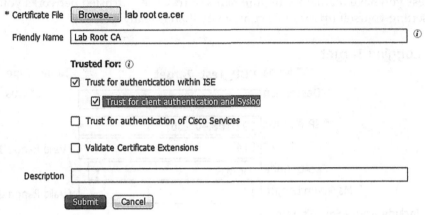

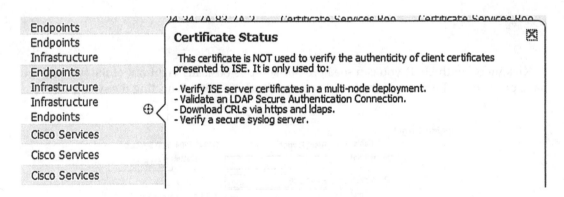

In order to set up a secure syslog target we first need to make sure that the CA certificate used by our syslog server is imported and trusted correctly. The first image shows an example of the settings needed when importing the certificate; make sure the highlighted section is checked off or else ISE won't actually trust the certificate for what we want to use it for. If you already have certificates imported and want to check them, then in Administration → System → Certificates → Trusted Certificates you can hover over the little "target" in your certificate's "Trusted For" column and if the last line says "Verify a secure syslog server" then you should be all set.

Logging Target

* Name **TLS_Test_Target**   Target Type **Secure SysLog**

Description [   ]   Status [☑] Enabled ▾

* IP Address [192.168.40.200]

* Port [6514]   (Valid Range 1 to 65535)

Facility Code [LOCAL6   ▾]

* Maximum Length [1024]   (Valid Range 200 to 8192)

Include Alarms For this Target [☐]

Buffer Messages When Server Down [☑]

Buffer Size (MB) [100]   (Valid Range 10 to 100)

Reconnect Timeout (Sec) [30]   (Valid Range 30 to 120)

Select CA Certificate [Lab Root CA   ▾]

Note:The CA certificates should be imported into the Certificate Store, enabled, and trusted for client authentication prior to configuring Secure Syslog. Ensure that a local certificate signed by the selected CA exists on the primary and secondary nodes. If a local certificate signed by the selected CA does not exist, the self-signed local certificate will be used.

Ignore Server Certificate validation [☐]

[Save] [Reset]

Setup wise our configuration here is going to look similar to the TCP target because that's what the secure target is based on, just with TLS added into the mix. We've got a different port setup here, similar to how you have TCP/80 for HTTP and TCP/443 for HTTPS, and we've selected the CA certificate that we imported previously as the certificate that will be used to verify the remote server. Like TCP we're also going to enable the message buffering so we don't lose anything should the syslog server go down for a short period of time.

After you have set up your remote targets you need to actually tell ISE what messages to send to the targets, which is done under the Logging Categories section. Select one of the categories, click the Edit button, and then move your configured target(s) to the right-hand column.

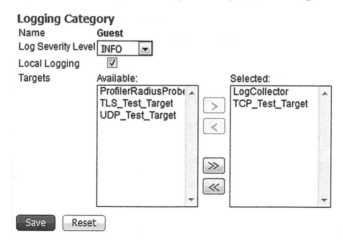

You can see we have started to send events from the Guest category to our syslog server using the TCP target we configured.

That's the basic setup for sending events to remote servers. Remember that less can be more here; you probably shouldn't go into each category and send it to your remote server unless you (a) really need it or (b) like to waste resources. Figure out what your remote servers need/support and send only what's needed; ISE and your remote targets will thank you for it!

Identity Firewall with Context Directory Agent

The Context Directory Agent (CDA) is an appliance that takes information from supported sources and uses that information to map IP addresses to usernames so that usernames can be used by consuming devices (e.g., ASAs, Web Security Appliances (WSAs)) to make policy decisions. For example, using usernames on an ASA could let you limit access to a financial application to only users in a specific AD group without them needing to be in a separate VLAN. Most times CDA is configured to pull login events from AD and depending on your users that might be enough. However, there are some downsides to this, the main one being lag time for users moving between wired and wireless connections. A user moving from their desk (wired) to a conference room (wireless) won't generate any events that CDA can use to map the new wireless IP to the user. The result is that unless the user has access to a fallback web-UI to generate a login event (either on the device or something centralized) there will be a period of time the user won't have access to the resources they should. Both of the two outcomes here are undesirable: either users have to go through an extra step or they can't do their job until a login event is generated.

With ISE though we have the advantage that as a user moves around the network we can almost immediately glean the IP of the user and then pass that information on to the CDA, ensuring that users always have access to their resources.

The process to set up ISE/CDA integration is pretty straightforward. The first thing we'll want to do is configure CDA to receive events from PSNs.

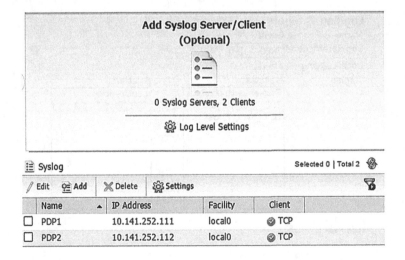

This shows part of the dashboard from a CDA appliance that already has two ISE policy nodes configured as syslog clients. These clients are using TCP to maintain packet order for some larger syslog messages but you have the option to use UDP or TLS-secured TCP as well.

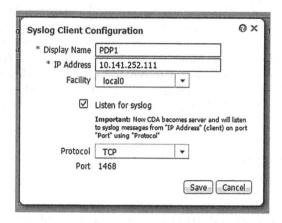

The key part to configuring these clients is checking off the "Listen for syslog" for each one. This tells CDA to listen for events instead of sending mapping events/updates to the IP address you define.

Once you have CDA configured to get syslogs, it's time to configure ISE to send them. First, you need to define the CDA appliance as a remote log target similar to how we went over previously. Once you do that, you want to add that new target into three ISE logging categories: AAA Audit, Passed Authentications, and RADIUS Accounting. Save your changes and go back to the CDA appliance and look at the Live Log and you should start to see events coming in that indicate mappings are being created/updated from RADIUS information.

▶	2015-02-09 18:44:03.808-05:00	ⓜ	ContextManager	Updated Mapping Record From Radius Client	👁
▶	2015-02-09 18:44:02.564-05:00	ⓜ	ContextManager	Updated Mapping Record From Active Directory	👁
▶	2015-02-09 18:44:01.807-05:00	ⓜ	ContextManager	Added Mapping Record From Radius Client	👁
▶	2015-02-09 18:44:01.807-05:00	ⓜ	ContextManager	Updated Mapping Record From Radius Client	👁

Here we see CDA adding/updating mappings from ISE as well as a traditional AD integration. Both can be configured side by side and work together.

If you see warning events about messages being in the wrong format, be sure that both ISE and CDA have NTP properly configured and that you are using message sizes large enough to accommodate the information CDA needs to perform mappings. Clicking on the "eye" will give you more information about those warnings. In a distributed deployment you may also see warnings about messages from unknown servers. This is normal and it's likely from not having the Admin/monitor nodes defined as syslog clients. The messages they are sending aren't critical to identity mapping so they are safe to leave off but if you want to get rid of the errors feel free to define them.

Set Up a Remote Syslog Server

The term SIEM has been thrown around a couple of times in this chapter but we understand that not everyone will have the funds to purchase one. Luckily with a couple of open-source packages you can put together a fairly easy-to-use and flexible log management system for ISE as well as other devices on your network. We'll be making use of rsyslog, elasticsearch, and kibana to create our log system; rsyslog will be receiving the syslog data, formatting it, and then sending it to elasticsearch where it will be stored and indexed for our searching needs. Finally kibana will give us a nice web-UI where we can search the log data.

Required packages are as follows:

- Rsyslog (tested with 8.6.0)
- Elasticsearch (tested with 1.4.4)
- Kibana (tested with 4.0.0)

Depending on your preferred distribution how you go about getting these packages will differ but the configurations should still be the same. There are some minor changes that could be made to this setup; the use of Logstash with elasticsearch is very common but in terms of ease of setup rsyslog is both easier to configure and possibly even already installed depending on your chosen distribution. If you are planning on creating a truly universal logging system, then Logstash might be a better option but for our purposes rsyslog provides a lot of flexibility with the ease of use we need to get started quickly.

Configuring Rsyslog

The first thing we'll want to do is configure rsyslog to listen for events from remote servers as well as configure the output of those events to our elasticsearch instance. Listening for remote events is a simple two-line affair in /etc/rsyslog.conf:

```
module(load="imtcp")
input(type="imtcp" port="6514")
```

This tells rsyslog to load the module needed to listen on TCP ports and then creates a listener on port 6514. If you want to use UDP instead, change "tcp" to "udp" in the lines above.

Next we have to tell rsyslog to output our logs to elasticsearch but since elasticsearch is expecting a structure format we need to create that format and use it, else our logs won't get parsed correctly/at all. Place the following into "/etc/rsyslog.d/55-elasticsearch .conf":

```
# Load Elasticsearch Output Module
module(load="omelasticsearch")

# Logstash index template
template(name="index-template"
  type="list") {
    constant(value="logstash-")
    property(name="timereported" dateFormat="rfc3339" position.from="1" position.to="4")
    constant(value=".")
    property(name="timereported" dateFormat="rfc3339" position.from="6" position.to="7")
    constant(value=".")
    property(name="timereported" dateFormat="rfc3339" position.from="9" position.to="10")
}

# Syslog message template
template(name="plain-syslog"
  type="list") {
    constant(value="{")
      constant(value="\"@timestamp\":\"")       property(name="timereported"
dateFormat="rfc3339")
      constant(value="\",\"host\":\"")          property(name="hostname")
      constant(value="\",\"severity\":\"")      property(name="syslogseverity-text")
      constant(value="\",\"facility\":\"")      property(name="syslogfacility-text")
      constant(value="\",\"tag\":\"")      property(name="syslogtag" format="json")
      constant(value="\",\"message\":\"")       property(name="msg" format="json")
    constant(value="\"}")
}

# Send events to local elasticsearch instance. Also enables the Bulk API for optimization
# and sets the retry count so that if elasticsearch goes offline we'll keep trying to reach it
action(type="omelasticsearch"
    template="plain-syslog"
    searchIndex="index-template"
    dynSearchIndex="on"
    bulkmode="on"
  action.resumeretrycount="-1")
```

That should cover the basics for rsyslog; at this point (re)starting the daemon will give you a working syslog server listening on a TCP port of your choice and sending all events to the elasticsearch instance we'll set up next.

Configuring Elasticsearch

Now we need to set up elasticsearch, which luckily for us is fairly simple. The default configuration provided works well enough for us in this example; just copy the example files that come with the package into /etc/elasticsearch/. The only change we'll need to make is an addition in "elasticsearch.yml" to support kibana, which is our next step:

```
# Kibana Settings
http.cors.allow-origin: "/.*/"
http.cors.enabled: true
```

Configuring Kibana

The newest version of kibana simplifies our start-up a little bit since we no longer need to worry about the web server part. After installation you just need to start the application, probably with your distribution choice of init script/systemd. Assuming you haven't made any changes to the default elasticsearch configuration other than the ones we specified the default kibana settings will give you a log interface located at http://<serverFQDN>:5601.

The first time you access the UI you will need to select the format the indices are in so that they can be read correctly. We're replicating the naming scheme used by Logstash which means the configuration is easy. Check off both "Index contains time-based events" and "Use event times to create index names" while making sure that the "Index pattern interval" is set to Daily. Finally select the "@timestamp" as our time-field and click "Create" to finish the Index Pattern.

From here clicking the "Discover" tab will show you a nicely visualized and indexed system to search your ISE (or any other syslog source with the configuration we have here) logs with. In the upper left-hand corner you can click and select the time range you want to look in and if you want a refresh interval at all. The search bar at the top of the dashboard uses LUCENE query syntax and includes some contextual help, but here are some examples to get you started (use quotation marks if indicated):

- All events for the user "jdoe": "jdoe"
- All passed events for user "jdoe": "tag:CISE_Passed_Authentications AND jdoe"
- All profiling events: "tag: CISE_Profiler"

17

ISE CLI

INTRODUCTION

The large majority of your time with ISE will be spent in the GUI and obviously most of this book is dedicated to just that. However, the command-line interface (CLI) has its place and in fact if you stand up a new ISE environment (or if you did your current one) you will see that your first basic setup is CLI based.

ADE-OS—WHAT IS IT?

If you have used almost any prebuilt VM or installed medium from Cisco lately, you will probably notice that they all feel similar. There is good reason for this; all of them are built off of Cisco's Application Deployment Engine (ADE) OS which itself is built of Red Hat Enterprise Linux 6, 64-bit in its current iteration. Along with that comes a custom shell used when remote users log in that makes the system feel/act very much like IOS. This shell, named CARS (Cisco Application Restricted Shell —Cisco ADE Restricted Shell, who knows), limits what you can and cannot do to provide a little protection to the OS under it while still allowing you to do things you should without TAC support. If needed, you can obtain root access with the help of TAC but we'll cover that later on.

Anyone coming from IOS should feel right at home even though this is Linux and anyone else familiar with a Linux or Windows CLI should feel comfortable soon enough. The first thing you should do is type in "?" and as soon as you do you will be presented with a list similar to this.

Remember that "?" trick, since like IOS, it can be used after any command you type in to get more information about what else you can do or what you need to put after the command.

Also notice that the CLI will tell you if you are missing something and where your error starts. We first did a "show application" to see what the name of the application running on the VM was and obviously it was "ise."[1] Next we typed "?" to see if there was anything else we could look at and for the sake of argument here we were interested in the version. Unfortunately we typed the command wrong (on purpose) but we're told where we went wrong; something needs to be put *after* "version." "?" reveals that the CLI is expecting an application name to be put in (since you could technically have multiple applications installed) and then after putting that in we can see the version information for ISE running on this VM.

MANIPULATING OUTPUT

A key skill/tool to know about when working with the CLI is that nearly any output from any command can be manipulated in some way. These manipulations are accessed at the end of a command by typing the pipe character and then continuing the command by adding the manipulation and any needed commands to that. It's a little hard to describe but let's take a look at an example.

We can see the first thing we ran was "show logging | ?" and that the "?" did the same thing as with a normal command; it told us what other options we had available for use. There are six commands we can use to change the resulting output and they are all fairly self-explanatory but what are sometimes you might use them?

- begin: Good when you want to start looking at logs on a specific date. Depending on your setup logs could go back a ways so being able to run something like "show logging | begin 2015-05-08" to start on May 8 could be handy if you had an issue that started around then.

---

[1] Almost everything in the CLI is going to be case-sensitive. This means that if you type "show application version ISE," you will get an error back.

- count: This one isn't normally used by itself and is normally tracked onto the end of another modifier.
- end: Just like begin but this time we're going to spit out anything until that pattern matches. Could be used in a similar date-fashion or you can use it in conjunction with "begin" to pull out only sections of logs to look at.
- exclude: Removes any lines that match the pattern from being shown. Handy to remove stuff you know is normal and gets in the way of finding what you really want.
- include: The one you will probably use the most, displays only the lines you want and optionally, using the "next" and/or "prev" options, the specified number of lines before/ after a matching line. This means if you know you are looking for the string "restart failed on node," you can specify the full command "show logging | include "restart failed on node" next 5 prev 5" and you will get the five lines of the log file before and after that error, possibly giving you some important information about why the error happened.
- last: The second most used command, will display the last specified number of lines from the log file. The previous image shows this; if we're looking for stuff we know just happened, then this can save a lot of time.

Now in two places you just read that you could use something in conjunction with another command—what does that mean? It means that you can chain output modifiers together so that you can get exactly what you are looking for. Use both include and exclude to find what you need and then exclude some lines you know you don't. Use include multiple times to narrow down the output (since at this point we don't have access to regular expressions) and then track on count to see how many times that event took place. Manipulating output with these tools can save you a lot of time while troubleshooting any problems you may have.

SHOW COMMANDS

Running through all the possible "show" commands is a good place to start when you are looking at the ISE CLI for the first time since running them won't break anything; you can safely get a feel for things without worrying that ISE is going to burst into flames if you type something wrong. We won't go through all of the commands but here are some that will come in handy while you work with ISE:

- "show application status ise":
  - This command will show you the ISE processes, their state, and their ID. If you ever have anything go wrong/act weird, here would be a good place to start. It's normal to see processes listed as "disabled" here if you aren't using them (pxGrid) or if you are in a distributed deployment (PAP/PSNs won't have the MnT services running).

- "show backup history":
  - This command will give you a list of the backups that have run, the date they ran, the name of the file, and what repository it was copied to. Good to make sure your backups are running successfully.

- "show clock":
  - You can guess what this does but proper time keeping is a critical part of ISE and authentication in general. ISE and AD must be within 5 min of each other or authentications will fail. Certificate validity is based on dates/times and if they are off then valid certificates could be marked as invalid or vice versa. Keep good time!

- "show disks":
  - Disk space, one of those things you don't think about until it's gone. If you are running appliances or OVAs, then you should be fine here but if you customized at all then you could run into space issues. This command will not only tell you how much free space all the individual file systems have but also do a sanity check to ensure that the space is enough for ISE to operate normally.

- "show interface":
  - Linux people will recognize the output of this command right away since it's just redirected from "ifconfig." Here you can see the address assigned to each interface, its status and RX/TX packet counts, errors, dropped, etc. Can be useful when troubleshooting any network issues.

- "show ip route":
  - Displays the machine's routing table, another handy command for troubleshooting network issues.

- "show ntp":
  - Remember how we said time was important? This command will give you detailed info about your configured time servers, if you are synchronized, with which server, etc. If you are getting login/AD errors, then check this.

- "show running-config"/"show startup-config":
  - Network folks will recognize these; they show the current configuration and the saved configuration (used at boot up) of the ISE appliance. While not nearly as important as in the IOS/NX-OS worlds, this command will still show you the interface configurations, locally configured repositories, time zone, and some service info.

- "show tech-support":
  - A favorite for anyone troubleshooting, this command is more of a metacommand and runs a bunch of other commands to simplify collecting data needed for a TAC case. You probably don't want to just run it by itself but rather as "show tech-support file ⟨filename⟩" which will dump the output into the local disk where you can then grab it.

- "show udi":
  - Handy for licensing your ISE appliance(s) or troubleshooting why a license won't install (verifying the UDI).

- "show version":
  - A quick listing of version information for both the appliance level software and the running ISE package.

Now that's a large list but some commands are still not listed here. Their exclusion doesn't mean you won't use them, just that for most troubleshooting or day-to-day operations we haven't seen them used that often.

LOGGING

There is one command above you might notice isn't there and that's "show logging." Why isn't it there? Well, basically because it deserves its own section. Of all the "show" commands the logging one probably has the most depth and possibility for confusion.

First, we'll want to take a look at the base command. Running just "show logging" by itself will output information from the ADE-OS platform logs and ISE application log; the first will show you output from some system stuff such as the hourly cron jobs running, some Oracle DB output, Secure Shell (SSH) logins, etc., while the second will show you more ISE-specific logs about Tomcat, more Oracle output, patch output, ISE heartbeat node info and a whole bunch more. Here's the catch though: most of that information will not be useful to you at all. There is some info in there that can be helpful but the nonspecificity of it and the sheer amount of information (a PAP in a 6-node distributed deployment with ~4000 clients has >1.1 million lines from that output, a test month-old stand-alone node with 3 clients has ~250,000) make it impractical to sift through unless you know what you are looking for.

A better option is to look at the subcommands of the command and start targeting your searches a little bit.

```
ise.lab.local - PuTTY                              _  □  X

ise/admin# show logging ?
   >             Output Redirection.
   application   List application log files
   internal      Show syslog configuration internal
   system        List system log files
   |             Output modifiers.
   <cr>          Carriage return.

ise/admin# show logging
```

This shows what we have for options. "internal" won't be very helpful for us; it just shows you what the system log server is and if logging is enabled or not. Instead we'll want to concentrate on looking what "application" and "system" have to offer. Running each one of those commands will result in a list of log files you can look at being shown to you.

```
    92313 May 11 2015 22:00:01   appserver/catalina.out.2015-05-11
    92758 May 13 2015 00:00:01   appserver/catalina.out.2015-05-13
        0 May 05 2015 22:18:07   appserver/manager.2015-05-05.log
      112 Apr 26 2015 22:30:01   appserver/catalina.out.2015-04-26
      110 Apr 04 2015 14:41:07   appserver/catalina.2015-04-04.log
      353 May 20 2015 00:00:01   appserver/catalina.out.2015-05-20
   135459 May 05 2015 23:17:26   appserver/catalina.2015-05-05.log
      560 May 04 2015 00:00:01   appserver/catalina.out.2015-05-04
      448 Apr 16 2015 22:00:01   appserver/catalina.out.2015-04-16
        0 May 14 2015 07:45:22   appserver/manager.2015-05-14.log
        0 Apr 13 2015 20:13:47   appserver/manager.2015-04-13.log
     1154 May 14 2015 18:13:27   appserver/localhost.2015-05-14.log
      224 Apr 19 2015 22:30:01   appserver/catalina.out.2015-04-19
   135267 May 14 2015 23:24:20   appserver/catalina.2015-05-14.log
    65566 Apr 13 2015 20:20:21   appserver/catalina.2015-04-13.log
      224 May 19 2015 22:00:01   appserver/catalina.out.2015-05-19
      450 Apr 15 2015 00:00:01   appserver/catalina.out.2015-04-15
     4836 Apr 03 2015 12:56:33   appserver/catalina.2015-04-03.log
   440436 May 25 2015 23:59:58   localStore/iseLocalStore.log.2015-05-25-00-02-37-653
   380967 May 26 2015 20:35:54   localStore/iseLocalStore.log
   302260 May 18 2015 21:42:25   ca_appserver/catalina.out
ise/admin#
```

```
        0 May 18 2015 21:45:02   spooler.1
        0 Apr 02 2015 20:58:13   tallylog
    12462 May 23 2015 09:01:02   maillog.1
   497427 May 03 2015 01:00:01   cron.4
  1060682 May 26 2015 20:31:02   messages
  3276881 May 26 2015 20:35:54   secure
  8012048 May 03 2015 00:58:05   secure.4
        0 May 11 2015 21:45:01   spooler.2
   379735 May 11 2015 21:45:01   cron.3
   203715 May 26 2015 20:40:01   cron
   123204 May 18 2015 21:45:01   cron.2
  1887136 May 23 2015 23:59:53   messages.1
    16032 May 02 2015 13:51:50   faillog
     6877 May 26 2015 16:45:05   maillog
     7688 May 03 2015 00:00:02   messages.4
  1377562 May 11 2015 21:44:35   messages.3
      384 May 07 2015 21:31:12   btmp
    62278 Apr 02 2015 21:13:04   anaconda.log
     2657 Apr 02 2015 21:13:04   anaconda.ifcfg.log
    61440 May 26 2015 19:20:38   wtmp
     7735 May 14 2015 08:26:47   maillog.2
ise/admin#
```

The top image shows us the output of the "show logging application" command while the bottom one shows us the output of "show logging system"; *nix folks will love the latter since those file names are instantly familiar. In both cases you will want to put the full name of the file, including the preceding directory if there is one, at the end of the command you ran to get the list. For the application listing, if we wanted to see what was in the catalina.out file for the internal CA server, we would run the command "show logging application ca_appserver/catalina.out" and then similarly on the system side if we wanted to see what was in the messages file we would run "show logging system messages." Don't forget those output manipulation commands; you can throw them at the end of these commands too and find exactly what you are looking for.

CHANGING TIME ZONES

This topic comes up sometimes postinstallation and you wouldn't think it would be a big issue but it is, or rather it can be. If you need to change the time zone, do it before any configurations have been made and it's recommended to start fresh with the correct time zone if it's reasonable. Previous versions of ISE would perform a factory reset when moving between time zones but the latest versions are a little bit more forgiving but if you have made any major configurations it's highly recommended that you take a backup before executing the change.

```
ise/admin# conf t
Enter configuration commands, one per line.  End with CNTL/Z.
ise/admin(config)# clock timezone America/New_York

% On ISE distributed deployments, it is recommended all nodes be
% configured with the same time zone.
Continue with time zone change?  Y/N [N]: y
System timezone was modified. You must restart ISE for change to take effect.
Do you want to restart ISE now? (yes/no) yes
Stopping ISE Monitoring & Troubleshooting Log Collector...
Stopping ISE Monitoring & Troubleshooting Log Processor...
Stopping ISE Identity Mapping Service...
Stopping ISE pxGrid processes...
Stopping ISE Application Server...
Stopping ISE Certificate Authority Service...
Stopping ISE Profiler Database...
Stopping ISE Monitoring & Troubleshooting Session Database...
Stopping ISE AD Connector...
Stopping ISE Database processes...
Starting ISE Monitoring & Troubleshooting Session Database...
Starting ISE Profiler Database...
Starting ISE pxGrid processes...
Starting ISE Application Server...
Starting ISE Certificate Authority Service...
Starting ISE Monitoring & Troubleshooting Log Processor...
Starting ISE Monitoring & Troubleshooting Log Collector...
Starting ISE Identity Mapping Service...
Starting ISE AD Connector...
Note: ISE Processes are initializing. Use 'show application status ise'
      CLI to verify all processes are in running state.
ise/admin(config)#
```

The change itself is simple; first run "show timezones" and select your find new preferred zone. It's recommended that instead of selecting an exact zone (unless you are going to use Coordinated Universal Time (UTC)) you choose a zone named after a city in the time zone you are in, so instead of "EST" we would pick "America/New_York." This ensures that daylight savings time and any future changes happen automatically. Once you have your time zone, go into configure mode and enter "clock timezone ⟨new zone⟩." ISE will warn you that if you are in a distributed deployment, all nodes should be in the same time zone and then ask you if you want to continue. Once you agree, you will be prompted to restart the ISE services to apply the change.

APPLICATION COMMANDS

Chances are that if you are in the CLI, you are going to be looking at the "application" commands. Commands here are related to the configuration, upgrading, and general functioning of ISE.

The first application command you might use is "application configure ise".

```
ise.lab.local - PuTTY
ise/admin# application configure ise

Selection ISE configuration option
[1]Reset M&T Session Database
[2]Rebuild M&T Unusable Indexes
[3]Purge M&T Operational Data
[4]Reset M&T Database
[5]Refresh Database Statistics
[6]Display Profiler Statistics
[7]Export Internal CA Store
[8]Import Internal CA Store
[9]Create Missing Config Indexes
[10]Create Missing M&T Indexes
[11]Enable/Disable ACS Migration
[12]Generate Daily KPM Stats
[13]Generate KPM Stats for last 8 Weeks
[14]Exit
```

Now, most of these commands should be run *only* with the assistance/direction of TAC but some of them you will use on your own depending on the features you use. For example, the import/export of the internal CA store is required if you are running a redundant PAP node with an internal CA. Any of the commands to generate statistics won't hurt but they also shouldn't be needed during normal operation as they will be taken care of automatically by ISE.

The "application install/upgrade/remove" commands are all very similar in their execution and their use is fairly straightforward. The slight gotcha is that while the "upgrade" subcommand is used to upgrade ISE it's only used for moving between major versions such as 1.3 → 1.4 or if Cisco releases any Maintenance Release (MR) versions (1.2.1 was technically a major release even though the version numbering makes it look like a minor one). The only use for the "install/remove" subcommands we've found has been installing the root patch provided by TAC that opens up root access to the underlying OS. If you want to reinstall/reset your ISE configuration, you typically use the next command.

If you are ever stuck with a totally nonworking setup or, in a distributed environment, you want to rebuild a node or something similar, you can run "application reset-config ise" and your settings will be returned back to their defaults. You will be asked if you want to save the currently installed certificates before resetting to factory defaults too and that is highly recommended unless you know you don't want them. If you are refreshing any distributed nodes, this saves you time configuring the node but even a stand-alone node can benefit from this. After the node is reset it is in a stand-alone state and you can join it to an existing deployment or do whatever else you need to do.

The last important application command is "application reset-passwd" which is run in the format of "application reset-passwd ise ⟨admin user⟩" and will let you reset the password of a web UI admin if you have forgotten the password or it has become locked. This is usually only needed if you haven't set up AD (or another external login source) for authentication of your administrators since in that case the remote systems take care of handling locking/passwords. Like we mentioned in the Administration section, setting up external authentication is highly recommended. You can also reset/unlock accounts with other admin accounts so this is really a last resort action.

OTHER TOOLS

One of the more basic but helpful commands is "nslookup." DNS resolution is important for ISE so you can use this to check for normal A/PTR records but also for SRV records for something like AD by running "nslookup _ldap._tcp.lab.local querytype SRV." You have multiple DNS servers configured; you can also append "name-server ⟨ip⟩" to the end of the "nslookup" to target specific servers so that you can pinpoint if one of them is returning incorrect information and causing random problems. The "ping" and "traceroute" commands are also useful for ensuring you can correctly connect between nodes.

This next one might be a bit confusing and it's the "patch" command, which is used to install patch releases onto ISE. The confusing part here is that you should not use this command from the CLI unless you have very good reason to. The proper way to patch nodes is through the web UI, where you can upload the patch and ISE takes care of copying the code out to the nodes, installing the patch, and then rebooting the nodes in a sequential order so that your cluster stays in a functioning state while it's happening. The CLI "patch" command on the other hand only applies the patch to the one node you are currently on, a nonideal situation in most cases. If you are installing a patch, you probably want it everywhere. So when will you use this command? You can use this if you have to rebuild a node from scratch and need to bring it up to the same patch level as the rest of the cluster before you join it back. You might also want to use this if you want deterministic control over which nodes get a patch applied and when. The web UI will make sure that you never have all of your PSNs down at the same time but if you are a global company you will probably want to make sure that your PSNs are offline during maintenance windows for specific time zones. In that case you will need to manually install patches.

Telnet is provided by the CLI as well and while normally you should stay away from anything cleartext for running commands "telnet" here will actually give us a simple way to check (some) connectivity between nodes or even to other services such as AD. This image shows us some results.

You can see we are running the commands "telnet ⟨host⟩ port ⟨port⟩" in order to do this. In the first attempt we connect to port 80 which has an Apache web server listening and we can see that telnet connected and basically waited for us. Depending on the remote port you are testing it may act different but what's important here is the fact it did connect, which means we have established from our ISE node to the remote node/server the path is clear. The next two connections show the other possible (common) outcomes when testing ports with telnet. In both cases the ports can't connect so we know something is wrong; in the first case there is nothing listening on the port used. If you were running this test against another ISE node, you might get that error if the ISE services hadn't started yet. In the second attempt we used iptables to replicate what you would see with a host behind a firewall/ACL; you will notice the connection wasn't refused but rather telnet gave up connecting after a period of time.

It's normally not recommended but the commands under the "tech" commands can be helpful for people who have *nix experience and are familiar with top/iostat/vmstat. The nice thing about these commands is that the restricted shell just passes the output back to you without formatting/changing it so you get a more "raw" view of what's going on. The only command here you should probably avoid is "tech dumptcp" which outputs packets from a selected interface. In reality it's just running tcpdump but you can control only how many packets, if any, are captured before the command exits. Without any ability to filter packets you will, on anything other than a small lab deployment, be overrun with packets for clients or just normal traffic and miss what you are looking for. If there is a need to debug network communication, it's best to work with TAC and get the root patch installed so you have direct access to tcpdump.

EXAMPLES

Getting Tech Support Info

1. Run "show tech file" or redirect it depending on how you want to deal with the file.
2. Create repository in the web UI.
3. Copy file off.

At some point during your use of ISE you are probably going to have to open a TAC case; it's just a fact of life. As we discussed before the "show tech" command runs a bunch of other commands and gathers information for the TAC engineer to do further root cause analysis to try and determine what's wrong. If you are a first-time user, it can still seem like a daunting process especially if the pressure of a nonworking ISE install is on you so let's go through the steps right here. It might also be helpful to run through these before such a situation comes up so you are familiar with them.

First step is that we'll need to create a remote repository that we can copy the resulting file to. ISE supports a number of protocols including FTP/SCP/TFTP/NFS so you can pick whichever one works best for you; in this example we'll be using the FileZilla FTP server[2] and assuming you have already downloaded and installed it.

[2]http://bit.ly/1W2RPQn.

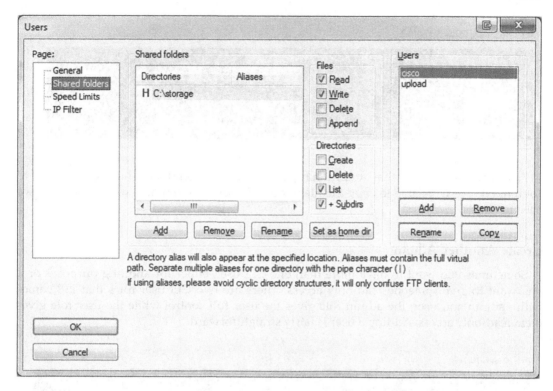

The first image shows that we created a new user called "cisco" and gave the account a password; next we added a directory "C:\storage" as a directory (and since it's the only one it will be the users' home directory things go into by default) and gave the user write access by checking off the "Write" box.

We're ready to run the "show tech" command at this point. There are two different ways to run this and each one will depend on how you want to deal with the file:

- "show tech file output.txt": This will result in a file being created in the default disk:/ location called "output.txt.tar.gz." Use this if you just want to get the file to TAC.
- "show tech > output.txt": This will also create a file in the disk:/ location but it will just be called "output.txt," no compression involved so it's a bit easier to jump into if you want to debug yourself.

The first option results in a file that's about 118 kB, and the second option gives you a file that's about 1.7 MB—neither of them break the bank these days but the choice is yours.

After you have run whichever version of "show tech" works for you, it's time to copy it off. You will need to know the URL format of the protocol you chose to use; most of the time it's just "⟨protocol⟩://," so in the case of our FTP server the URL is "ftp:// ⟨ip address⟩/."

```
ise.lab.local - PuTTY
ise/admin# show tech > output.txt
ise/admin# copy disk:/output.txt ftp://192.168.0.30/
Username: cisco
Password:
ise/admin#
```

Finally we can see here that after running the command to send the "show tech" output to "output.txt" we were able to copy the file to our FTP server. From here we can do what we need to with it.

Create Another Admin

Sometimes you want to have more than one CLI user, either for auditing purposes or if you want to give someone read-only access. There are two CLI user roles that ISE comes with—admin and user; the admin role gives the user full control while the user role gives them read-only access. Adding a user is fairly straightforward.

```
ise.lab.local - PuTTY
ise/admin# show run | inc username
username admin password hash $5$T692kVXu$f9OApF5Hw63ptKk84nLyuQKQPGMRCWqeJ4LomhtwH09 role admin
ise/admin# conf t
Enter configuration commands, one per line.  End with CNTL/Z.
ise/admin(config)# username readonly password plain P@ssw0rd role user
ise/admin(config)# username otheradmin password plain Adm!MPa$$ role admin
ise/admin(config)# exit
ise/admin# show run | inc username
username admin password hash $5$T692kVXu$f9OApF5Hw63ptKk84nLyuQKQPGMRCWqeJ4LomhtwH09 role admin
username readonly password hash $5$7ad942U3$irYFPkgkiCRpOCfTqFMsPPbTGB5D3QgbqCPNPAHV5V0 role user
username otheradmin password hash $5$9OIxU/pX$aECh3mMMD1xVh8.XAkjEPd1KQAraDkD45c.XpsiDa/. role admin
ise/admin#
```

Here we've demonstrated adding two different accounts, one that is a full admin and another for read-only access. The general format when you add these accounts will be "username ⟨username⟩ password plain ⟨password⟩ role ⟨admin | user⟩." You can also add email addresses for each user if you want or disable existing accounts by appending "disabled" to the end of the username command.

As you can see, while not as in-depth as the web UI sections, ISE still has plenty of important things to offer via the CLI and you should make use of them when possible. Don't be afraid of the CLI!

ISE Administration

You've got the basics of ISE set up but chances are you won't be the only one using it. Even if you are the primary user, wouldn't you rather log in with your directory password? Administering ISE is an important step in your deployment since doing it wrong could make tracking changes more difficult at best and at worse potentially lead to a compromised ISE infrastructure.

AUTHENTICATING TO ISE

By default users are authenticated against an internal store and during setup a single user, "admin" by default, is created that has access to both the CLI and GUI of ISE. This user will always be there and cannot be deleted from the GUI. You can delete the user from the CLI but you need to have another administrator account to do that and you can't delete your own user account so you shouldn't be able to be left without at least one CLI administrator account. Typically you would select the same identity store, like Active Directory, that you are authenticating your users against. Doing this sets the default identity source seen during log-in to that external source but it also means that you can select "internal store"; so if you have issues with your external directory or need to log in as the local admin user, you still can.[1]

The password policies that you define apply only to local administrators but they, mostly, span both GUI and CLI users. Settings such as custom denied words and lock out emails apply only to GUI users and password history is limited to one past password for CLI users but everything else applies to both. Since these policies apply only to local administrators it's likely that they will end up only applying to the admin user created during setup and in that case it's recommended to not lock the accounts after a number of login attempts and instead suspend the account or disable the "Suspend or Lock Account with Incorrect Login Attempts" option entirely. Locking the account is OK for the GUI since an externally authenticated admin can log in and unlock the local admin but if you have only a single CLI admin and that account gets locked you need to boot off the ISE ISO and reset the CLI admin's password in order to log in again. If you have a system running vulnerability scans, it can quickly lock you out from your entire CLI deployment when testing for default password, something this author knows all too well!

---

[1]You can configure administrators to authenticate to any external identity source you have configured, including RSA SecurID™ servers, so you can implement two factors into ISE Admin authentication if you desire it.

Besides there being different users for the different ISE interfaces there are also two types of users/groups for the ISE GUI—internal and external. Internal implies that the user or group is local to ISE only and is the default state when you click "Add" for either of those two objects. External implies that the user or group is linked to an external identity source in some way. A user can only be internal or external; when you create or edit an existing one, you will see a checkbox that lets you designate the account as "External." You could do this if you wanted your users to use their AD/RSA/LDAP credentials to log in but the downside is that you still manually need to create the accounts in ISE each time a new person comes on. If we look at the options for groups, we can see that by default they are marked as "internal" but that we can actually check both the "internal" and "external"–type boxes at the same time. This means that we can assign local users we create in ISE to the group as well as tie the local ISE group to a group in (in this case) Active Directory.

Admin Group

* Name	WG Helpdesk Admin
Description	Widget Group Helpdesk Users
Type	☐ Internal ☑ External

External Identity Source
Name LAB-AD

▼ **External Groups**

* lab.local/LAB/Employee/Group... ⌄   ➕

lab.local/LAB/Employee/Groups/Helpdesk

Save   Reset

Here we have created an external-only group and, since we selected a configured Active Directory source as our administration identity source, we were able to select a group that we had previously configured.[2] The big advantage here is that, assuming our account creation process handles it, we don't need to worry about provisioning access to new Helpdesk employees as they join us. When they log in, ISE validates that they are part of a configured group and grants them access. You won't see them listed in the Admin Users section but their username will show on all audit records so you don't lose anything.

You can't configure any of the built-in groups to be external only; they will always have the internal checkbox enabled.

RBAC

Once you have the authentication portion covered, we have to talk authorization—just like user access. Permissions for GUI users are broken down into menu access and data access; both need to line up in order to be effective. A user with menu access for the endpoint

---

[2]If you go to select an external group to tie an Admin Group to and you notice nothing comes up, make sure that you have selected an External Identity Source under the Authentication area.

identities area but no access to the data won't see anything. Likewise, a user with access to the endpoint data but no menu access won't be able to access the location to see the data they have access too. Combining these two types of access defines a role and that is the "R" in RBAC (role-based access control). ISE provides a set of RBAC policies by default that should cover most common organizations. The Helpdesk role grants the ability to look at the Home and Operations areas with the exception of the "Download Logs" and "Endpoint Protection Services" areas but provides no data access so users can't look at endpoints/users/administrators within ISE. The Policy Admin role grants access over user/endpoint data as well as the policy-relevant UI areas but prevents the administrator from making system-level changes. In total there are 11 default RBAC groups that an administrator could have in order to control their access.

Hopefully you won't need to make changes or additions to the RBAC area, but what if you do? Let's add a new set of permission for our Helpdesk to give them a bit more access so they can look at endpoints and utilize EPS. The first thing we want to do is duplicate the current "Helpdesk Admin Menu Access" permission so we can edit it without having to edit the default permissions. Go to Administration → System → Admin Access → Authorization → Permissions → Menu Access; check the box next to the above permission and then click the "Duplicate" button. ISE will bring us to a new area where it has duplicated the permissions and lets us edit them. First, you will want to give it a recognizable name and description so you (or someone else) will know what's different about it. Next in the Menu Access Privileges frame, change the status of the following from Hide to Show:

- Operations → Endpoint Protection Service
- Administration → Identity Management
- Administration → Identity Management → Identities

Your result should look like this:

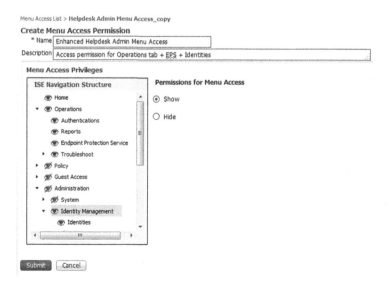

Submit the change and then go to the Data Access section. Now since the default Helpdesk Admin RBAC group doesn't have access to any data areas you will notice that there isn't a corresponding "Helpdesk Admin Data Access" permission prebuilt. We'll need to create a new one which is very similar to the duplicate process we just did. Click "Add," name the permission, and give it a good description. Next go to the "Endpoint Identity Groups" node and all of its subnodes and change their access to "Full Access"; unfortunately there isn't an easy way to mark all subnodes as "Full Access" from the top but if you haven't made many Endpoint Identity Group changes (which you shouldn't have since you are utilizing Logical Profiles right?) it should be a quick task. If you have made a number of changes, then you could duplicate the "Identity Admin Data Access" permission and then set all of the User Identity groups listed to "No Access."

An important note is that ISE currently does not provide the capability to give administrative users read-only permission over data. This means that expanding access for a group like your Helpdesk to allow them to do basic troubleshooting of client profiling issues by looking at endpoint identities will also give them the ability to delete one or all endpoints in the system.

Your final Data Access Permission should look like this:

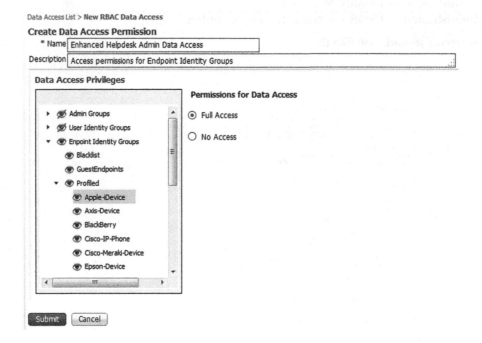

Save it and then go to the Policy area. Here we will map Admin Groups to their respective menu/data/both access permissions. The default policies show off the built-in RBAC policies as well as different ways to use menu/data permissions; looking at the External RESTful Services (ERS) examples you can see that it's possible to even just assign data permissions with no access to menu items. Like the access side of ISE where we build components and then join them into a policy to provide access, we need to do that same thing with the RBAC components we just created. We'll insert a new policy into the existing ones and then start filling in our values. Name can be anything you want, the Admin Groups will be one or more Admin Groups you want to grant access, and Permissions will be the menu and data permissions we customized.[3]

Your resulting policy line should look something like this:

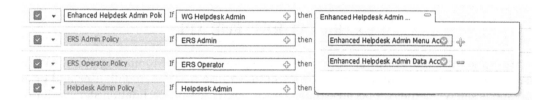

Now when users in the WG Helpdesk Admin group log in, they will have access to EPS actions as well as endpoint identity information. Since administrative policy's gets aggregated there is another way we could have gone about this; create an EPS group and an endpoint identity group, assign our users to those groups, create EPS and endpoint identity specific menu/data permissions, and then assign the EPS menu access/endpoint group the endpoint data/menu access. Technically that fits a little bit better into the RBAC way of thinking but it has a disadvantage in that it's hard to tell at a glance what access a single user would have. Add to that possibly nested groups within your external identity source and you can get a pretty complicated setup going on. Our recommendation would be to keep things role based like we initially designed for most deployments unless you have good reason too or if you have some sort of Identity and Access Management (IAM) system that can easily tell you who has what access.

API

ISE has three APIs available for you to use—Representational State Transfer (REST), ERS, and pxGrid. Programming with them is out of scope for the book, and probably could be a book in and of itself, but we'll hit on each one so you are better prepared to deal with them. There are some similarities between each one but overall each API specializes in a specific type of action so it would be worthwhile to align your API choice with your goal. For in-depth descriptions and examples check out the *ISE API Reference Guide*.

[3]RBAC policies are not first matched but instead built on each other so users in multiple groups will see their access match the total of what those groups have. Full access takes precedence over no access.

MONITORING REST API

The REST API is the simplest one of the three to utilize/query and is enabled OOTB with ISE.[4] Queries are simply HTTPS GET requests to specific URLs and ISE sends back the response in basic XML. You can technically use HTTP PUT but that is really only for special cases.

The REST API is open to any local administrative user but since data being queried is something that you have access to through the UI anyway it isn't an issue. If you are using Active Directory or some other external source, then any administrators you have set up won't be able to log in, a good or bad thing depending on how you look at it.

Ability wise there isn't a whole lot you can do through this API but you can perform CoA actions, retrieve session information, and get some basic troubleshooting info such as failure reasons.

EXTERNAL RESTFUL API

Also called the ERS API, this API is more complex than the Monitoring REST API but also provides more capabilities. ERS allows you to perform many endpoint, user, and group operations safely via the API because data goes through the same validation steps as it does when it's done via the GUI. This basically means that you don't need to worry about incorrect API calls causing damage, a little extra piece of mind. By default this API is disabled so if you want to use it you need to go to Administration → System → Settings → ERS Settings and enable it for at least your PAN[5].

ERS Settings

▼ General

External RESTful Services (ERS) is a REST API based on HTTPS over port 9060.
The ERS service is disabled by default.
An ISE Administrator with the "ERS-Admin" or "ERS-Operator" group assignment is required to use the API.
ERS on primary administration node or a stand alone node will allow the ERS client to perform read/write operations.
On all other nodes it allows only read access.
For more information, please visit the ERS SDK page at:
https://10.14.50.201:9060/ers/sdk

▼ ERS Setting for Primary Administration Node

◉ Enable ERS for Read/Write
○ Disable ERS

▼ ERS Setting for All Other Nodes

○ Enable ERS for Read
◉ Disable ERS

[Save] [Reset]

[4]In ISE 1.3 the REST API URL's changed from what they were in previous versions. The old URLs are still available for compatibility but are depreciated and will be removed in a future release.
[5]After any major ISE version upgrades, not patch installs, ERS is disabled and you will have to perform these steps again to re-enable it. Upgrade guides should mention this but it's worth noting on the front end of an API implementation as well.

If you want to run read-only queries against your other nodes, then you can enable that here as well. As noted on that page, you will need to be in the "ERS Admin" or "ERS Operator" groups in order to utilize the API, so we do have some separation between different users of the API:

- *ERS Admin*: Can perform all API operations
- *ERS Operator*: Can perform only read-only operations

Also notice the reference in the previous image to https://<PANIP>/ers/sdk. That takes you to a bunch of documentation about the API including some basic setup, how to perform all the available actions in the API, example use cases, and even a Java-based demo application. Heed the warnings in those pages however; most of the examples don't perform proper certificate verification and should never be deployed as they are in a production application without changes to fix that.

Once ERS is enabled, you actually need to assign users to those groups; even Super Admins aren't permitted to use the API by default. The "admin" user cannot use the ERS API at all either; this prevents people from "just using the admin account because it's easier" and opening themselves up to any security issues down the road. If you are using ERS, you will need to have/create at least one new account to utilize it.

ERS groups are set to be internal only OOTB and while you can technically set them to be "External" as well and add users, those users will not work. As seen in the next image, we can create users and assign them to multiple Admin Groups which would allow a user to be both a GUI administrator and an ERS API administrator.

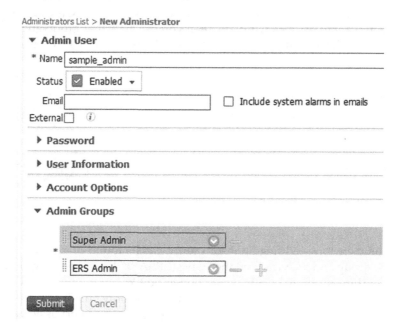

If you are planning on using ERS though, we highly recommend dedicated API users for your applications that have only ERS-level access. Multiple accounts might be more work on the front-end but better auditability and separation of privilege are always a good thing!

The other side of ERS is the Guest component and it requires separate configuration than the rest of the ERS API. You still need to enable ERS globally like we did under Administration → System → Settings → ERS Settings but the user will need to be added to a User Identity group that will have access to a Guest Sponsor group that has ERS enabled. That means for user creation we'll actually create a local network access user and not an administrative user. Now technically you could ERS enable an existing Sponsor group but like previously stated, privilege separation is always a good thing. We're going to create a new Sponsor group just for ERS usage, a new User Identity group that will be assigned to that Sponsor group, and finally our Guest ERS API user.

First let's create our new User Identity group; go to Administration → Identity Management → Groups and click "Add" and create a new group with a fitting description like this.

Identity Group

* Name	GuestERSAPI
Description	Guest ERS API Users

Save   Reset

Once we have that group created we'll want to create our Sponsor group that will be ERS enabled. Go to Guest Access → Configure and then go to "Sponsor Groups." If you already have a group you want to use as a template, then you can click that group and select "Duplicate" or start fresh with a brand new group; we'll do the latter so click "Create".

Sponsor group name:*	Guest_ERS_Group
Description:	Guest ERS Sponsor Group

Members...

Sponsor Group Members

Search

Name

GuestERSAPI

More info about creating/editing Sponsor groups can be found in Chapter 9 but here you can see our new group and we've added the "GuestERSAPI" User Identity group we just created. Settings for this group can be whatever you would like but they should align with what your ERS application will be doing. If you are going to be only creating users one at a time, you can safely disable the "Import" and "Random" guest creation permissions.

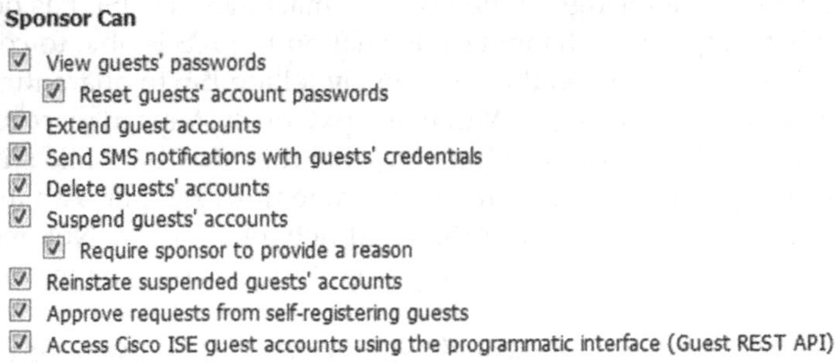

Sponsor Can

- ☑ View guests' passwords
  - ☑ Reset guests' account passwords
- ☑ Extend guest accounts
- ☑ Send SMS notifications with guests' credentials
- ☑ Delete guests' accounts
- ☑ Suspend guests' accounts
  - ☑ Require sponsor to provide a reason
- ☑ Reinstate suspended guests' accounts
- ☑ Approve requests from self-registering guests
- ☑ Access Cisco ISE guest accounts using the programmatic interface (Guest REST API)

The last piece for the ERS Sponsor group is that we need to enable the API. Ensure that the very last checkbox is checked so that the user we're about to create will be able to perform the needed actions.

Our last step will be to create our Guest ERS API user so go to Administration → Identities and click "Add." Create your user like you normally would but make sure you add them to the group we created in the first step of this process. The next image shows the user we created for this example.

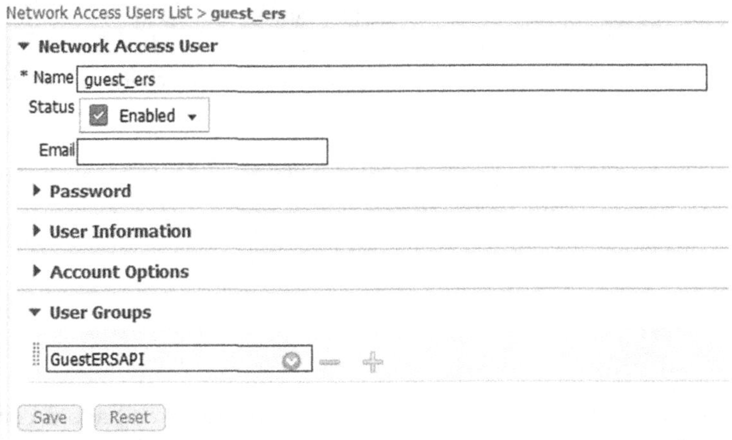

Network Access Users List > **guest_ers**

▼ **Network Access User**

* Name | guest_ers

Status ☑ Enabled ▾

Email |

▶ **Password**

▶ **User Information**

▶ **Account Options**

▼ **User Groups**

⦙ GuestERSAPI ⊘ ― ✛

[Save] [Reset]

From here you will want to reference the ISE API guide or the previously mentioned software development kit (SDK) so that you can start programming your own applications!

pxGRID

The final option for getting data out of ISE is also the newest, pxGrid. This is more than just an API and is really a data exchange mechanism that is meant to share different types of data across a wide range of systems. A typical example using an IPS and ISE would be that separately the IPS has no knowledge of the users on machines and ISE has no knowledge of the actions a user is taking. By exchanging information the IPS is able to correlate users to events it sees and then take action on those events by telling ISE to quarantine the user until actions are taken to remediate the issue. With many pxGrid systems in place all sharing information it allows those systems to concentrate on what they do best while still gaining other valuable context about what they are doing at the same time. ISE plays an important role in pxGrid because of what it provides—user data and network control. Not every device may have data ISE wants but chances are almost any pxGrid device is going to want identity data from ISE.

Setup wise it's a little bit more complicated than the other APIs. You need to enable and assign the pxGrid role to one or two nodes in your deployment before you are able to use it. You can do this from Administration → System → Deployment and then clicking on the nodes you want to enable the service on. In simple, single- or dual-node deployments the choice is pretty simple but in a distributed deployment which nodes should have the pxGrid role? Technically any of them can be, but we recommend that you use one or two of your PSNs to house the role since those nodes are already open to end users and integration with other systems should be easier.

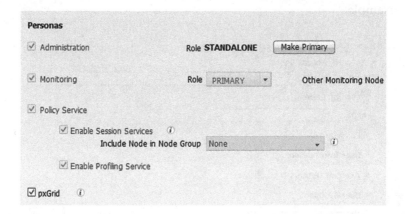

pxGrid handles authentication via certificates so you need to have a certificate that is bound to the pxGrid service. After enabling the pxGrid persona ISE will try and utilize the certificate that is already assigned to the nodes you selected but if you have multiple certificates on your pxGrid node(s) then you may have to manually select which certificate you want or possibly even generate a new one. The important thing to note is that the pxGrid certificate must have both the "Server Authentication" and "Client Authentication" usage values in order to be used[6].

---

[6]If you are using certificates from most public CAs, then you are probably already good to go; we checked a number of them and certificates had server/client authentication object identifiers (OIDs).

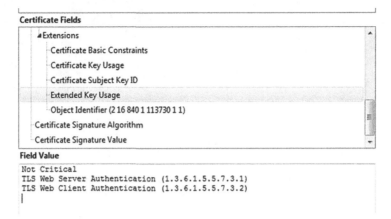

Certificate Fields

- ⊿Extensions
  - Certificate Basic Constraints
  - Certificate Key Usage
  - Certificate Subject Key ID
  - Extended Key Usage
  - Object Identifier (2 16 840 1 113730 1 1)
- Certificate Signature Algorithm
- Certificate Signature Value

Field Value

```
Not Critical
TLS Web Server Authentication (1.3.6.1.5.5.7.3.1)
TLS Web Client Authentication (1.3.6.1.5.5.7.3.2)
```

Once you have the certificates squared away, you should be able to see the client screen under Administration → pxGrid Services. There won't be anything here at first but once you start to tie applications to it they will begin to show up.

Unfortunately going into application development with pxGrid is complex and probably an entire book on its own. Cisco provides a wealth of information at their Developer site and there is an excellent guide on configuring the pxLog application from Cisco as well.

Cisco pxGrid Developer site: http://bit.ly/1LOU0oD
pxLog example application: http://bit.ly/1PhjKKO

Subject Index

Printed in the United States
By Bookmasters